Anthology of MOVIE SONGS

PIANO • VOCAL • GUITAR

gold EDITION

ISBN 978-1-4234-9087-6

HAL • LEONARD® CORPORATION

7777 W. BLUEMOUND RD. P.O. BOX 13819 MILWAUKEE, WI 53213

Visit Hal Leonard Online at
www.halleonard.com

THE ADDAMS FAMILY THEME
Theme from the TV Show and Movie

Music and Lyrics by
VIC MIZZY

Moderately

They're creep-y and they're kook-y, mys-te-ri-ous and spook-y, they're

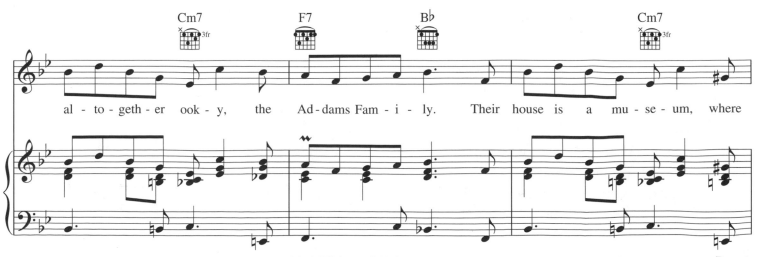

al-to-geth-er ook-y, the Ad-dams Fam-i-ly. Their house is a mu-se-um, where

peo - ple come to see 'em, they real - ly are a scree - um, the Ad - dams Fam - i - ly.

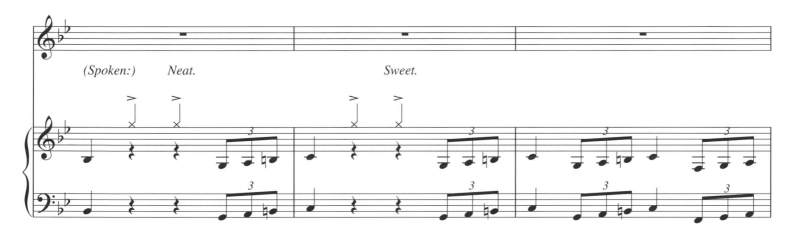

(Spoken:) Neat. Sweet.

Petite. So get a witch - 's shawl on, a broom - stick you can crawl on, we're

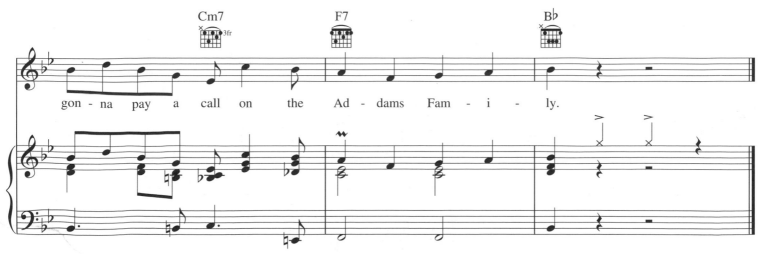

gon - na pay a call on the Ad - dams Fam - i - ly.

ALL FOR LOVE
from Walt Disney Pictures' THE THREE MUSKETEERS

Words and Music by BRYAN ADAMS,
R.J. LANGE and MICHAEL KAMEN

Moderately, not too fast

be there when ___ you're old, to have and ___ to
from the wind and ___ the rain, from the hurt and ___
When hon - or's ___ at stake, this vow I ___ will

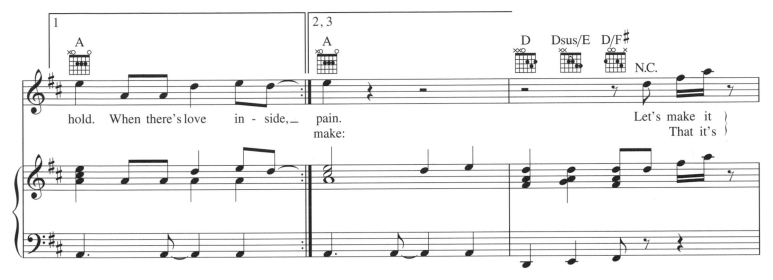

hold. When there's love in - side, ___ pain.
make:

Let's make it
That it's

all for one and all for love. ___

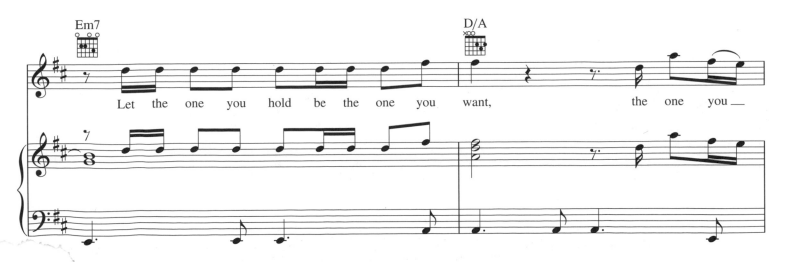

Let the one you hold be the one you want, the one you ___

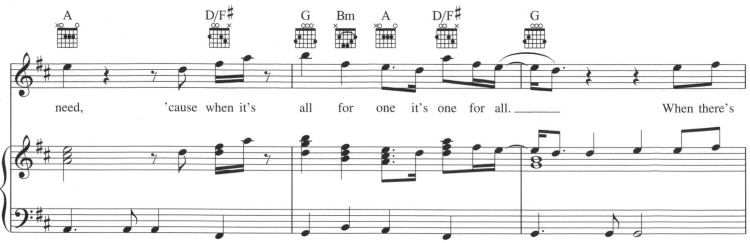

need,   'cause when it's   all   for   one   it's   one   for   all. _____   When there's

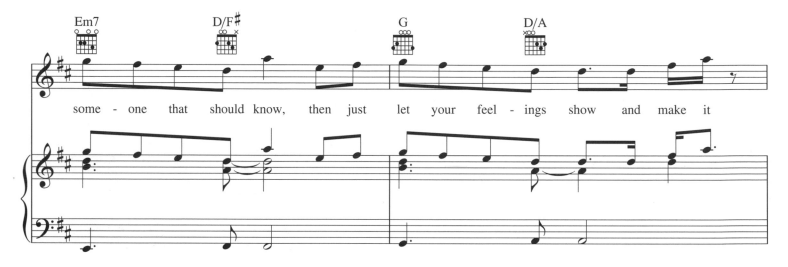

some - one   that   should   know,   then   just   let   your   feel - ings   show   and   make   it

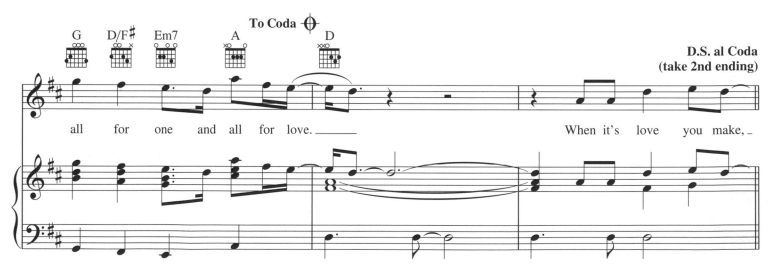

all   for   one   and   all   for   love. _____   When   it's   love   you   make, _

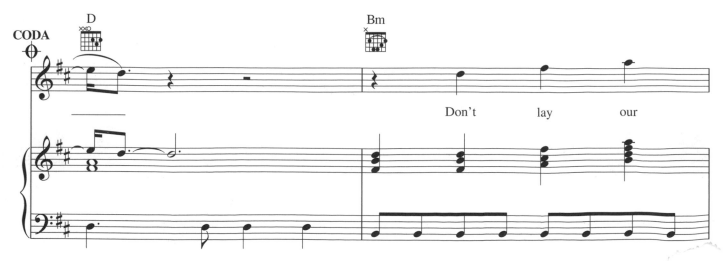

Don't   lay   our

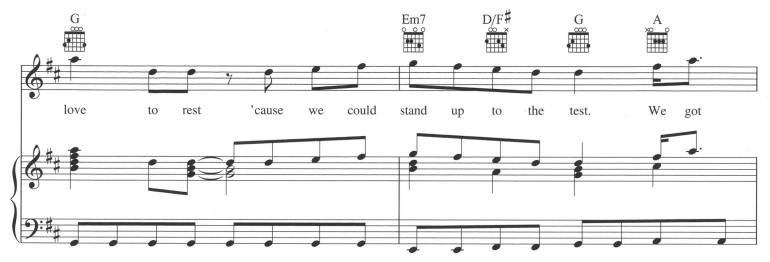

love to rest 'cause we could stand up to the test. We got

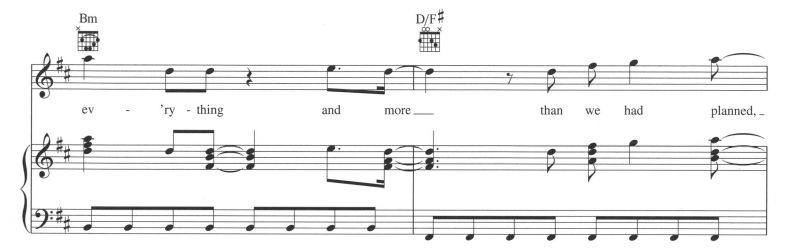

ev - 'ry - thing and more _____ than we had planned, _

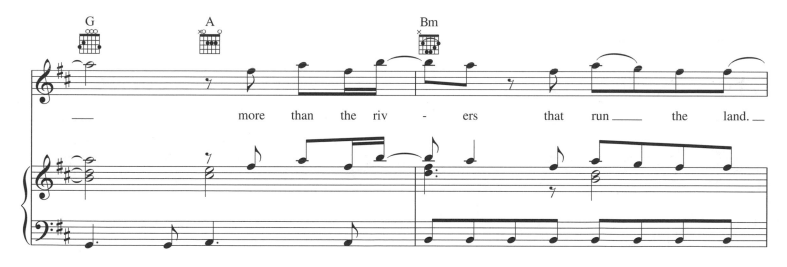

_____ more than the riv - ers that run _____ the land. _

We've got it all _____ in our hands.

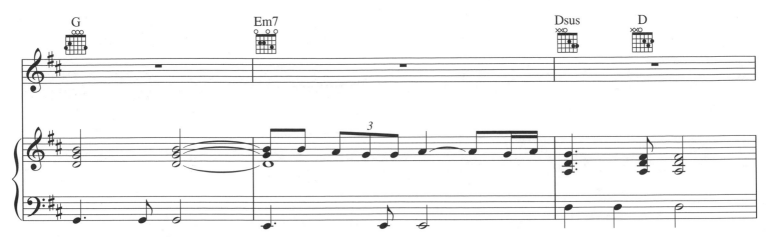

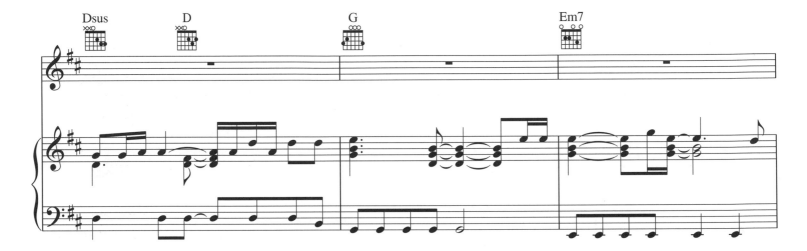

Now it's all for one and all for love. __

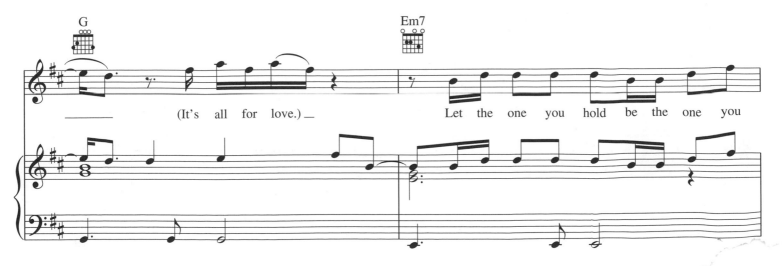

__ __ (It's all for love.) __   Let the one you hold be the one you

ALL THE WAY
from THE JOKER IS WILD

Words by SAMMY CAHN
Music by JAMES VAN HEUSEN

When some-bod-y loves you, it's no good un-less he loves you all the
When some-bod-y needs you, it's no good un-less she needs you all the

way. Hap-py to be near you, when you need some-one to cheer you
way. Thru the good or lean years and for all the in-be-tween years,

all the way. Tall-er _____ than the tall-est tree is,
come what may. Who knows _____ where the road will lead us,

AMERICA

from the Motion Picture THE JAZZ SINGER

Words and Music by
NEIL DIAMOND

Moderately bright

Far,   we've been trav - el - ing far, ___

___ with - out ___ a   home, ___

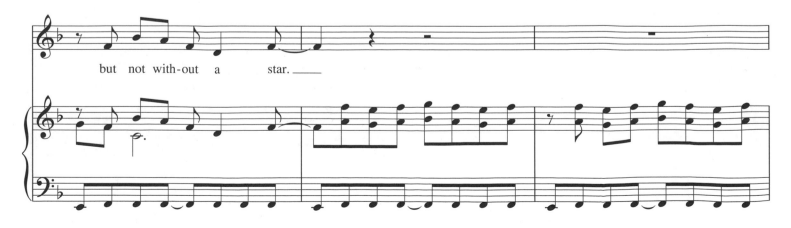

but not with-out a   star. ___

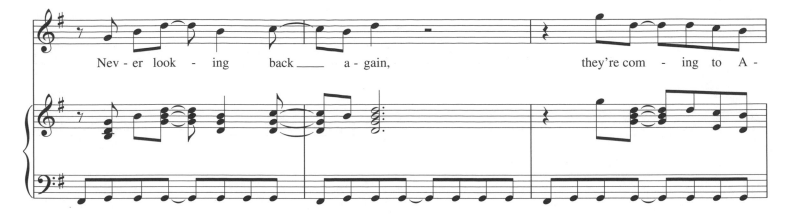

Nev - er look - ing back _____ a - gain, they're com - ing to A -

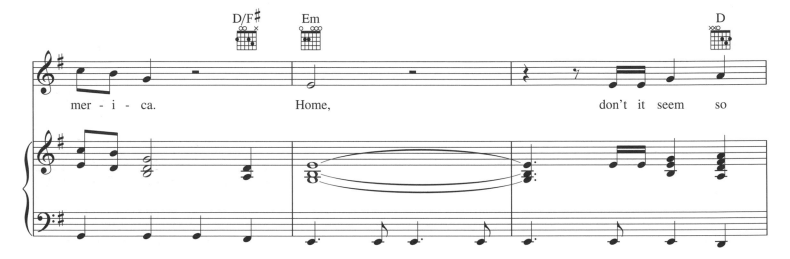

mer - i - ca. Home, don't it seem so

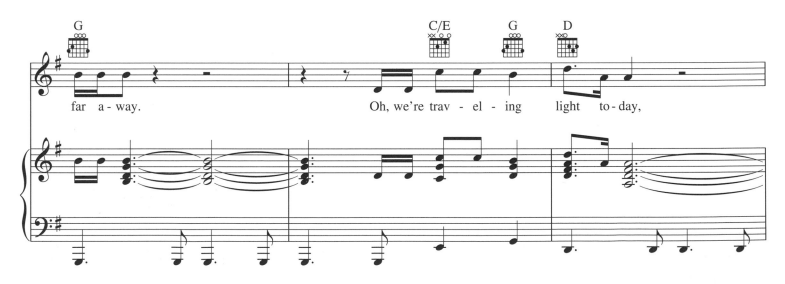

far a - way. Oh, we're trav - el - ing light to - day,

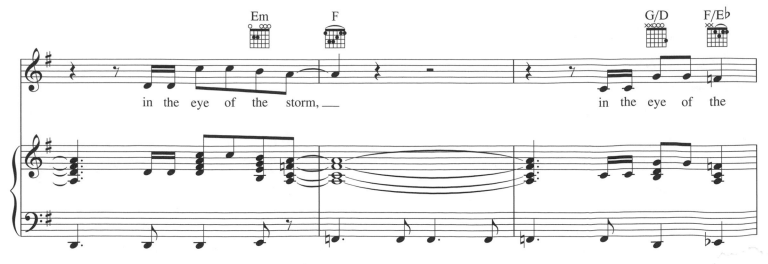

in the eye of the storm, _____ in the eye of the

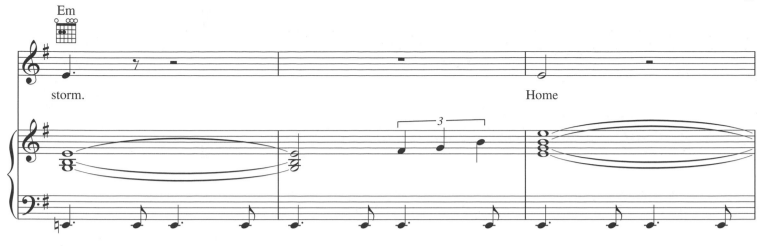

storm.   Home

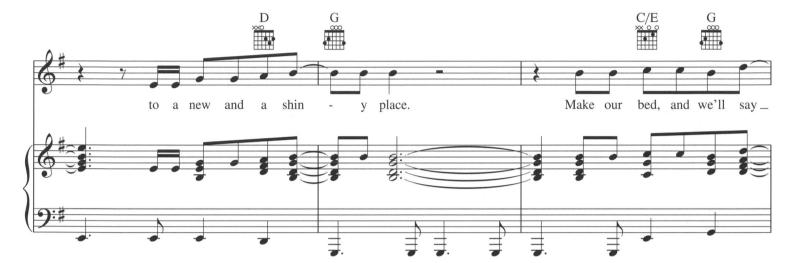

to a new and a shin - y place.   Make our bed, and we'll say

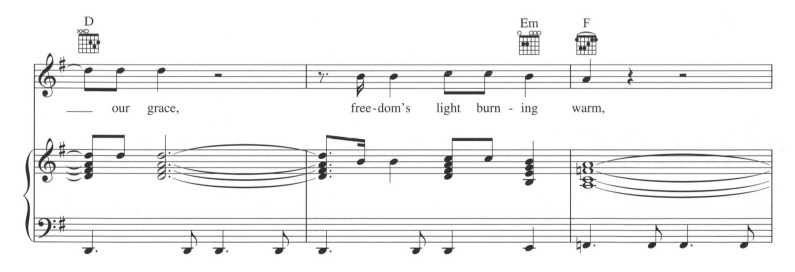

our grace,   free-dom's light burn - ing warm,

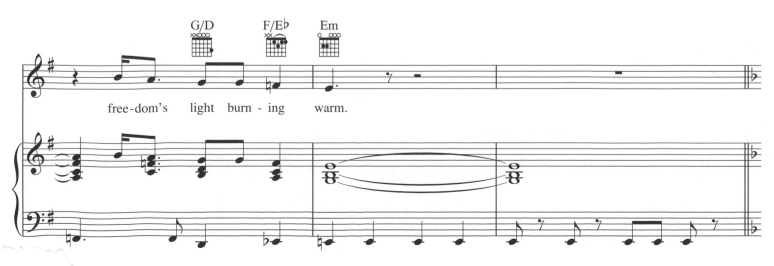

free-dom's light burn - ing warm.

Ev -'ry-where   a - round ___ the world,

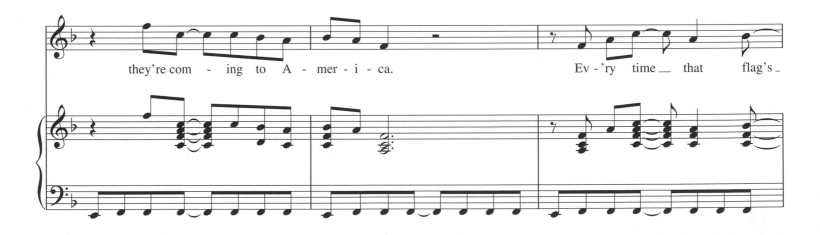

they're com - ing to A - mer - i - ca.   Ev -'ry time ___ that   flag's _

___ un - furled, _   they're com - ing to A - mer - i - ca.

Got a dream to take _____ them there. They're com - ing to A -

mer - i - ca. Got a dream, _ they've come _____ to share.

They're com - ing to A - mer - i - ca. They're com - ing to A -

mer - i - ca. They're com - ing to A - mer - i - ca.

They're com - ing to A - mer - i - ca.   They're com - ing to A -

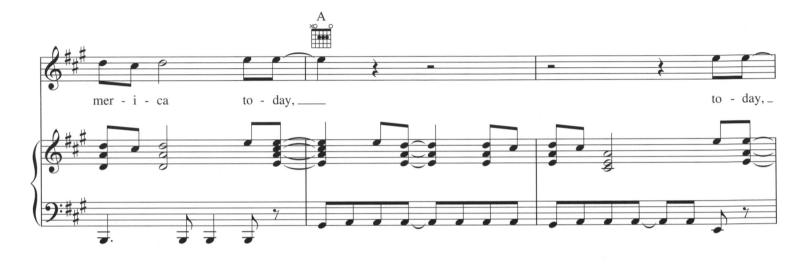

mer - i - ca   to - day, ____   to - day, ____

____   to - day, ____

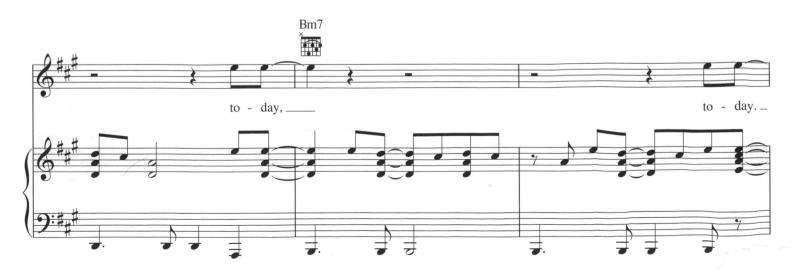

to - day, ____   to - day. ____

My coun-try 'tis of thee (to - day), ___ sweet ___ land of

lib-er-ty (to - day), ___ of thee I sing ___ (to - day), ___

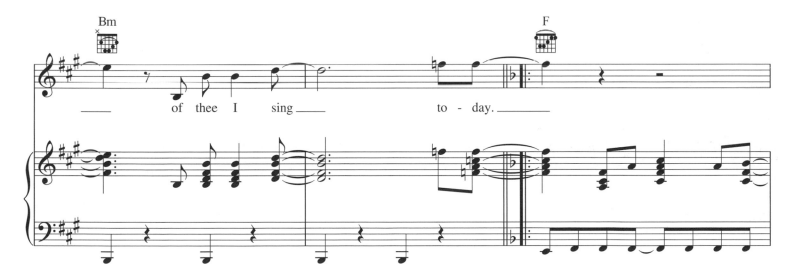

___ of thee I sing ___ to - day. ___

Repeat and Fade

To - day, ___ to - day. ___

AND ALL THAT JAZZ

from CHICAGO

Words by FRED EBB
Music by JOHN KANDER

nois - y hall __ where there's a night - ly brawl __ and all that

jazz!

Slick your hair __ and wear your

buck - le shoes __ and all that jazz! __ I hear that Fa - ther Dip __ is gon - na

blow the blues __ and all that jazz! __ Hold on, hon, __ we're gon - na

bun - ny hug, _ I bought some as-pi - rin _ down at U - nit-ed Drug. _ In case we shake a - part _ and want a

brand new start _ to do that jazz! ___

Oh, ___ I'm gon-na see my She - ba shim-my shake. _ (And all that jazz!) _

Oh, ___ she's gon-na shim-my till her gar-ters break. _ (And all that jazz!) _ Show ___

Come on, babe, _ we're gon-na brush the sky. _ I bet-cha luck-y Lin - dy nev - er

all that jazz! _ Show ____ me where to park my gir - dle, Oh, ____

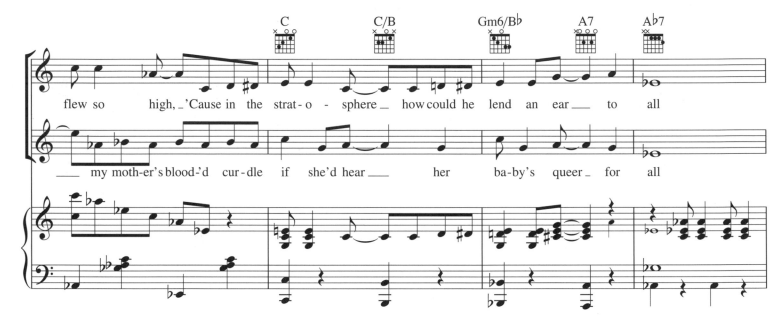

flew so high, _ 'Cause in the strat-o - sphere _ how could he lend an ear _ to all

____ my moth-er's blood'd cur-dle if she'd hear ____ her ba-by's queer _ for all

that jazz!

No, I'm no one's wife, _ but oh, I

love my life _ and all _____ that _____

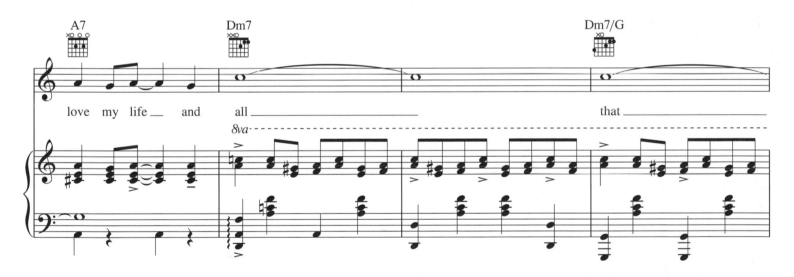

_____ jazz! _____ That jazz!

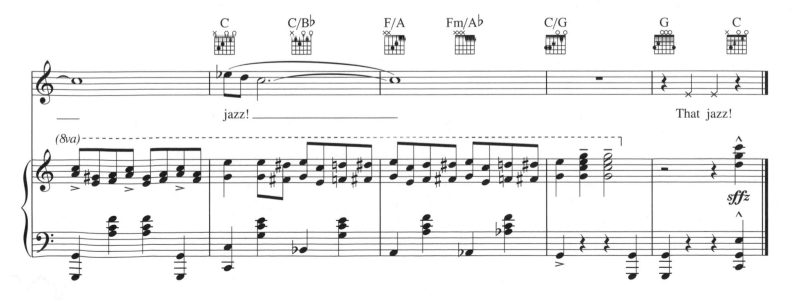

BABY ELEPHANT WALK

from the Paramount Picture HATARI!

Words by HAL DAVID
Music by HENRY MANCINI

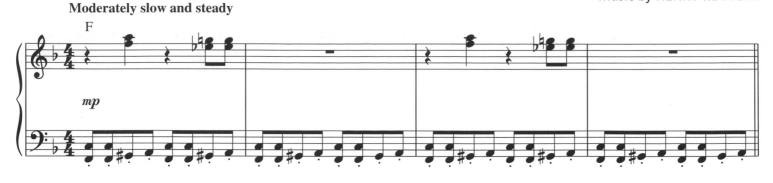

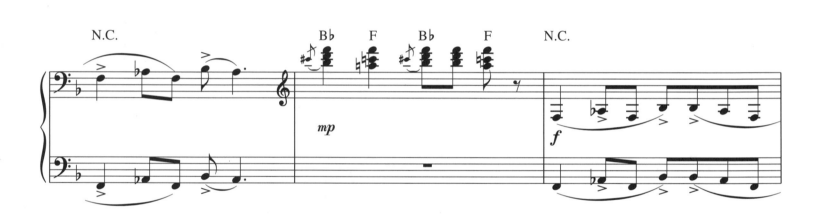

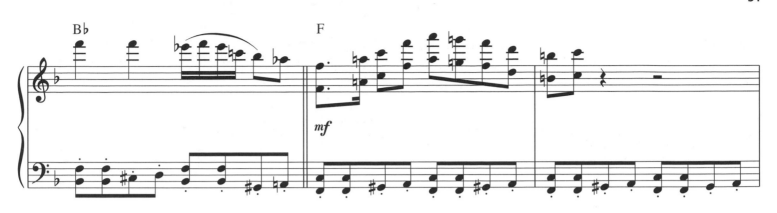

BACK IN THE SADDLE AGAIN

from BACK IN THE SADDLE AGAIN

Words and Music by GENE AUTRY
and RAY WHITLEY

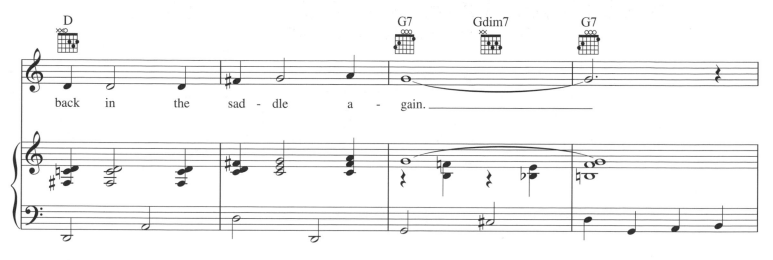

back in the sad - dle a - gain. _____

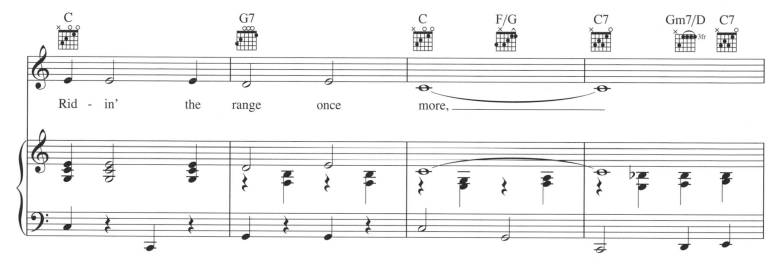

Rid - in' the range once more, _____

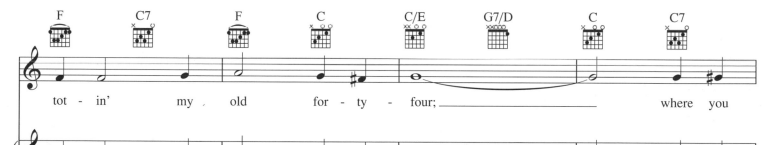

tot - in' my old for - ty - four; _____ where you

sleep out ev - 'ry night, where the on - ly law is right, I'm

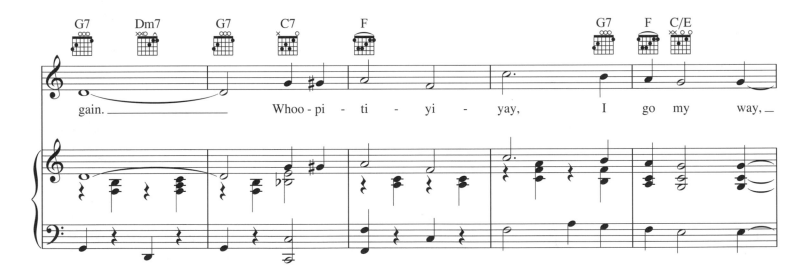

BELLA'S LULLABY
from the Summit Entertainment film TWILIGHT

Composed by CARTER BURWELL

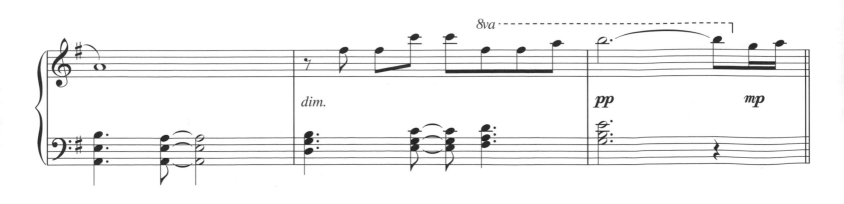

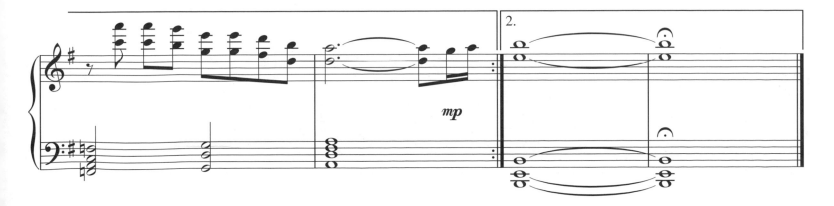

BEAUTIFUL CITY
from GODSPELL

Music and Lyrics by
STEPHEN SCHWARTZ

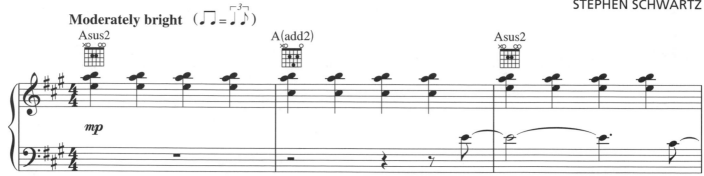

Out of the ruins and rub - ble,
We may not reach the end - ing,

out of the smoke, ___ out of our night
but we can start ___ slow - ly but tru -

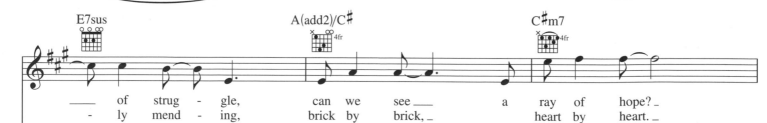

___ of strug - gle, can we see ___ a ray of hope? ___
- ly mend - ing, brick by brick, _ heart by heart. _

One / Now,
pale thin ray, / may-be now, ___
reach-ing for the day. ___ / we start learn-ing how. ___

___ }
We can build _____ a beau-ti-ful cit - y,

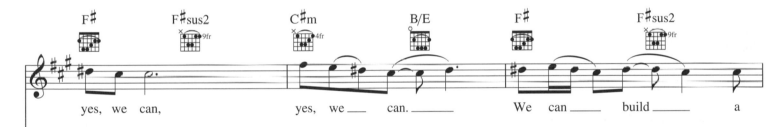

yes, we can, yes, we ___ can. _____ We can ___ build ___ a

beau-ti-ful cit - y, ___ not a cit-y of ___ an - gels, but we can ___ build a cit-y ___ of

man. _____ man. _____

_____ When your trust _____ is all but shat - tered, when your faith _

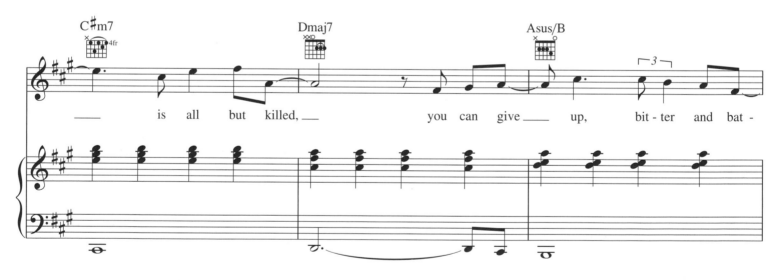

_____ is all but killed, ___ you can give _____ up, bit - ter and bat -

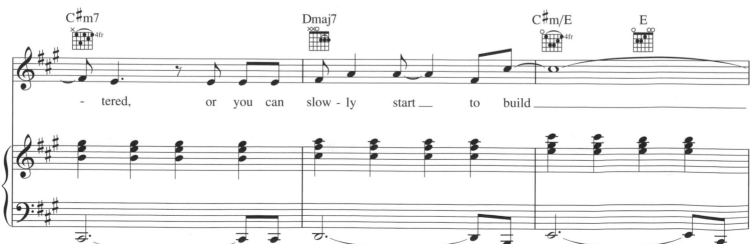

- tered, or you can slow - ly start __ to build _____

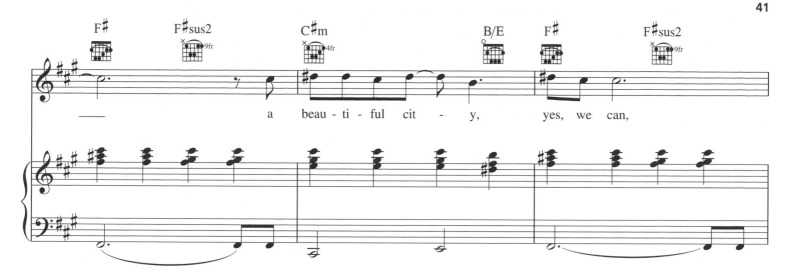

a beau - ti - ful cit - y, yes, we can,

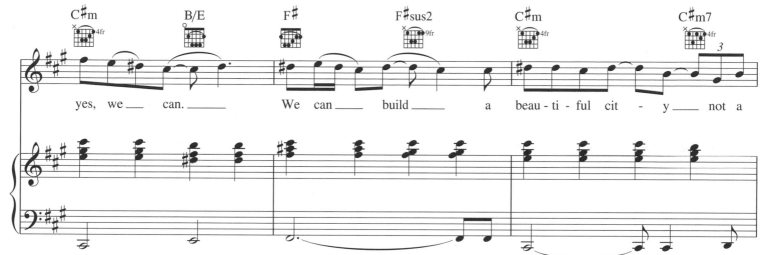

yes, we can. We can build a beau - ti - ful cit - y not a

cit - y of an - gels, but fi - nal - ly a cit - y of

man.

rall.

BEN
from BEN

Words by DON BLACK
Music by WALTER SCHARF

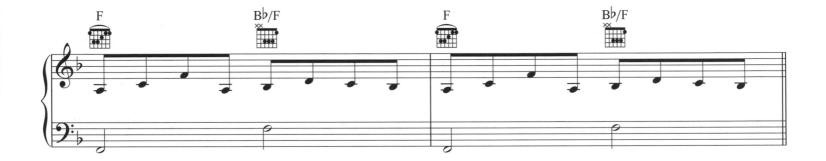

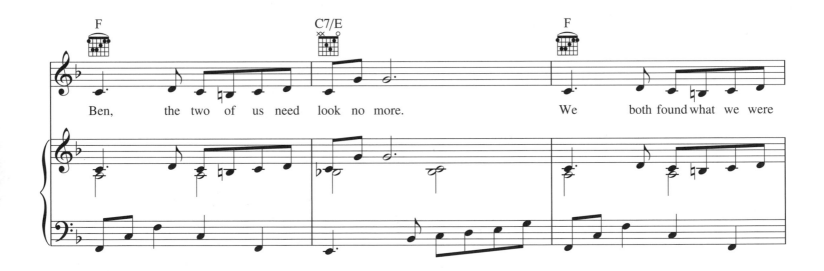

Ben, the two of us need look no more. We both found what we were

look- ing for. With a friend to call my own, I'll nev- er be a-

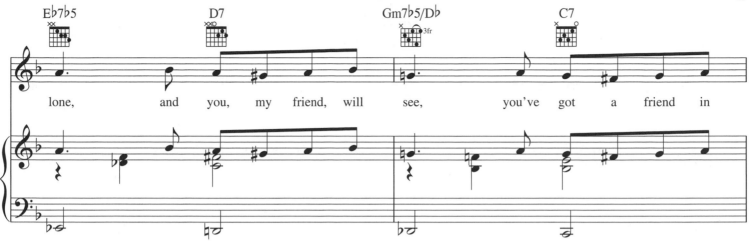

lone, and you, my friend, will see, you've got a friend in

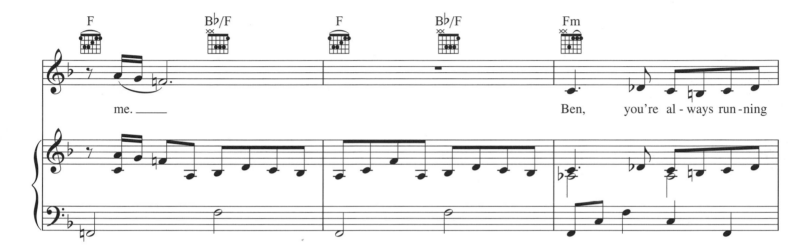

me. _____ Ben, you're al - ways run - ning

here and there. You feel you're not want - ed an - y - where.

If you ev - er look be - hind and don't like what you find, there's some - thing you should

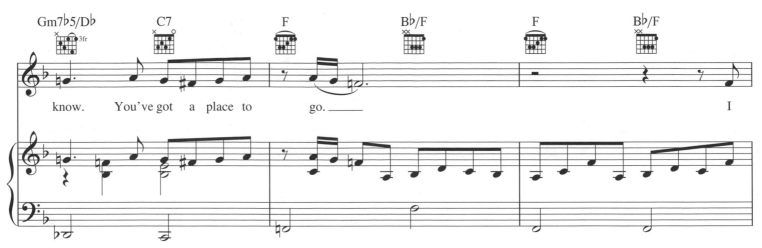

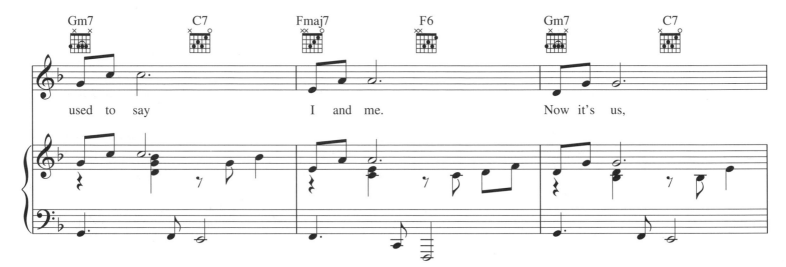

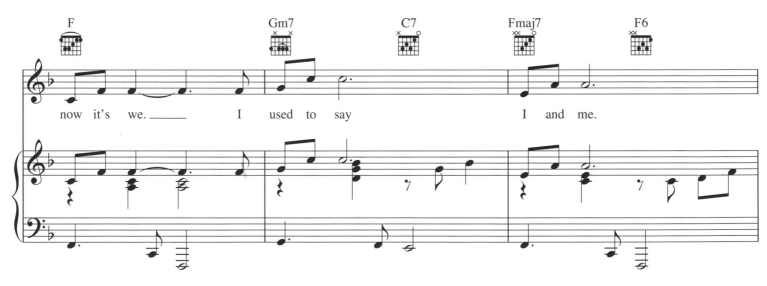

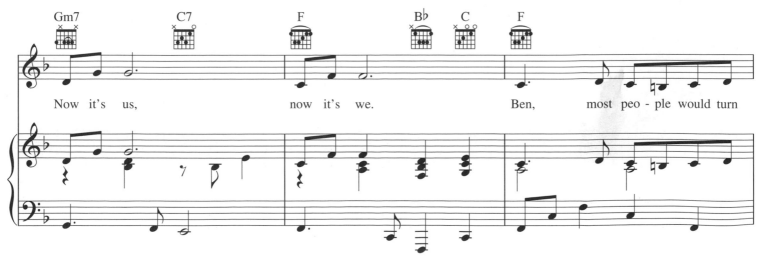

you a-way. I don't lis-ten to a word they say.

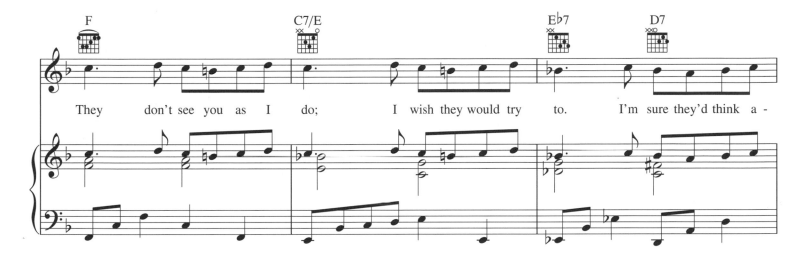

They don't see you as I do; I wish they would try to. I'm sure they'd think a-

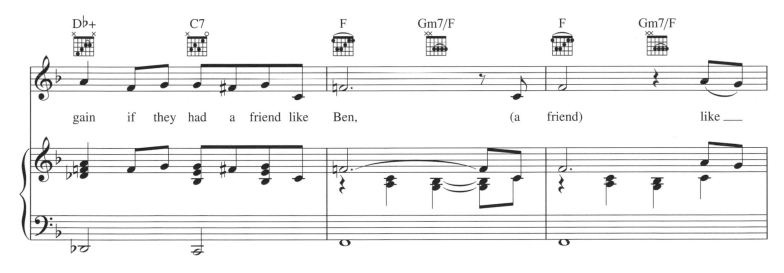

gain if they had a friend like Ben, (a friend) like _____

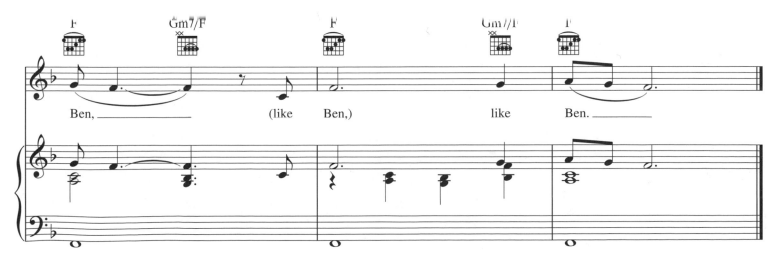

Ben, _____ (like Ben,) like Ben. _____

BIBBIDI-BOBBIDI-BOO
(The Magic Song)
from Walt Disney's CINDERELLA

Words by JERRY LIVINGSTON
Music by MACK DAVID and AL HOFFMAN

Sa - la - ga - doo - la men-chic - ka boo - la bib - bi - di - bob - bi - di - boo. Put 'em to-geth-er and what have you got bib - bi - di - bob-bi - di - boo. Sa - la - ga - doo - la men-chic - ka boo - la bib - bi - di - bob-bi - di - boo. It -'ll do mag-ic be-lieve it or not,

BIG SPENDER
from SWEET CHARITY

Music by CY COLEMAN
Lyrics by DOROTHY FIELDS

Moderately, with a beat

The min-ute you walked in the joint, I could see you were a man of dis-tinc-tion, a

real big spend-er! Good look-ing, so re-fined. Say,

would-n't you like to know what's go-ing on in my mind? So let me get right to the point,

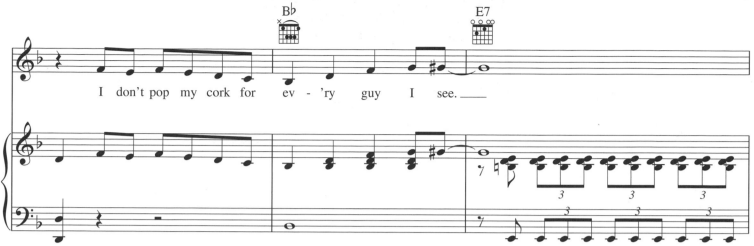

I don't pop my cork for ev - 'ry guy I see. ___

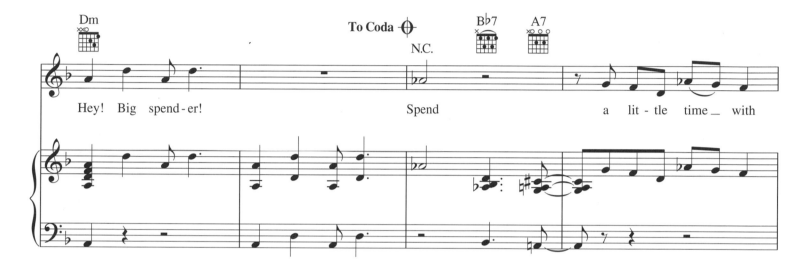

Hey! Big spend - er! Spend a lit - tle time ___ with

me. Do you like to have

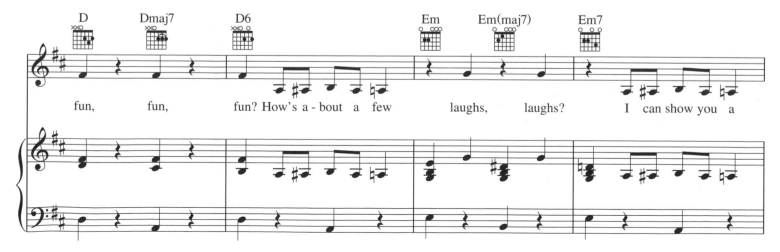

fun, fun, fun? How's a - bout a few laughs, laughs? I can show you a

BREAKING FREE

from the Disney Channel Original Movie HIGH SCHOOL MUSICAL

Words and Music by
JAMIE HOUSTON

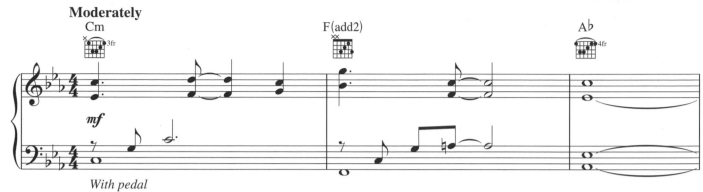

Moderately

With pedal

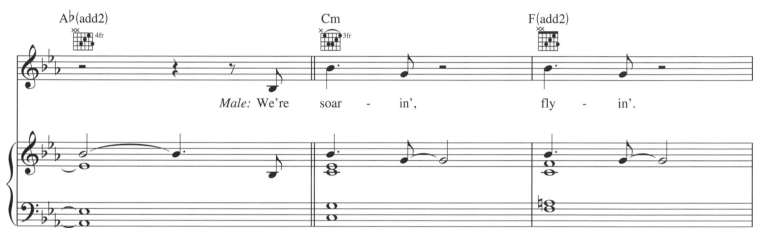

Male: We're soar - in', fly - in'.

There's not a star — in heav - en that we — can't reach. — *Female:* If we're try -

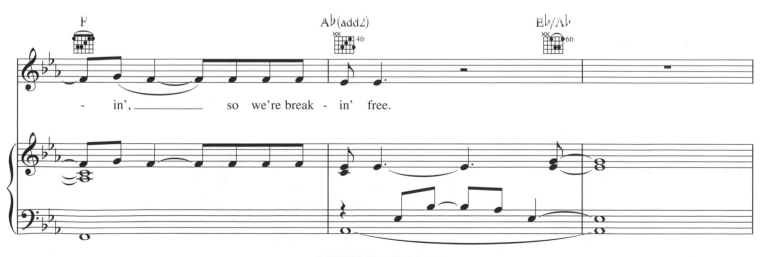

- in', _____ so we're break - in' free.

CAN YOU FEEL THE LOVE TONIGHT

from Walt Disney Pictures' THE LION KING

Music by ELTON JOHN
Lyrics by TIM RICE

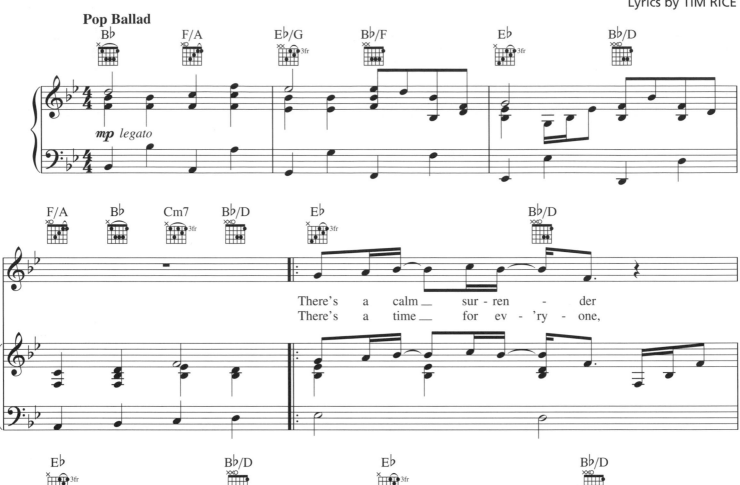

Pop Ballad

There's a calm __ sur-ren-der
There's a time __ for ev-'ry-one,

to the rush __ of day, __ when the heat __ of the roll-ing world __
if they on-ly learn __ that the twist-ing ka-lei-do-scope __

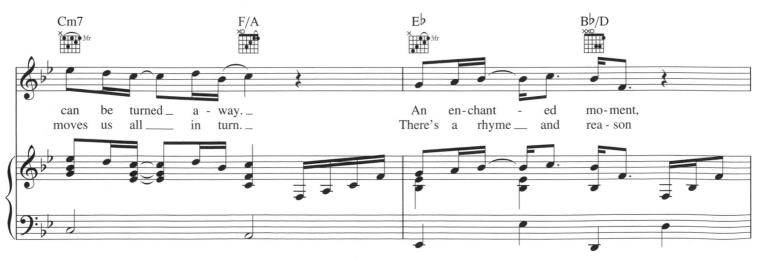

can be turned __ a-way. __ An en-chant-ed mo-ment,
moves us all __ in turn. __ There's a rhyme __ and rea-son

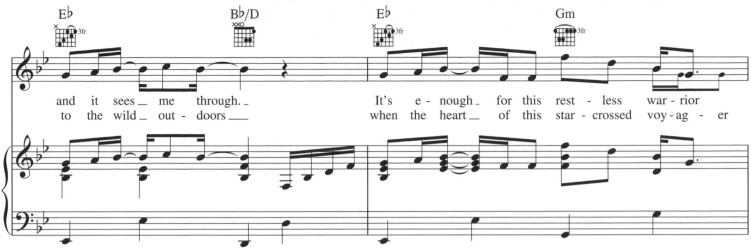

and it sees __ me through. __ It's e - nough __ for this rest - less war - rior
to the wild __ out - doors __ when the heart __ of this star - crossed voy - ag - er

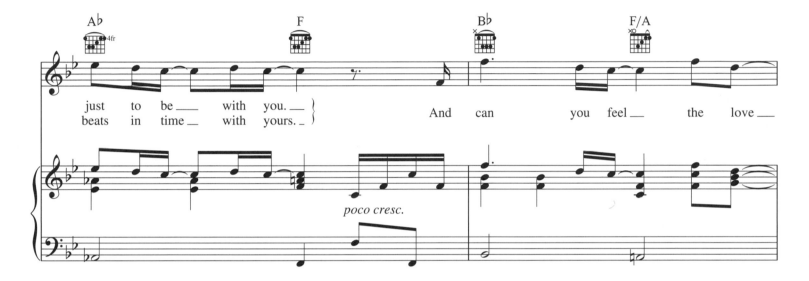

just to be __ with you. __ And can you feel __ the love __
beats in time __ with yours. __

poco cresc.

__ to - night? __ It is where __ we are. __

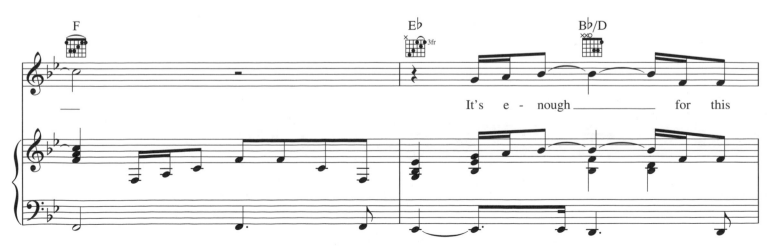

__ It's e - nough __ for this

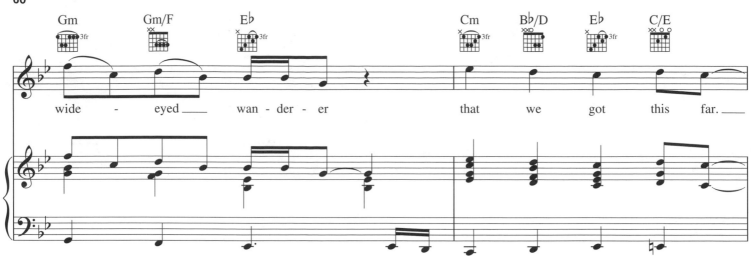

wide - eyed ___ wan - der - er   that   we   got   this   far. ___

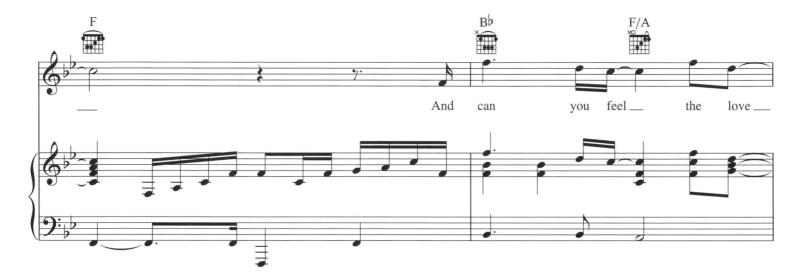

___   And   can   you   feel ___ the   love ___

___   to - night, _____   how   it's   laid ___   to   rest? ___

It's   e - nough _____   to   make

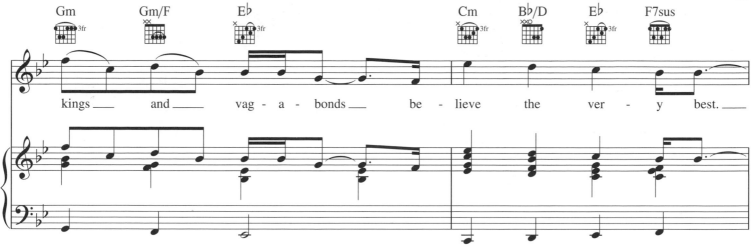

kings ___ and ___ vag - a - bonds ___ be - lieve the ver - y best. ___

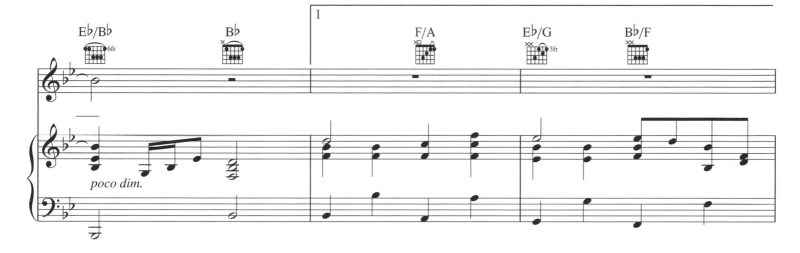

poco dim.

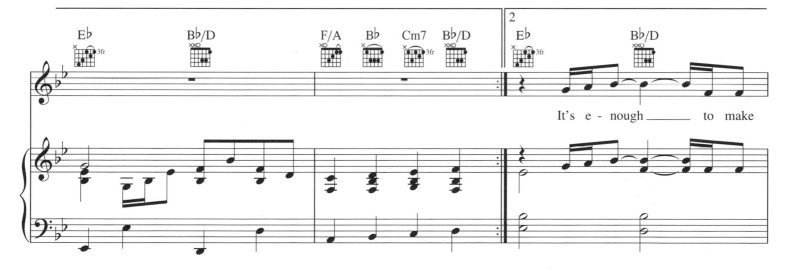

It's e - nough ___ to make

kings __ and __ vag-a-bonds __ be-lieve the ver - y best. ___

molto rit.

THE CANDY MAN

from WILLY WONKA AND THE CHOCOLATE FACTORY

Words and Music by LESLIE BRICUSSE
and ANTHONY NEWLEY

Brightly

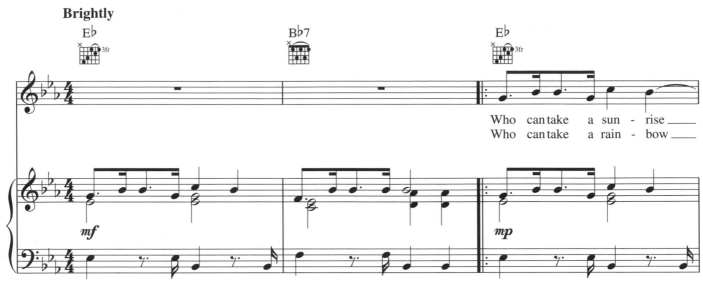

Who can take a sun - rise ____
Who can take a rain - bow ____

sprin - kle it with dew, ____
wrap it in a sigh, ____

cov - er it in choc - 'late and a mir - a - cle or two?
soak it in the sun and make a straw - b'ry lem - on pie?

The

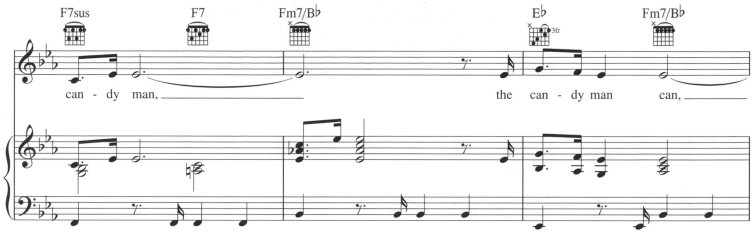

can - dy man, _____ the can - dy man can, _____

___ the can - dy man can 'cause he mix - es it with love and makes the

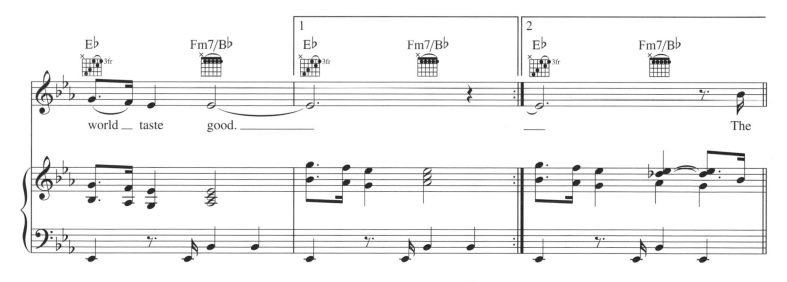

world __ taste good. _____ ___ The

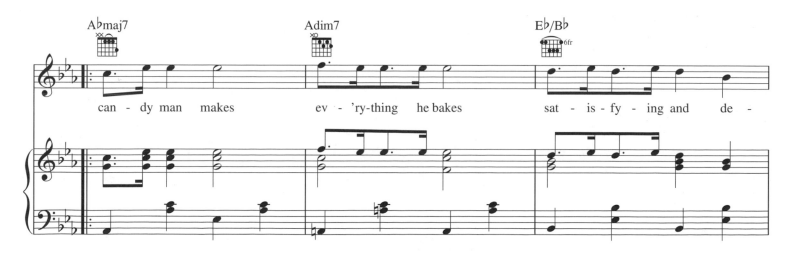

can - dy man makes ev - 'ry-thing he bakes sat - is - fy - ing and de -

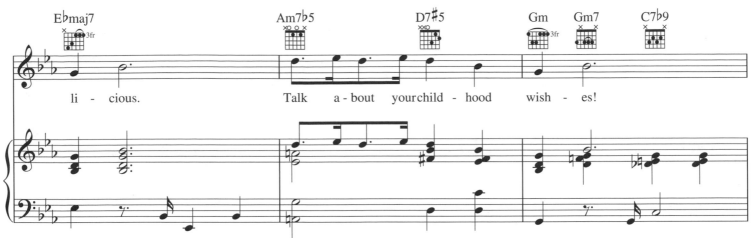

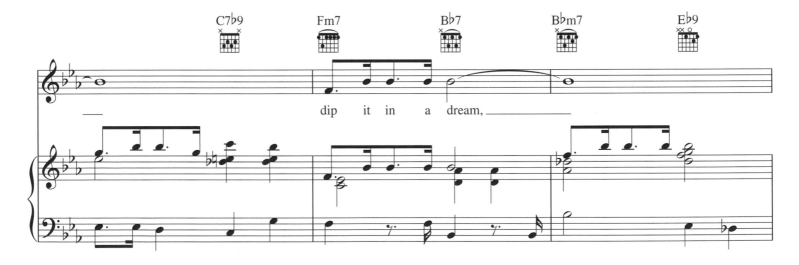

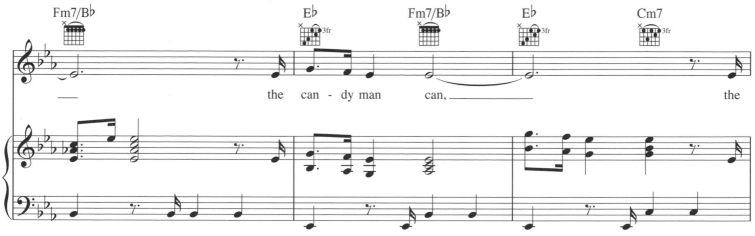

the can - dy man can, _____ the

can - dy man can 'cause he mix - es it with love and makes the world __ taste good. _____

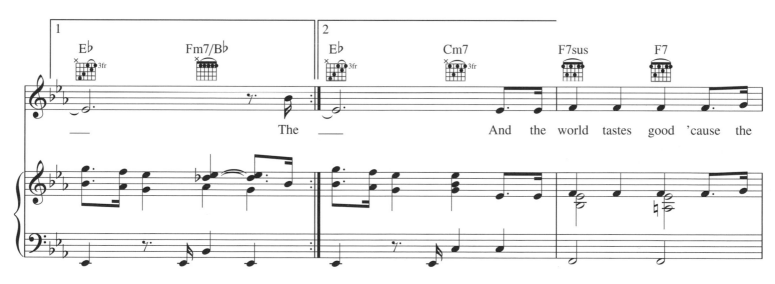

1

__ The __ And the world tastes good 'cause the

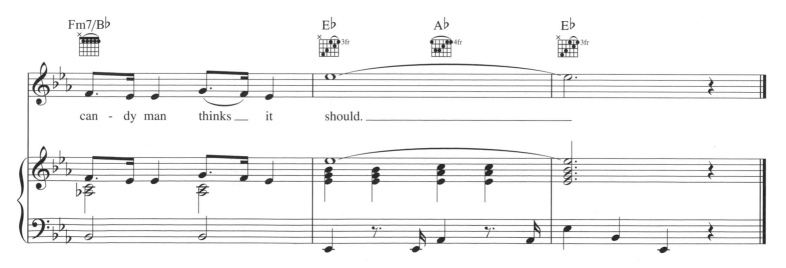

can - dy man thinks __ it should. _____

CHIM CHIM CHER-EE

from Walt Disney's MARY POPPINS

Words and Music by RICHARD M. SHERMAN
and ROBERT B. SHERMAN

Lightly, with gusto

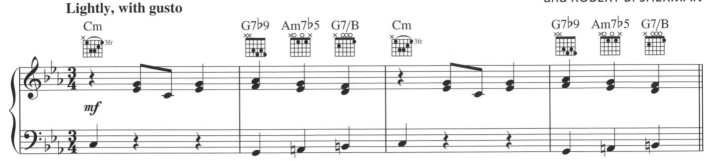

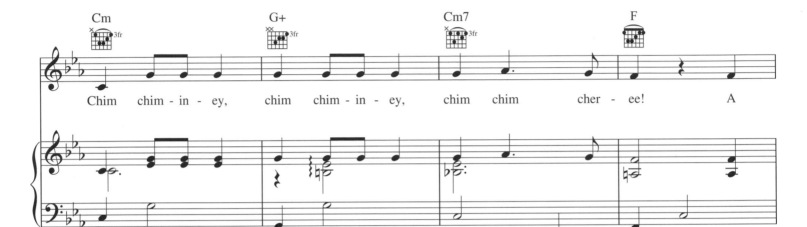

Chim chim-in-ey, chim chim-in-ey, chim chim cher-ee! A

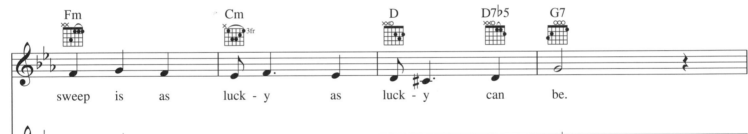

sweep is as luck-y as luck-y can be.

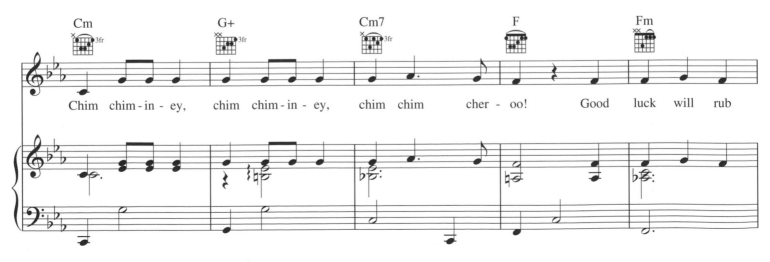

Chim chim-in-ey, chim chim-in-ey, chim chim cher-oo! Good luck will rub

off when I shakes 'ands with you, or blow me a kiss and

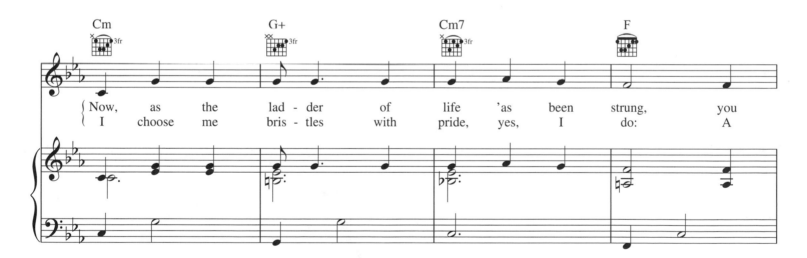

that's luck - y, too.

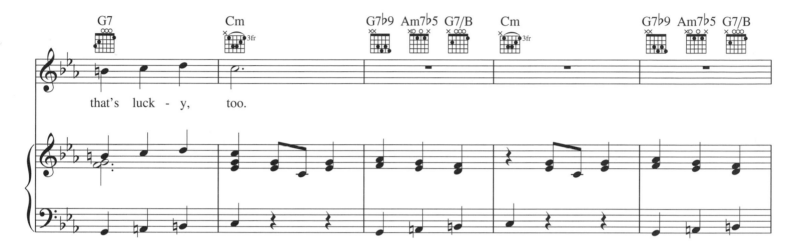

Now, as the lad - der of life 'as been strung, you
I choose me bris - tles with pride, yes, I do: A

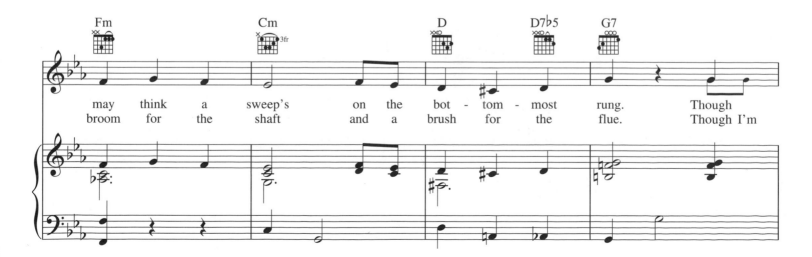

may think a sweep's on the bot - tom - most rung. Though
broom for the shaft and a brush for the flue. Though I'm

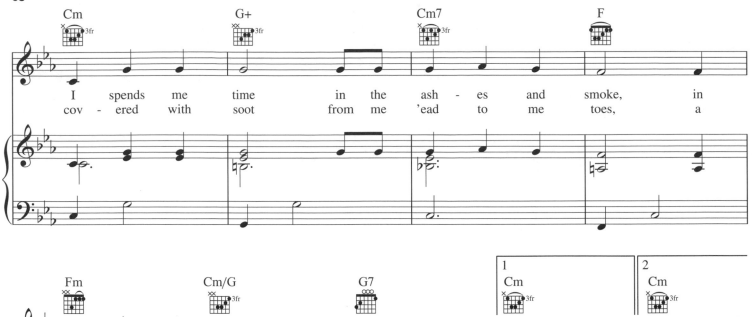

Cm · G+ · Cm7 · F

I spends me time in the ash - es and smoke, in
cov - ered with time soot from me 'ead to me toes,

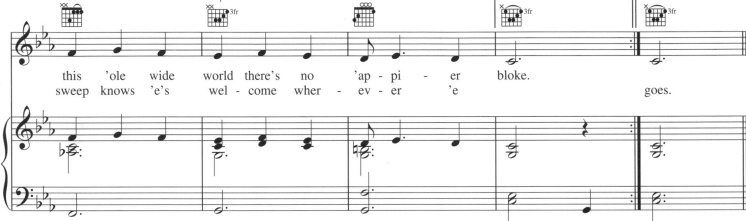

Fm · Cm/G · G7 · | 1. Cm | 2. Cm

this 'ole wide world there's no 'ap - pi - er bloke.
sweep knows 'e's wel - come wher - ev - er 'e goes.

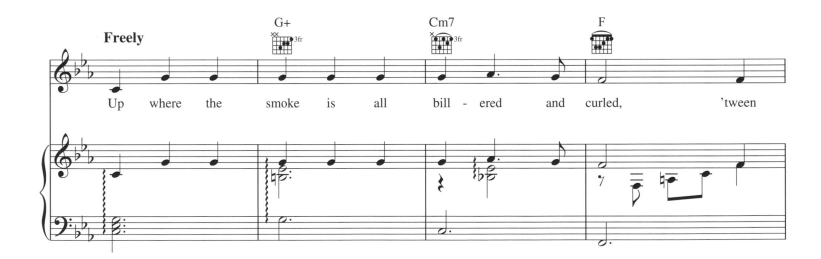

Freely · G+ · Cm7 · F

Up where the smoke is all bill - ered and curled, 'tween

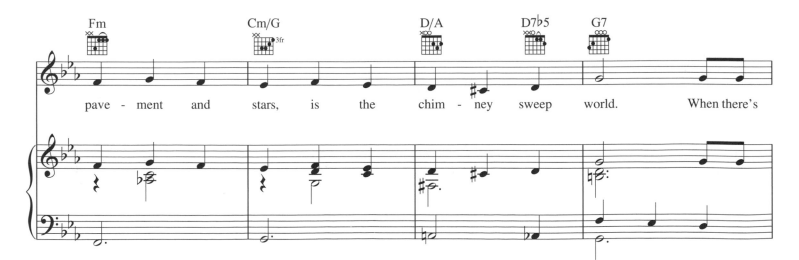

Fm · Cm/G · D/A · D7♭5 · G7

pave - ment and stars, is the chim - ney sweep world. When there's

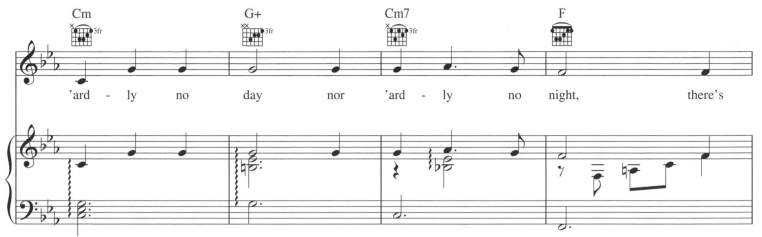

'ard - ly no day nor 'ard - ly no night, there's

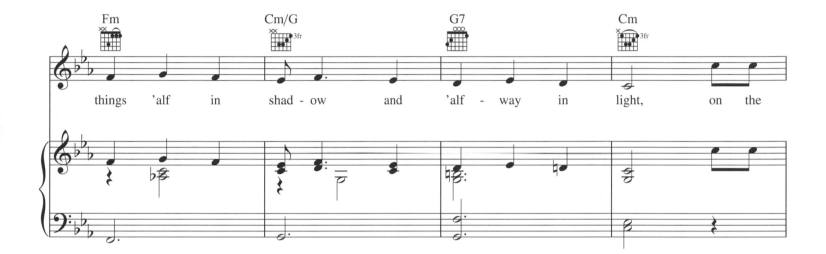

things 'alf in shad - ow and 'alf - way in light, on the

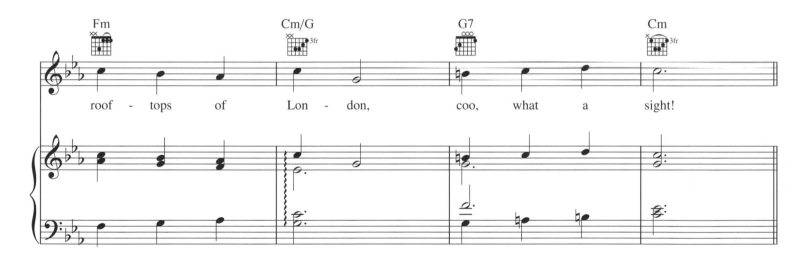

roof - tops of Lon - don, coo, what a sight!

Tempo I

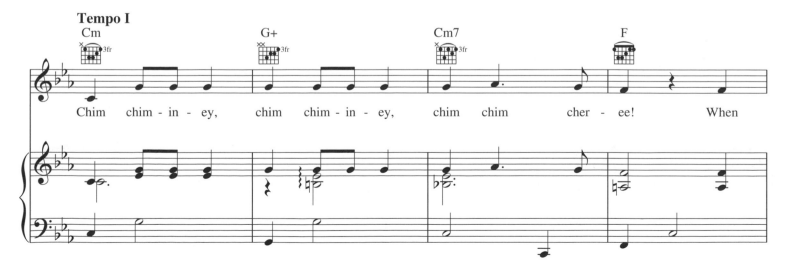

Chim chim - in - ey, chim chim - in - ey, chim chim cher - ee! When

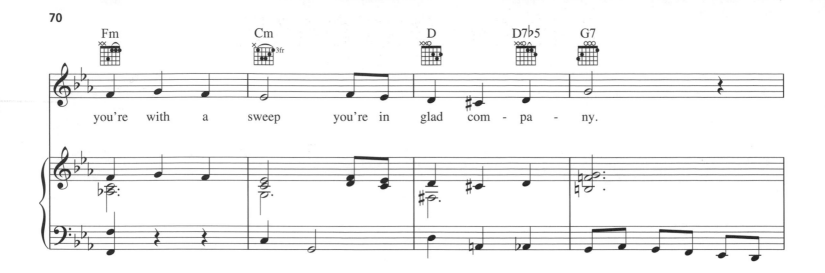

you're with a sweep you're in glad com - pa - ny.

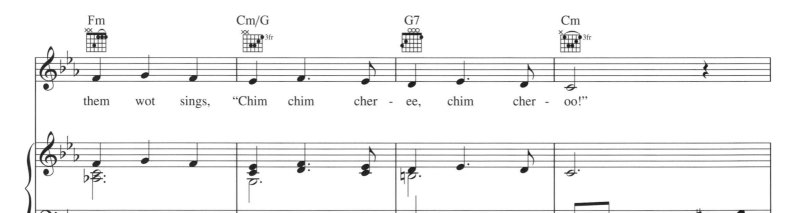

No - where is there a more 'ap - pi - er crew than

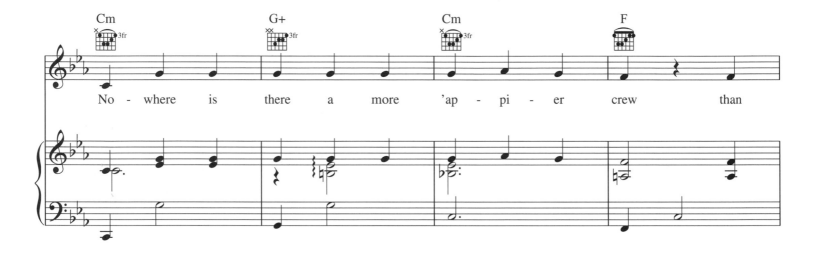

them wot sings, "Chim chim cher - ee, chim cher - oo!"

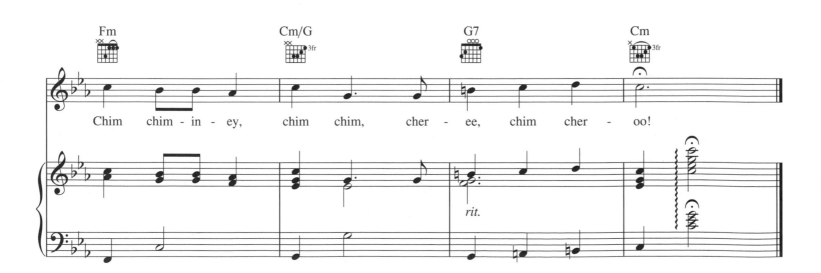

Chim chim - in - ey, chim chim, cher - ee, chim cher - oo!

rit.

THE CRYING GAME
from THE CRYING GAME

Words and Music by
GEOFF STEPHENS

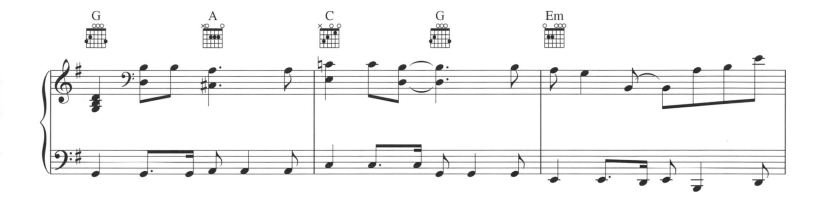

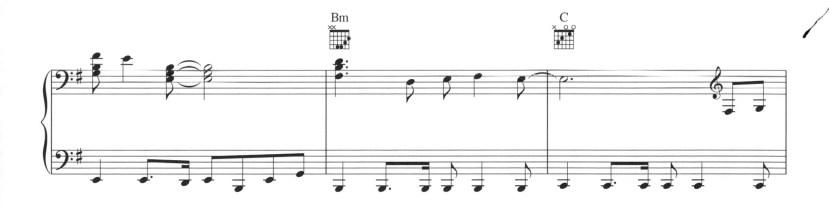

I know _ all there
Instrumental solo

is to know __ a - bout the cry - ing game. __

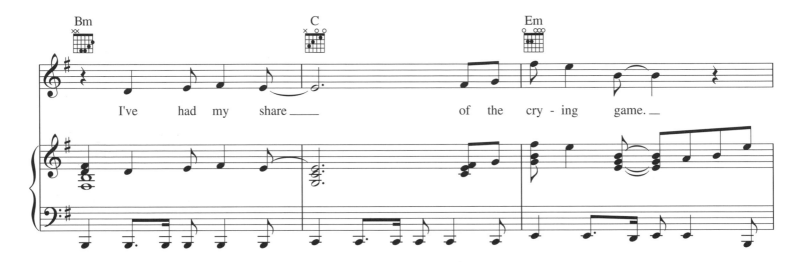

I've had my share _____ of the cry - ing game. __

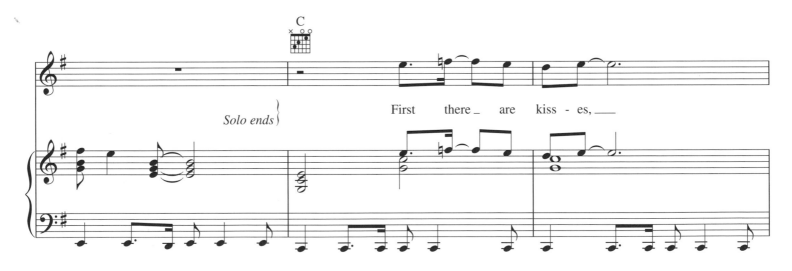

Solo ends

First there _ are kiss - es, __

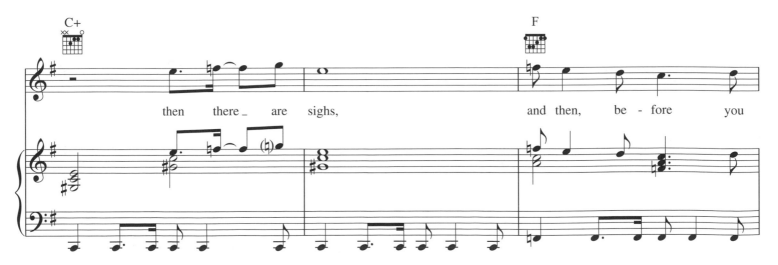

then there _ are sighs,   and then, be - fore you

To Coda ⊕

know where_ you are, you're say-ing good-bye. ____

One day_ soon, I'm gon-na tell the moon_ a-bout the

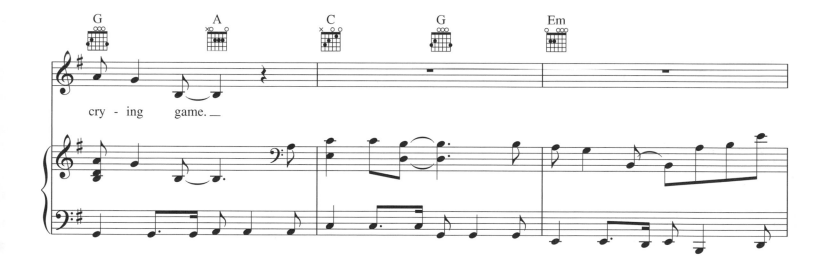

cry-ing game. _

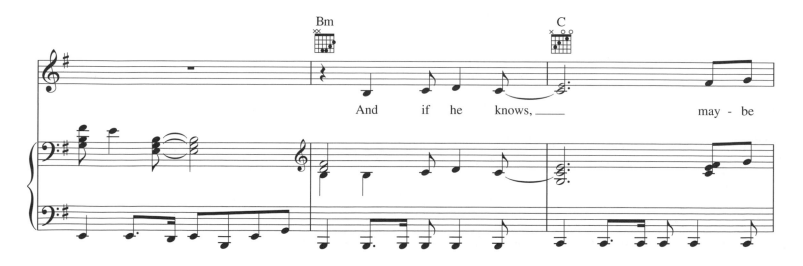

And if he knows, ____ may-be

he'll ex - plain ___ why there ___ are

heart - aches, ___ why there ___ are tears,

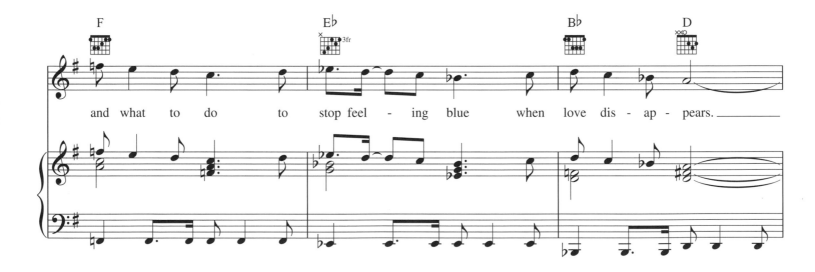

and what to do to stop feel - ing blue when love dis - ap - pears. _____

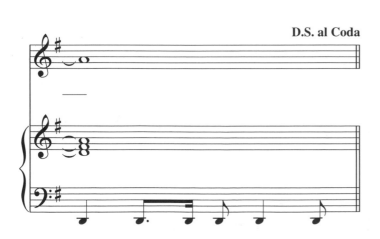

___

D.S. al Coda

CODA

Don't want no more _____

of the cry - ing game._____ I

don't want no more_____ of the cry - ing game._____

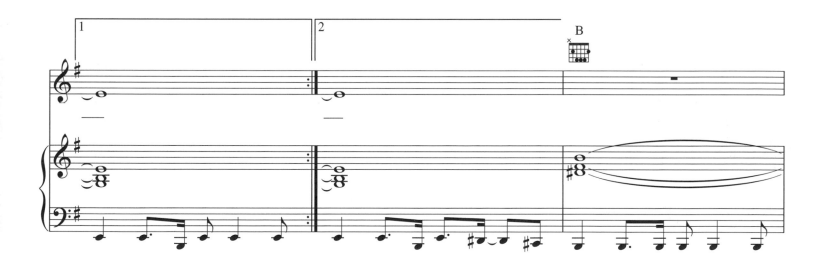

Oh! _____

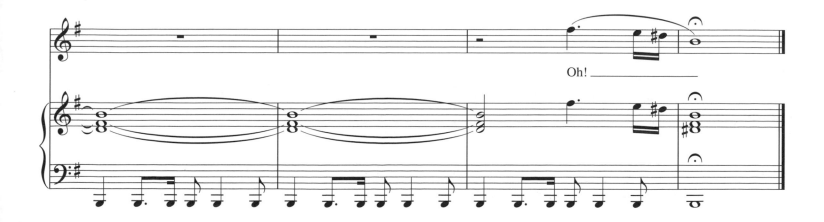

CINEMA PARADISO

from CINEMA PARADISO

Music by ENNIO MORRICONE

Simply, with feeling

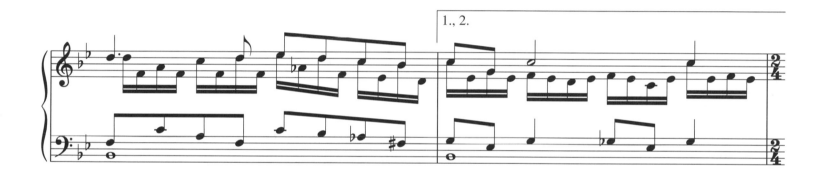

DANCING QUEEN

from MAMMA MIA!

Words and Music by BENNY ANDERSSON,
BJÖRN ULVAEUS and STIG ANDERSON

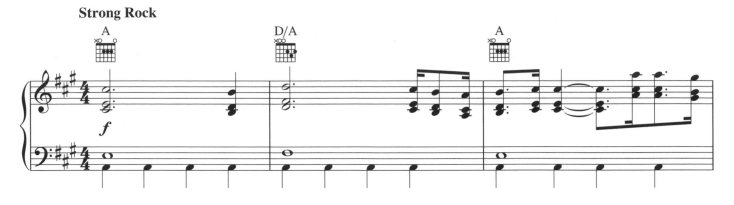

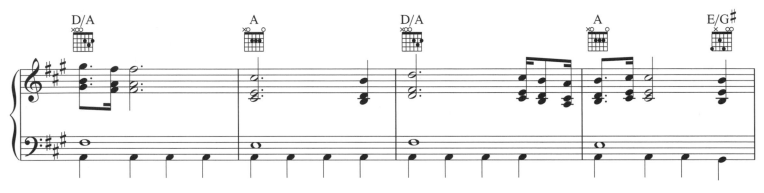

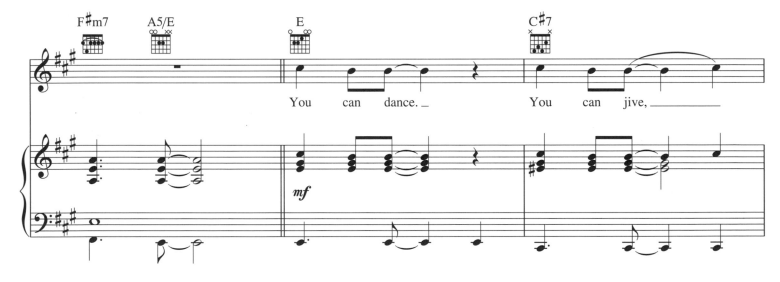

You can dance. You can jive, having the time of your life. Oh, see that girl.

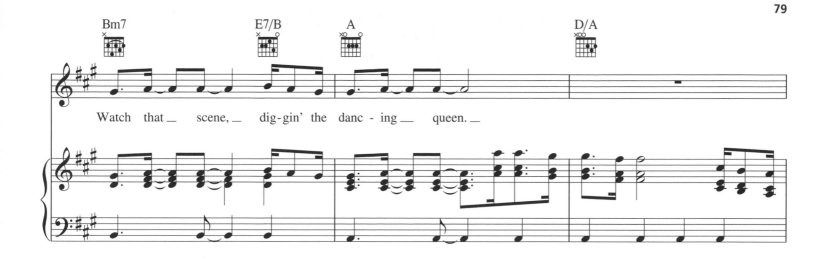

Watch that __ scene, __ dig-gin' the danc-ing __ queen. __

Fri - day night __ and the lights are low. __

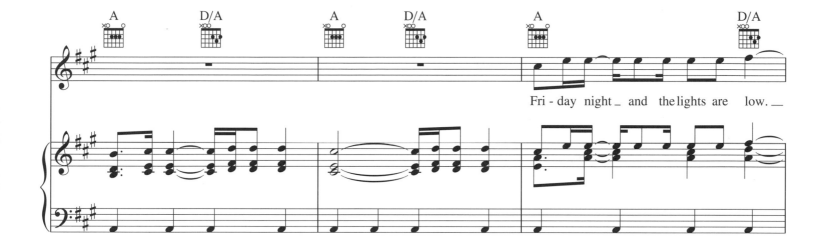

__ Look-ing out __ for a place to go, __ oh, __

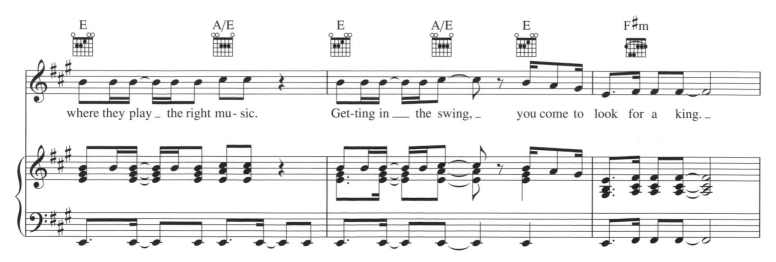

where they play __ the right mu - sic. Get-ting in __ the swing, __ you come to look for a king. __

An - y - bod - y could be that guy. ____
You're a teas - er, you turn 'em on; ____

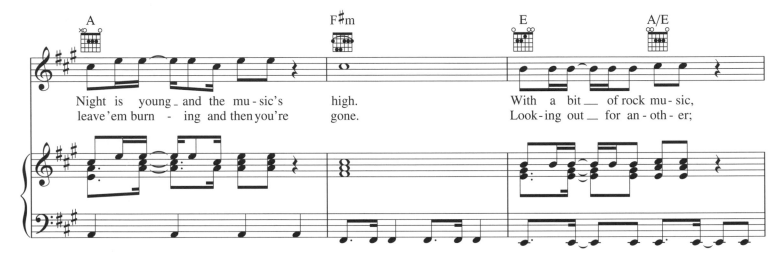

Night is young ___ and the mu - sic's high.
leave 'em burn - ing and then you're gone.

With a bit ___ of rock mu - sic,
Look - ing out ___ for an - oth - er;

ev - 'ry - thing ___ is fine. ⎱ You're in the mood for a dance, ___
an - y - one ___ will do. ⎰

and when ___ you

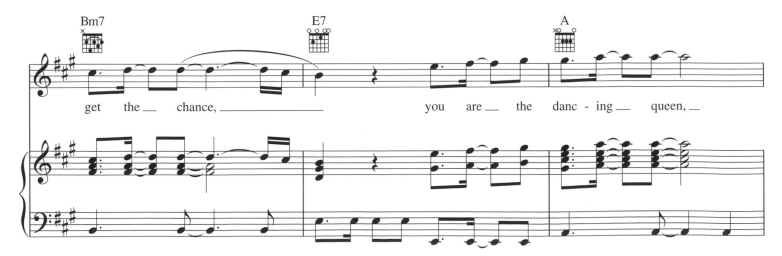

get the ___ chance, _____ you are ___ the danc - ing ___ queen, ___

young and__ sweet,__ on - ly sev - en - teen.__

Danc - ing__ queen,__ feel the__ beat__ from the tam - bou - rine.__

You can dance.__ You can jive,__

hav - ing__ the time of__ your life.__ Oh,__ see that__ girl.__

Watch that ___ scene, ___ dig-gin' the danc - ing ___ queen. ___

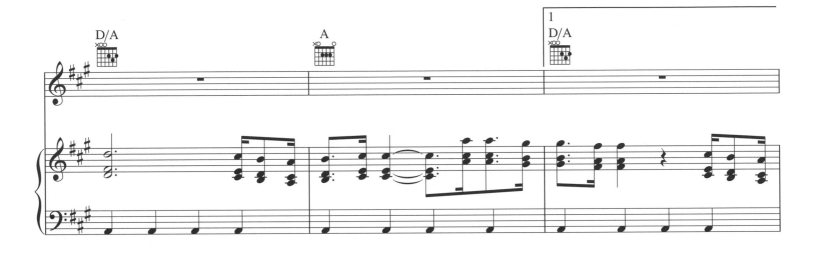

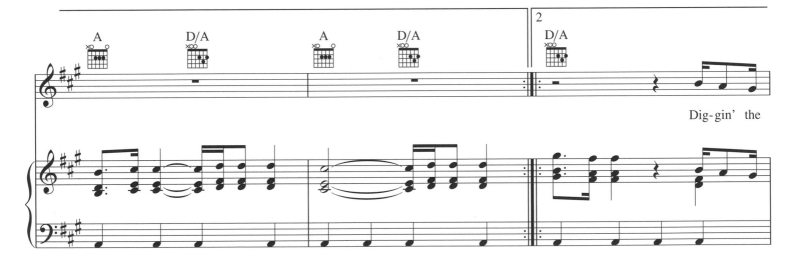

Dig-gin' the

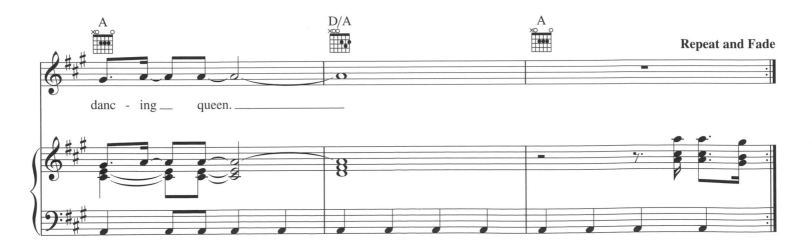

danc - ing ___ queen. _____

Repeat and Fade

DOMINIQUE

from THE SINGING NUN

English Lyrics and Arrangement by NOEL REGNEY
By SOEUR SOURIRE, O.P.

ask - ing for re - ward, he just talks a - bout the
che - mins, en - tous lieux, Il ne parle que du bon

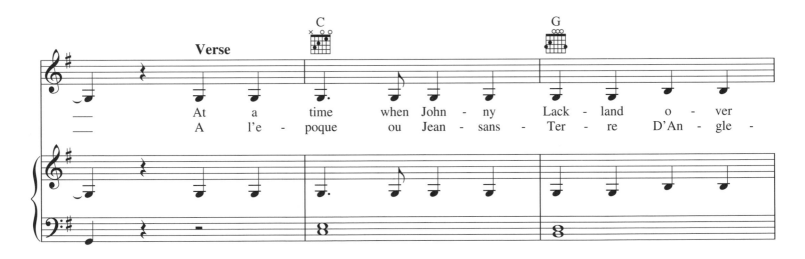

Lord, he just talks a - bout the Lord.
Dieu, Il ne parle a que du bon Dieu.

To Coda

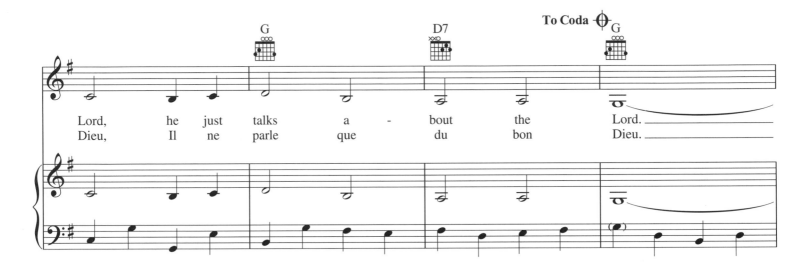

Verse

At a time when John - ny Lack - land o - ver
A l'e - poque ou Jean - sans - Ter - re D'An - gle -

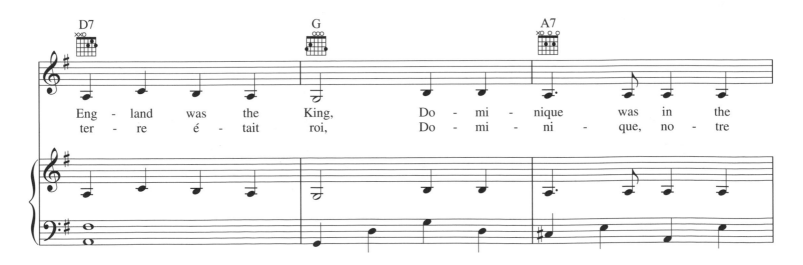

Eng - land was the King, Do - mi - nique was in the
ter - re é - tait roi, Do - mi - ni - que, no - tre

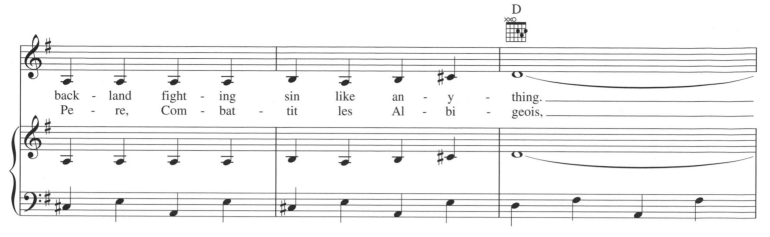

ENGLISH	FRENCH
2. Now a heretic, one day, Among the thorns forced him to crawl. Dominique with just one prayer, Made him hear the good Lord call. (To Refrain)	2. *Certain jour un hérétique* *Par des ronces le conduit* *Mais notre Père Dominique* *Par sa joie le convertit. (Au refrain)*
3. Without horse or fancy wagon, He crossed Europe up and down. Poverty was his companion, As he walked from town to town. (To Refrain)	3. *Ni chameau, ni diligence* *Il parcourt l'Europe à pied.* *Scandinavie ou Provence* *Dans la sainte pauvreté. (Au refrain)*
4. To bring back the straying liars And the lost sheep to the fold, He brought forth the Preaching Friars, Heaven's soldiers, brave and bold. (To Refrain)	4. *Enflamma de toute école* *Filles et garçons pleins d'ardeur,* *Et pour semer la Parole* *Inventa les Frères-Prêcheurs. (Au refrain)*
5. One day, in the budding Order, There was nothing left to eat. Suddenly two angels walked in With a load of bread and meat. (To Refrain)	5. *Chez Dominique et ses frères* *Le pain s'en vint à manquer* *Et deux anges se présentèrent* *Portant de grands pains dorés. (Au refrain)*
6. Dominique once, in his slumber, Saw the Virgin's coat unfurled Over Friars without number Preaching all around the world. (To Refrain)	6. *Dominique vit en rêve* *Le prêcheurs du monde entier* *Sous le manteau de la Vierge* *En grand nombre rassemblés. (Au refrain)*
7. Grant us now, oh Dominique, The grace of love and simple mirth, That we all may help to quicken Godly life and truth on earth. (To Refrain)	7. *Dominique, mon bon Père,* *Garde-nous simples et gais* *Pour annoncer à nos frères* *La Vie et la Vérité. (Au refrain)*

DO-RE-MI
from THE SOUND OF MUSIC

Lyrics by OSCAR HAMMERSTEIN II
Music by RICHARD RODGERS

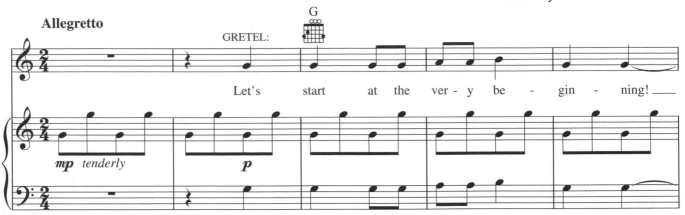

GRETEL: Let's start at the ver-y be-gin-ning! ___

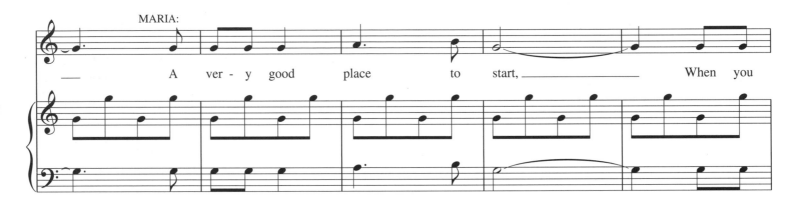

MARIA: ___ A ver-y good place to start, _____ When you

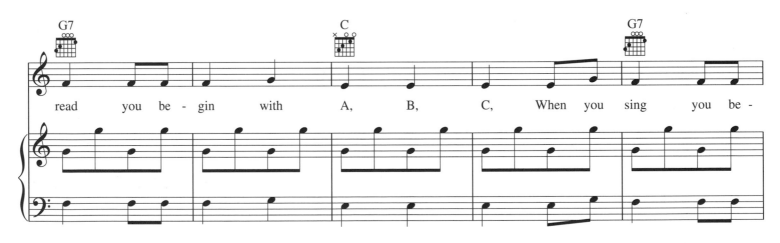

read you be-gin with A, B, C, When you sing you be-

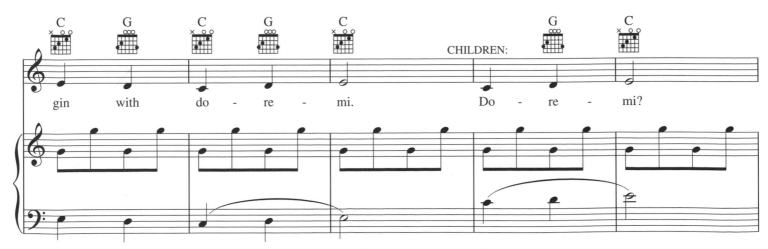

gin with do-re-mi. **CHILDREN:** Do-re-mi?

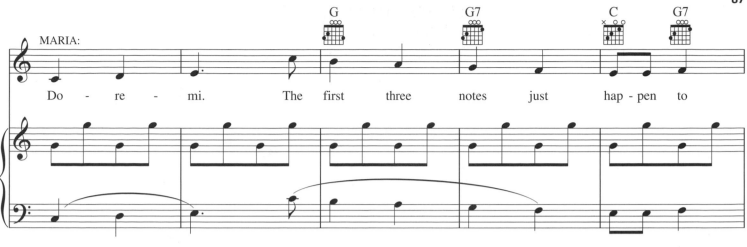

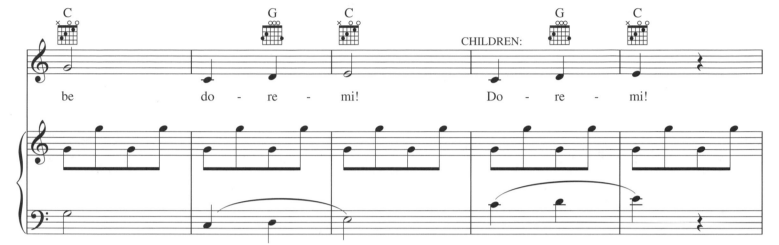

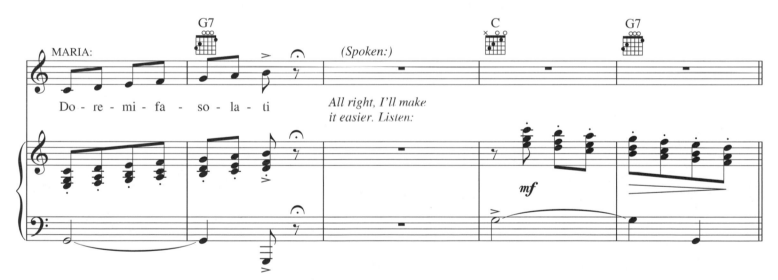

Refrain *(in spirited tempo)*

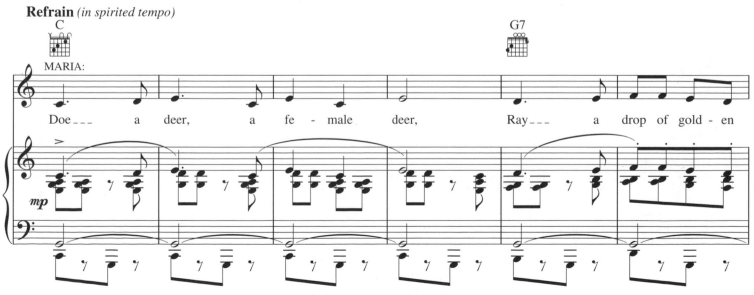

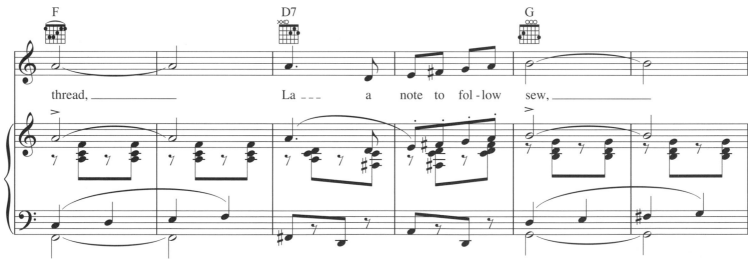

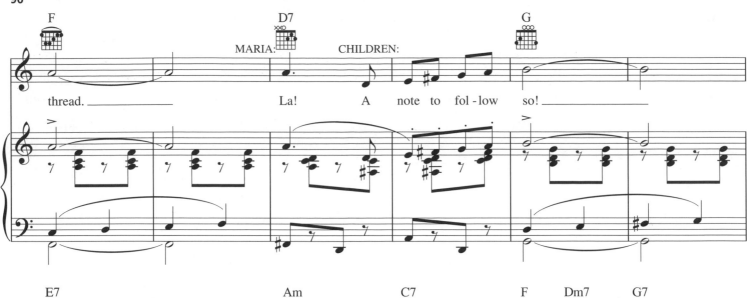

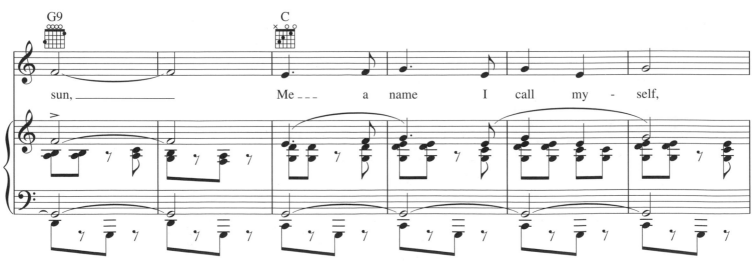

Far___ a long, long way to run.___ Sew___ a nee-dle pull-ing

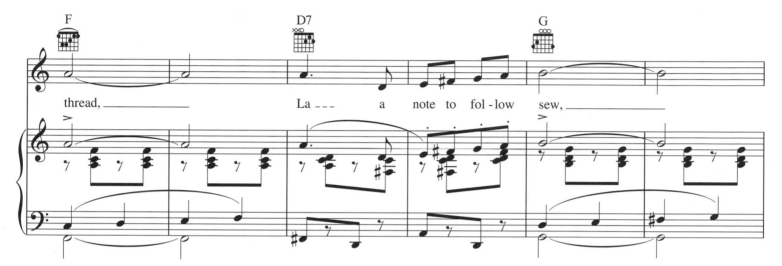

thread,___ La___ a note to fol-low sew,___

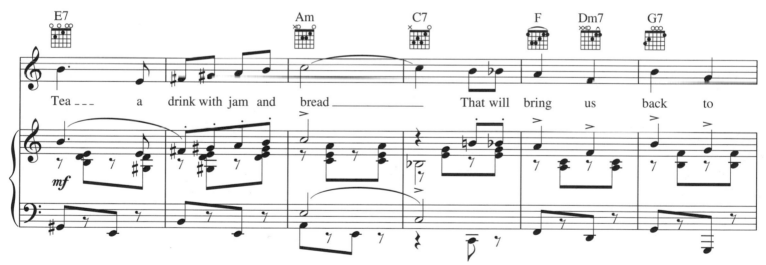

Tea___ a drink with jam and bread___ That will bring us back to

doe!___ Do-re-mi-fa-so-la-ti-do!___

DREAMS TO DREAM
(Finale Version)
from the Universal Motion Picture AN AMERICAN TAIL: FIEVEL GOES WEST

Words and Music by JAMES HORNER
and WILL JENNINGS

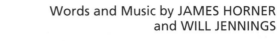

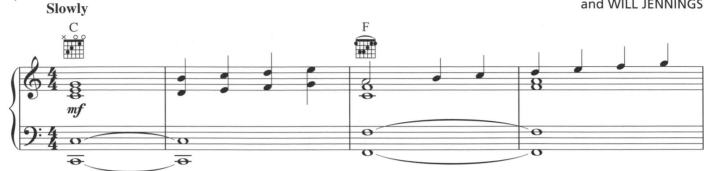

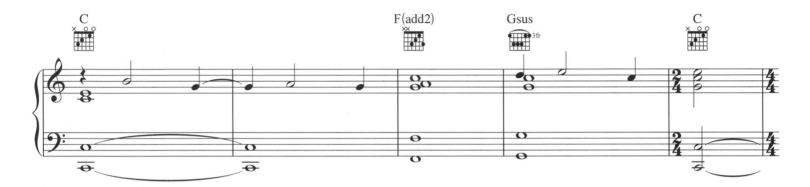

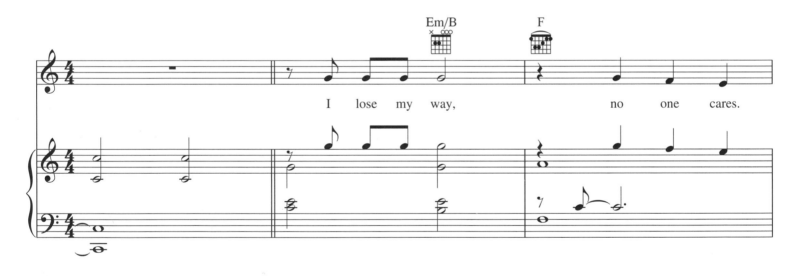

I lose my way, no one cares.

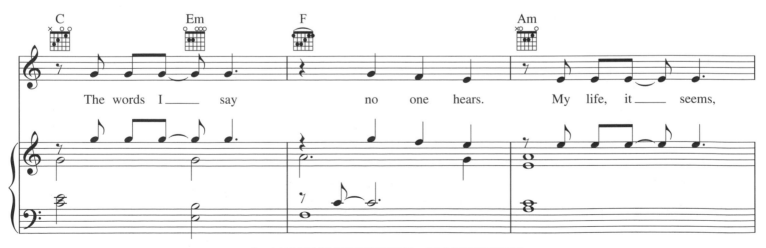

The words I ___ say no one hears. My life, it ___ seems,

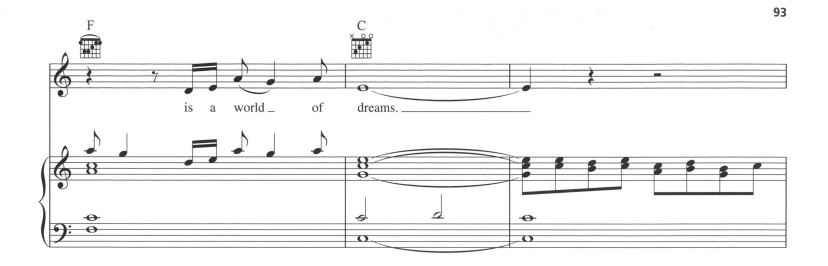

is a world __ of dreams. _____

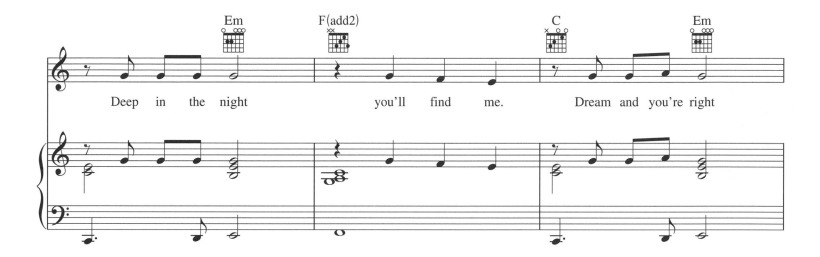

Deep in the night __ you'll find me. Dream and you're right

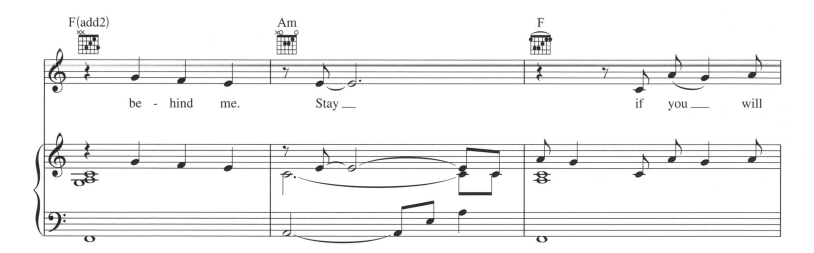

be - hind me. Stay __ if you __ will

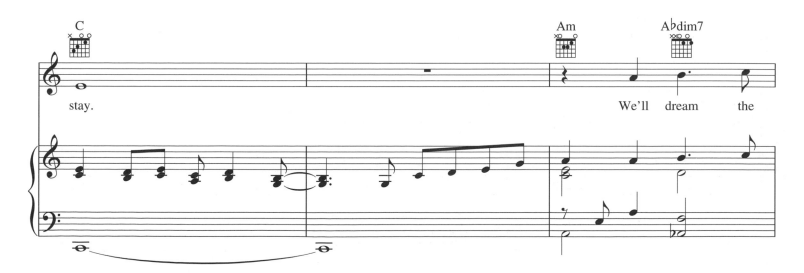

stay. We'll dream the

Slightly faster

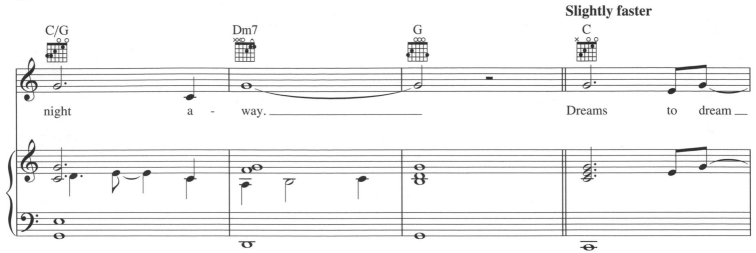

night a - way. _____ Dreams to dream _____

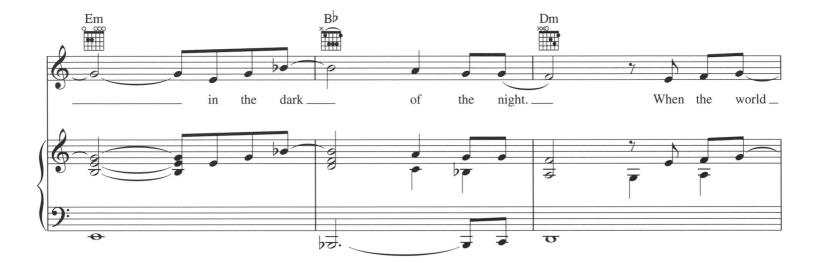

_____ in the dark _____ of the night. _____ When the world _____

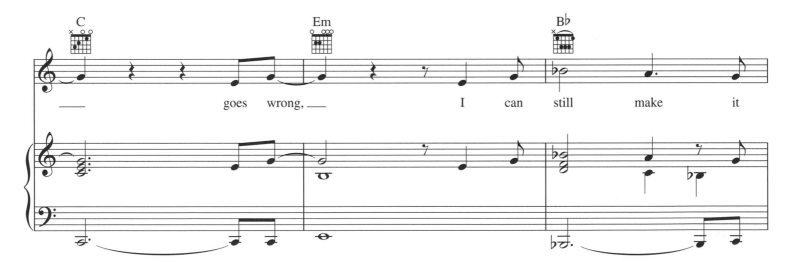

_____ goes wrong, _____ I can still make it

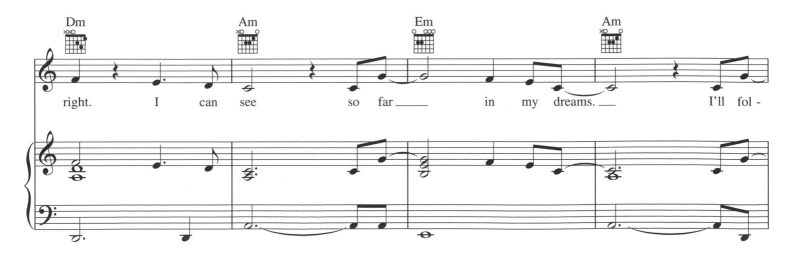

right. I can see so far _____ in my dreams. _____ I'll fol -

-low my dreams ___ un - til ___ they come ___

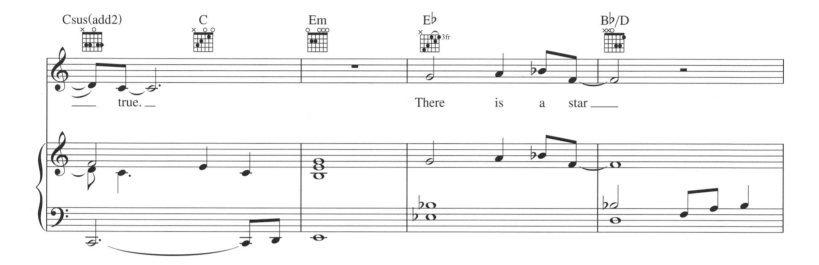

___ true. ___ There is a star ___

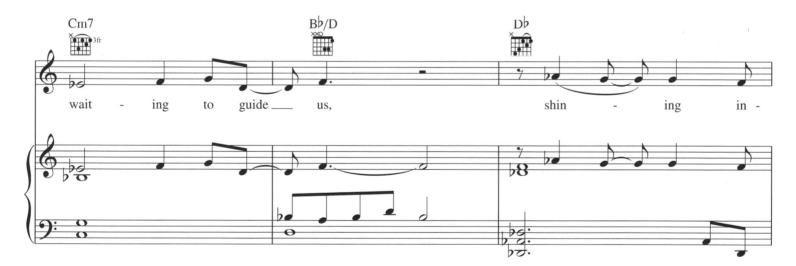

wait - ing to guide ___ us, shin - ing in -

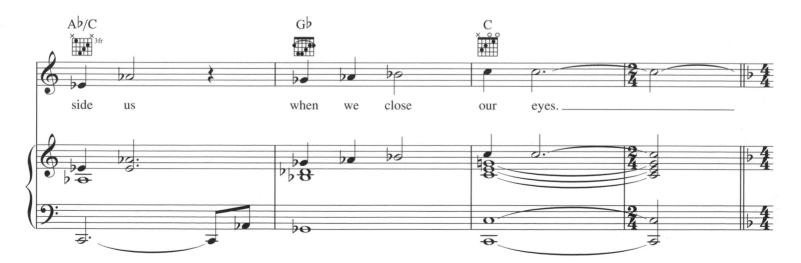

side us when we close our eyes. ___

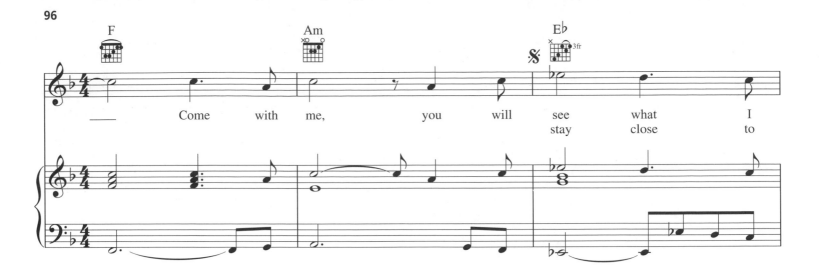

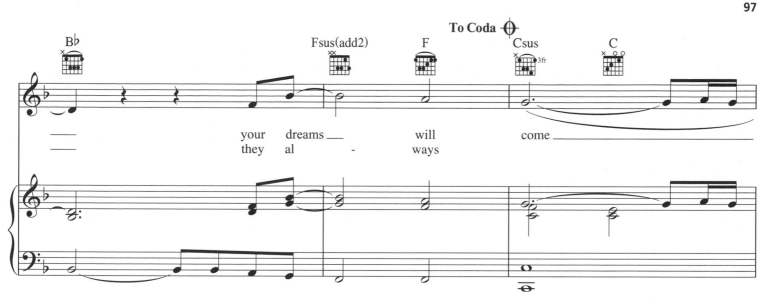

your dreams ___ will come _____
they al - will ways

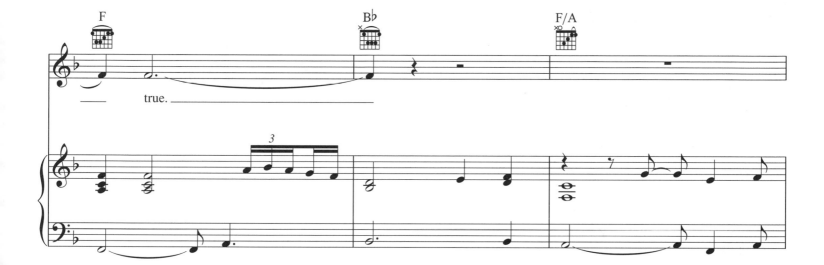

___ true.

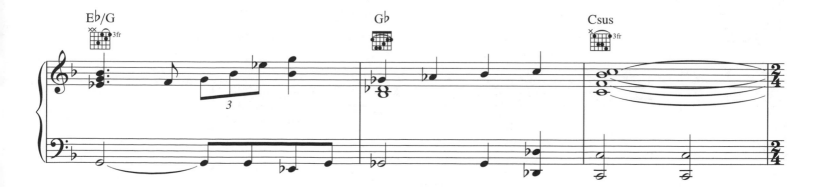

D.S. al Coda

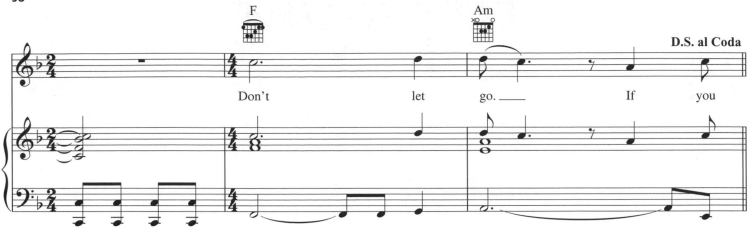

Don't let go. ___ If you

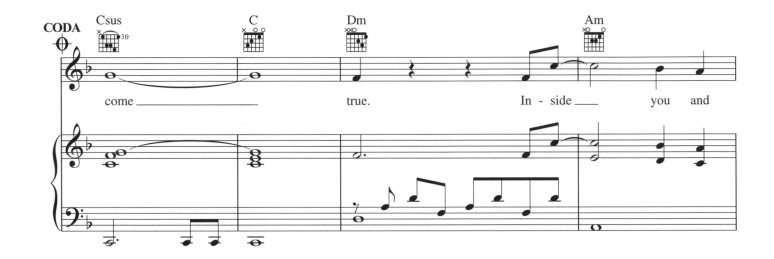

CODA

come _____ true. In - side ___ you and

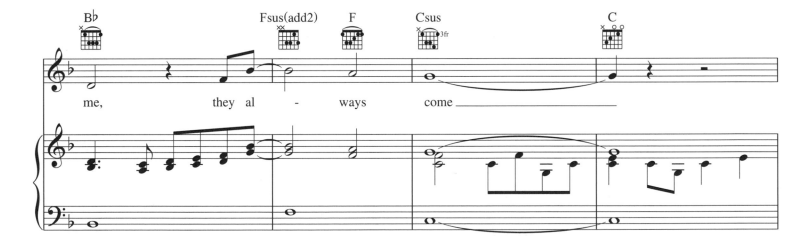

me, they al - ways come _____

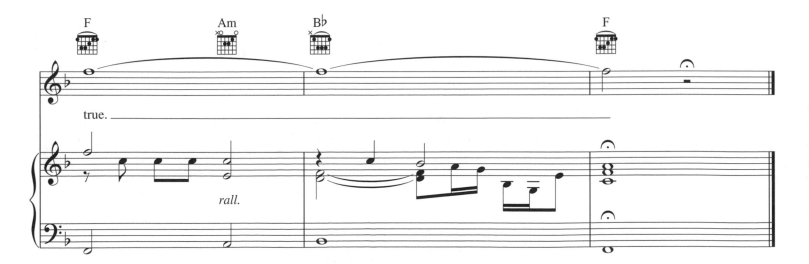

true. _____

rall.

EASY TO LOVE
(You'd Be So Easy to Love)
from BORN TO DANCE

Words and Music by
COLE PORTER

Moderately

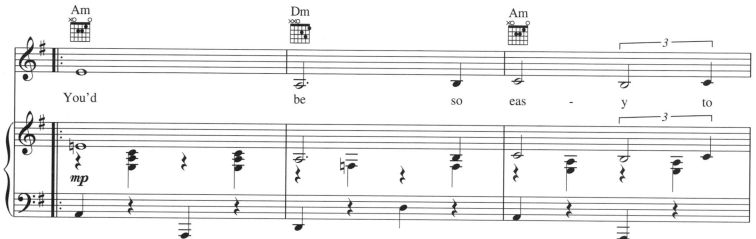

You'd   be   so eas - y to

love,   so eas - y to i - dol - ize, all

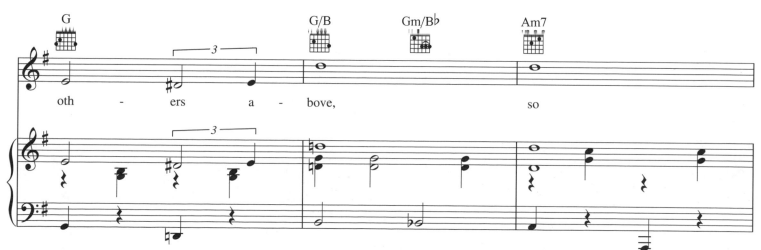

oth - ers a - bove,   so

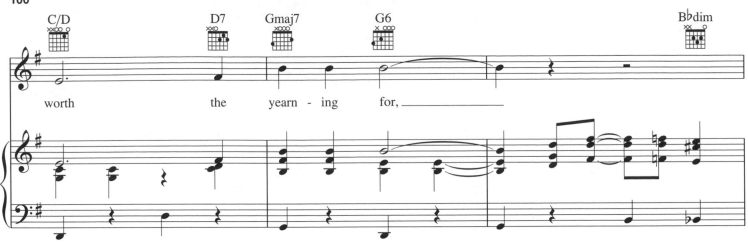

worth the yearn - ing for, _____

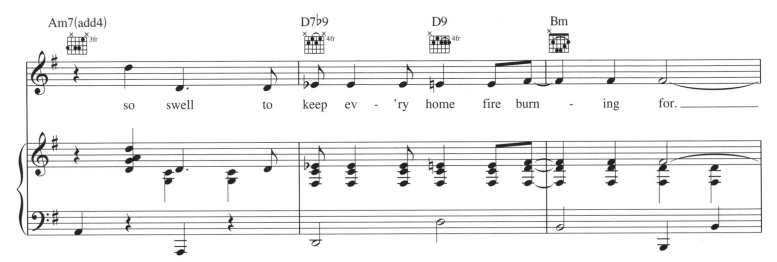

so swell to keep ev - 'ry home fire burn - ing for. _____

We'd be so

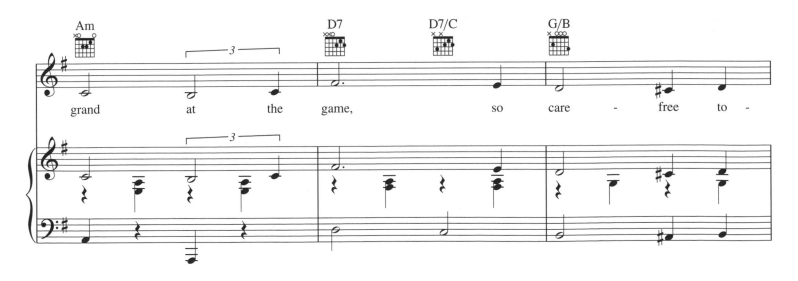

grand at the game, so care - free to -

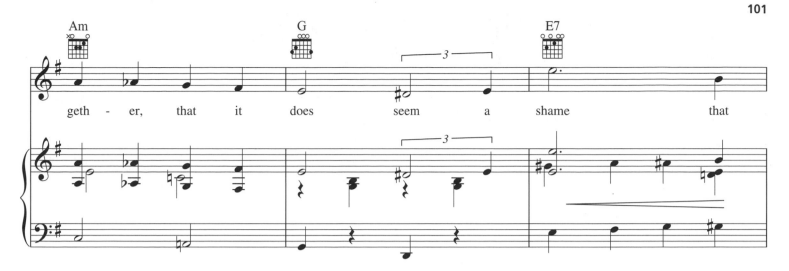

geth - er, that it does seem a shame that

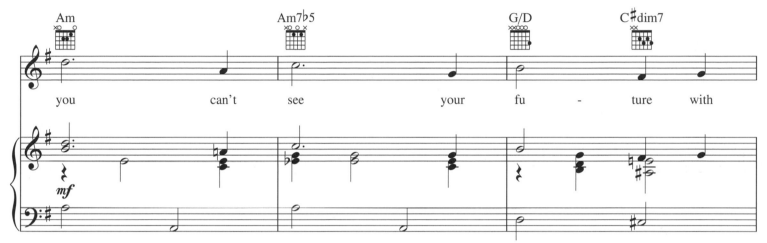

you can't see your fu - ture with

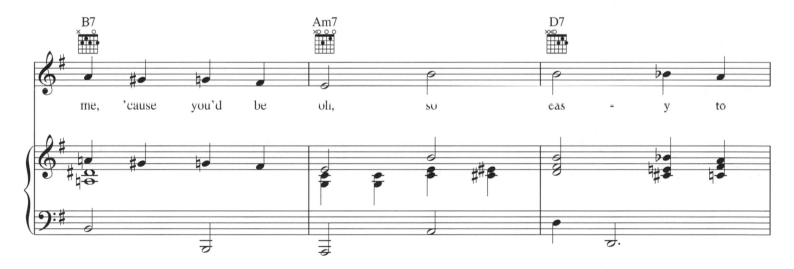

me, 'cause you'd be oh, so eas - y to

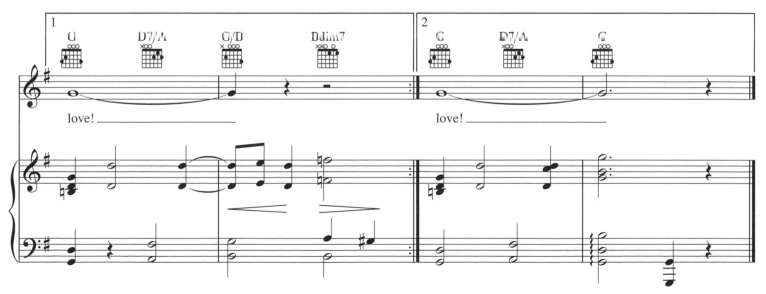

love! _____

love! _____

THE ENGLISH PATIENT
from THE ENGLISH PATIENT

Written by
GABRIEL YARED

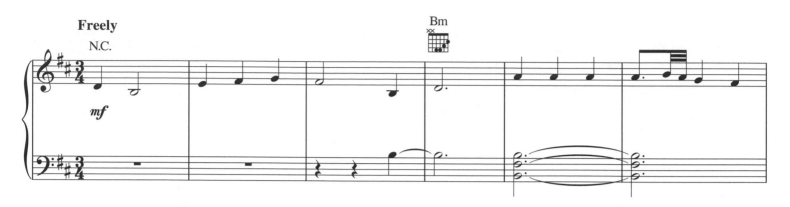

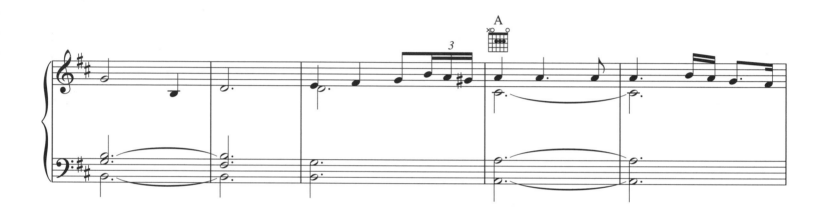

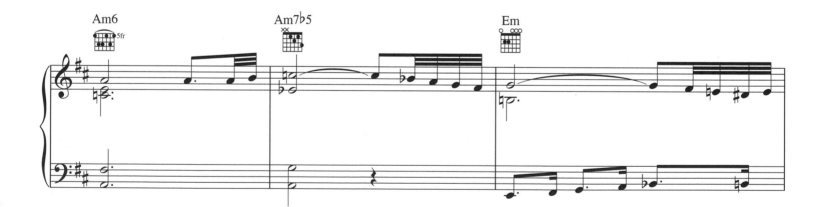

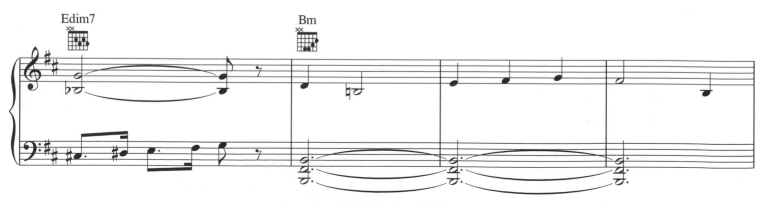

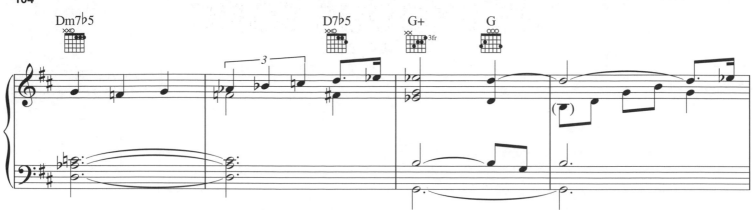

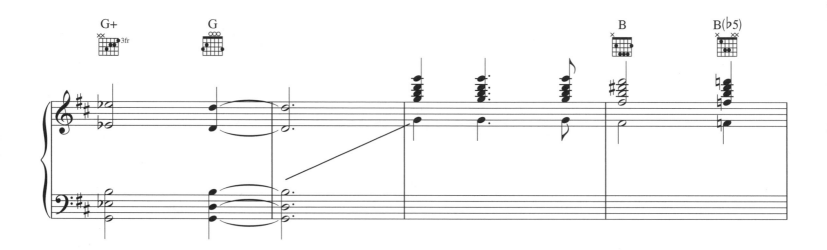

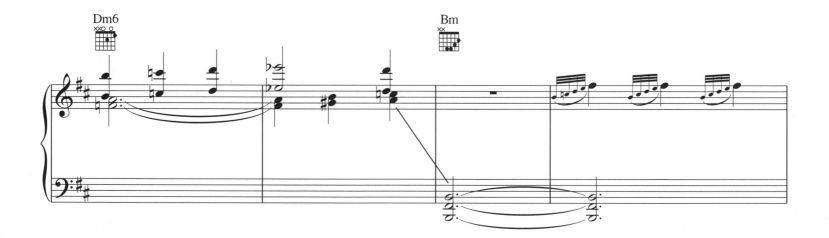

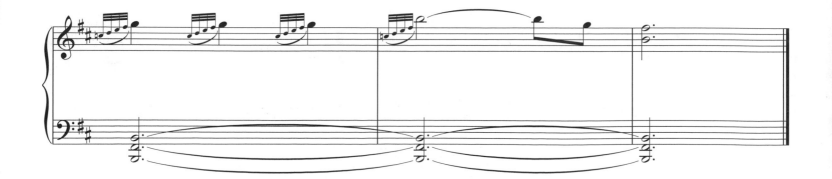

THE EXODUS SONG

from EXODUS

Words by PAT BOONE
Music by ERNEST GOLD

help of God I know I can be strong. So strong. To

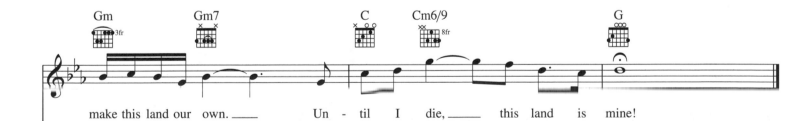

make this land our home, _____ if I must fight, _____ I'll fight to

make this land our own. _____ Un - til I die, _____ this land is mine!

THEME FROM E.T.
(The Extra-Terrestrial)
from the Universal Picture E.T. (THE EXTRA-TERRESTRIAL)

Music by
JOHN WILLIAMS

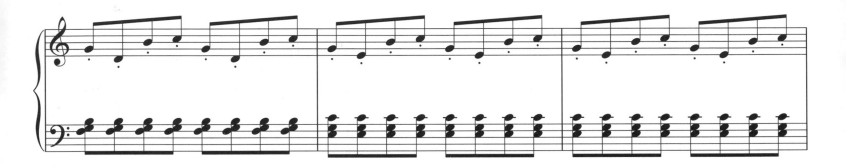

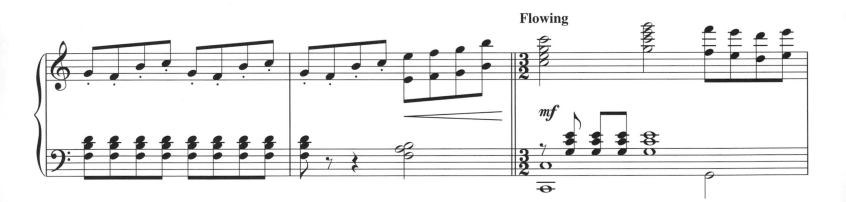

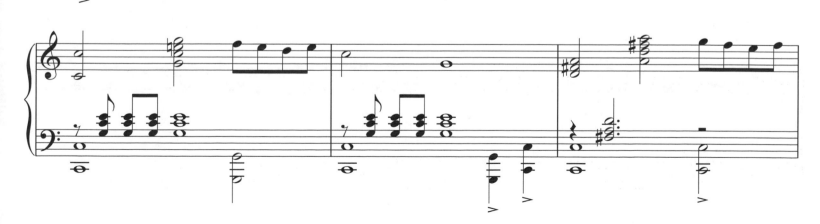

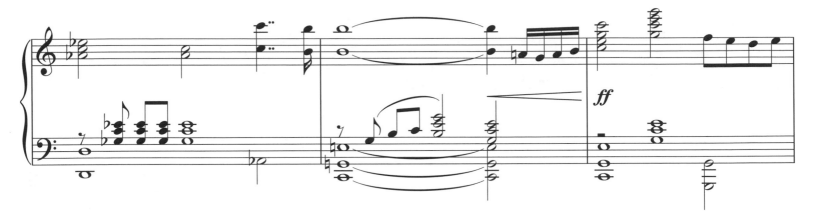

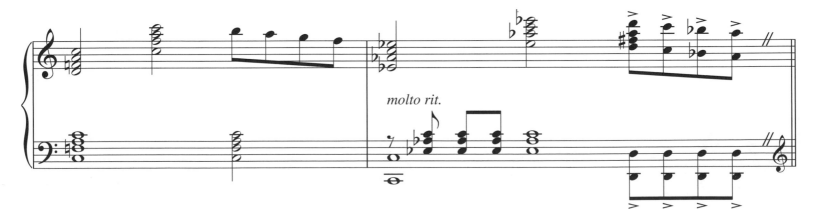

Meno mosso (In 3)

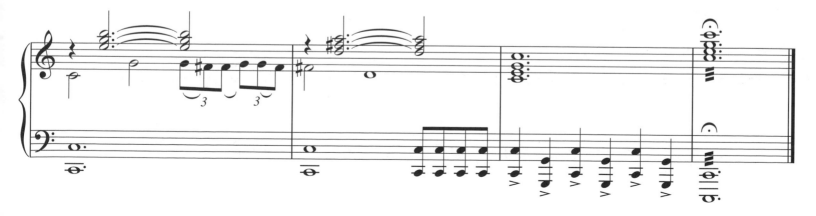

FORREST GUMP – MAIN TITLE
(Feather Theme)
from the Paramount Motion Picture FORREST GUMP

Music by ALAN SILVESTRI

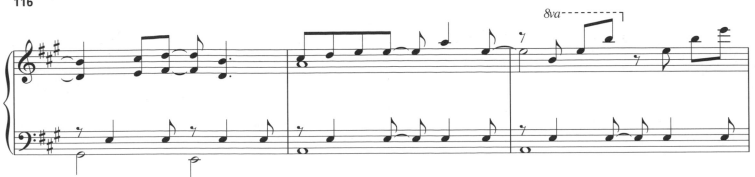

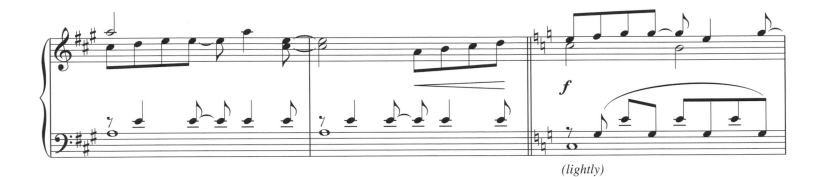

(lightly)

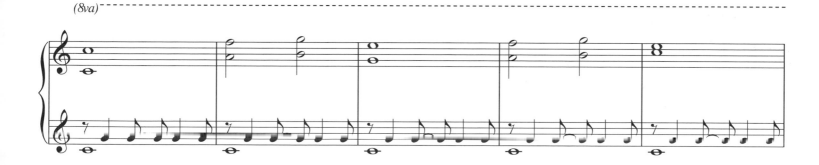

GEORGIA ON MY MIND

from RAY

Words by STUART GORRELL
Music by HOAGY CARMICHAEL

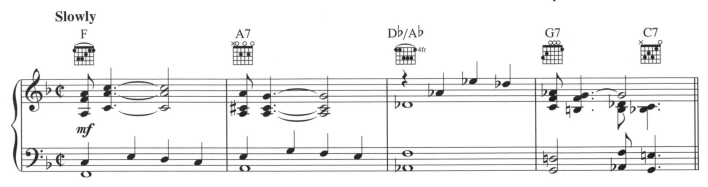

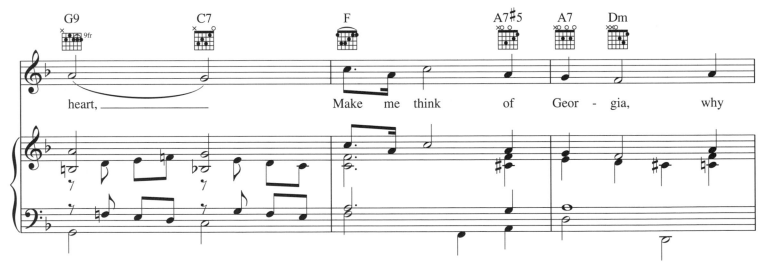

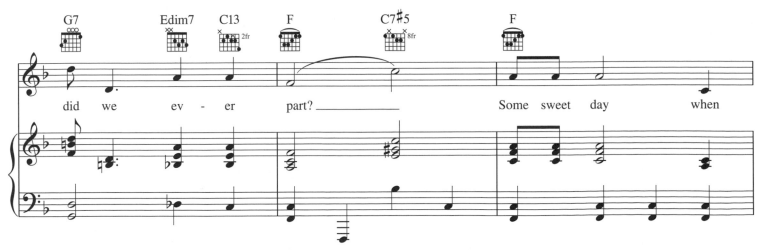

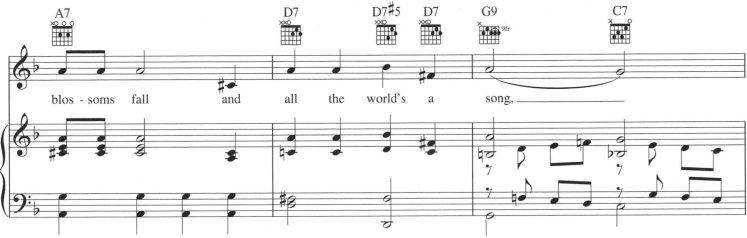

blos - soms fall and all the world's a song,

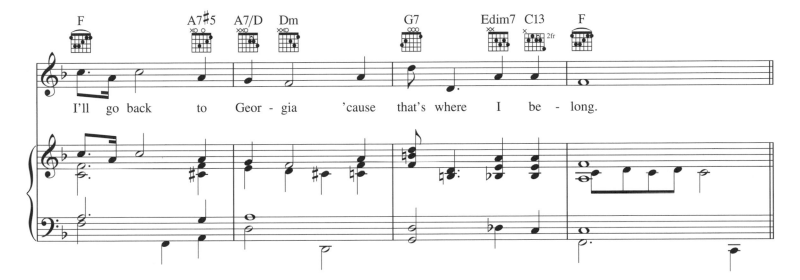

I'll go back to Geor - gia 'cause that's where I be - long.

Geor - gia, Geor - gia, the whole day

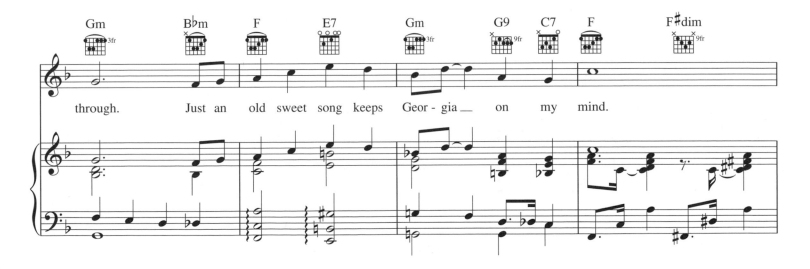

through. Just an old sweet song keeps Geor - gia on my mind.

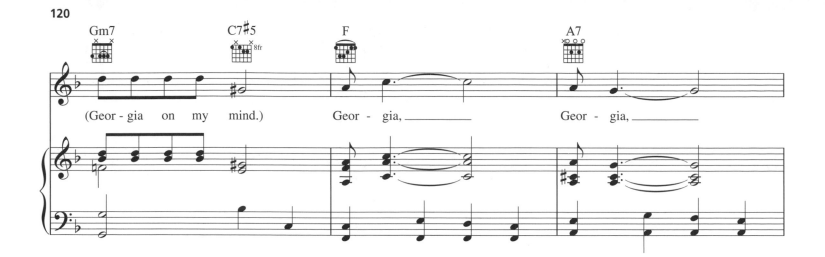

(Geor-gia on my mind.) Geor-gia, _____ Geor-gia, _____

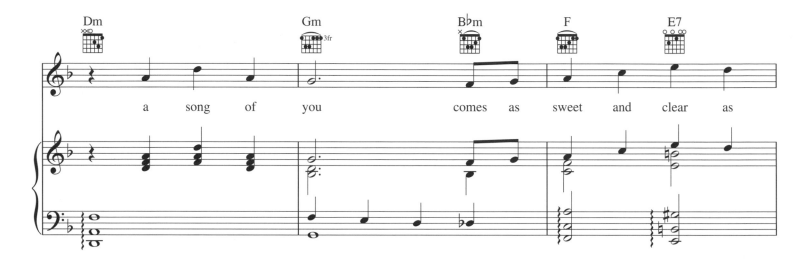

a song of you comes as sweet and clear as

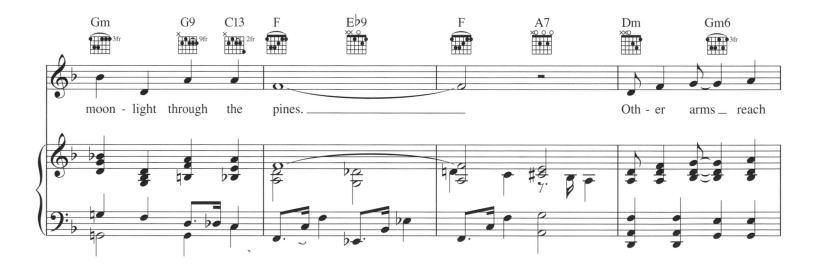

moon-light through the pines. _____ Oth-er arms_ reach

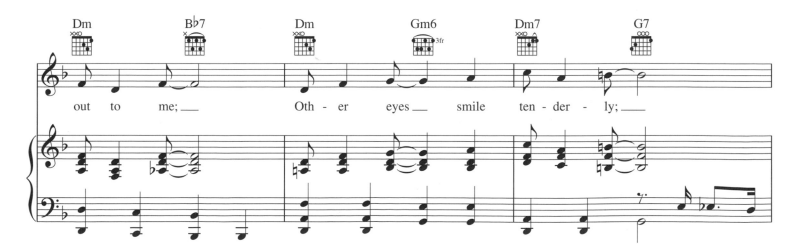

out to me; __ Oth-er eyes_ smile ten-der-ly; __

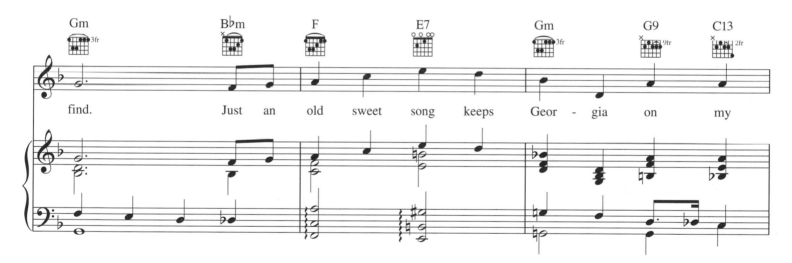

GEORGY GIRL
from GEORGY GIRL

Words by JIM DALE
Music by TOM SPRINGFIELD

Moderately

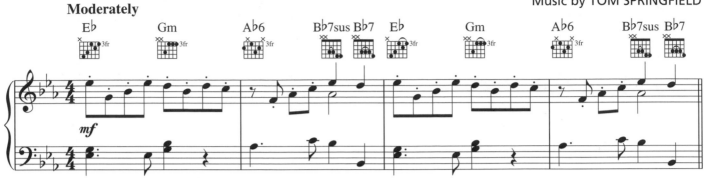

Hey there! __ Geor- gy Girl, __ swing- ing down the street so

fan- cy free. No- bod- y you meet could ev- er see the

lone- li- ness there in- side you. Hey there! __ Geor- gy Girl, __

why do all the boys just pass you by? Could it be you just don't
dream-ing of the some-one you could be. Life is a re-al-i-

try, or is it the clothes you wear? _____ You're al-ways
ty, you can't al-ways run a-way. _____ Don't be so

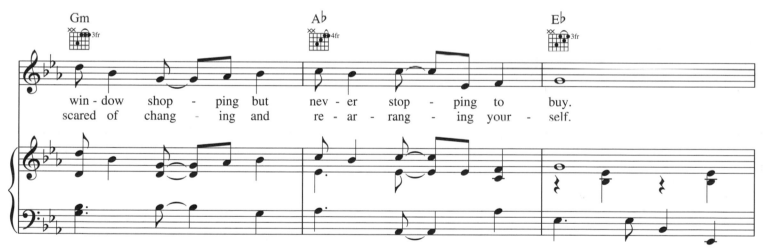

win-dow shop-ping but nev-er stop-ping to buy.
scared of chang-ing and re-ar-rang-ing your-self.

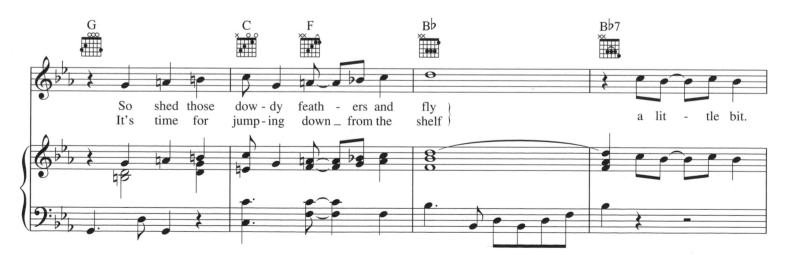

So shed those dow-dy feath-ers and fly
It's time for jump-ing down from the shelf } a lit-tle bit.

Hey there! __ Geor - gy Girl, __ there's an - oth - er Geor - gy deep in - side.

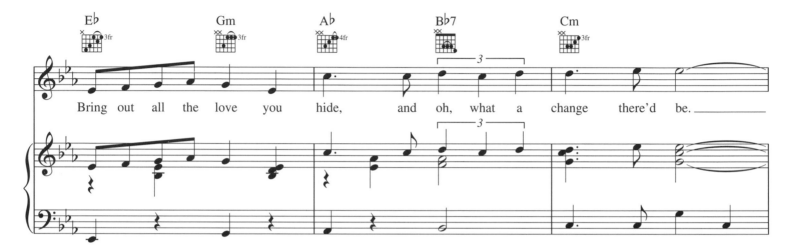

Bring out all the love you hide, and oh, what a change there'd be. __

__ The world would see a new __ Geor - gy Girl. __

Repeat and Fade

__ Girl. A new __ Geor - gy

HOPELESSLY DEVOTED TO YOU

from GREASE

Words and Music by
JOHN FARRAR

Moderate 2

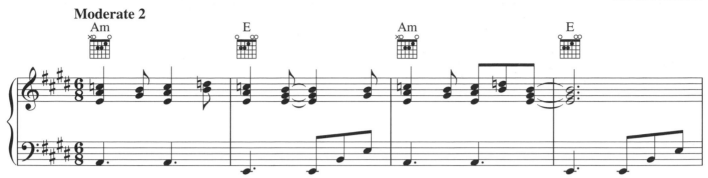

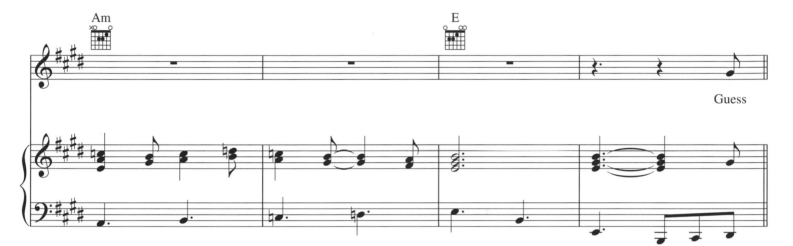

Guess

mine is not the first _____ heart bro - ken, _____ my
know I'm just a fool _____ who's will - in' _____ to
head is say - in', "Fool, _____ for - get him." _____ My

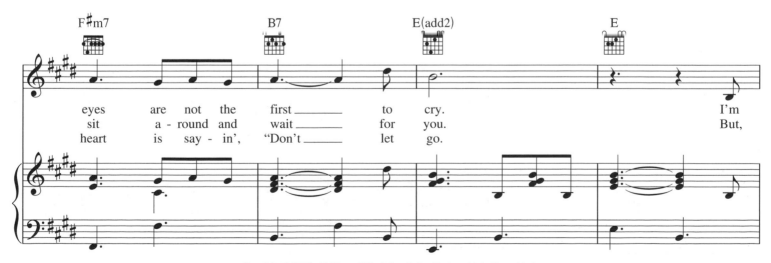

eyes are not the first _____ to cry.
sit a - round and wait _____ for you.
heart is say - in', "Don't _____ let go.

I'm
But,

126

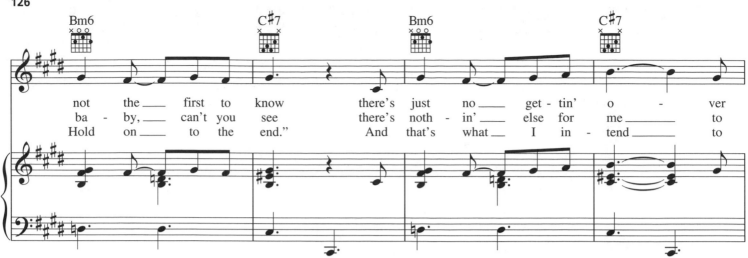

not the ___ first to know there's just no ___ get-tin' o - ver
ba - by, ___ can't you see there's noth-in' else for me ___ to
Hold on ___ to the end." And that's what ___ I in-tend ___ to

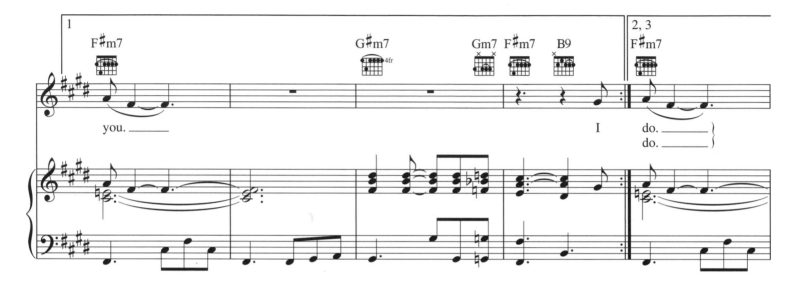

you. ___

I do. ___
do. ___

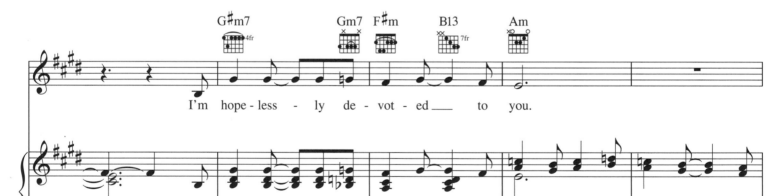

I'm hope-less - ly de - vot-ed ___ to you.

But now there's no - where to hide ___ since you

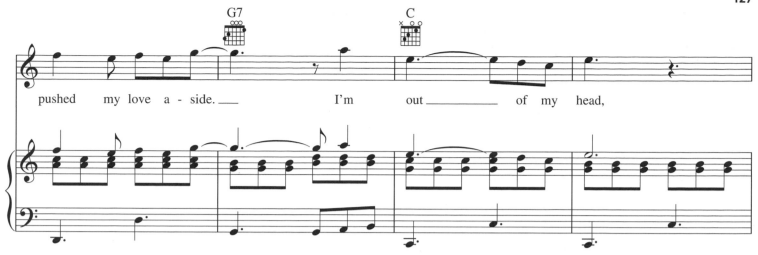

pushed my love a-side.___ I'm out_____ of my head,

hope - less-ly de - vot - ed ___ to you,_____

To Coda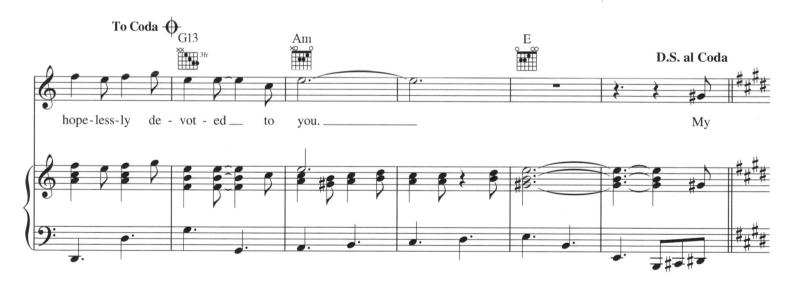

hope-less-ly de - vot - ed ___ to you._____ My

D.S. al Coda

CODA

vot - ed ___ to you._____

HELP!
from HELP!

Words and Music by JOHN LENNON
and PAUL McCARTNEY

Moderately, with a driving beat

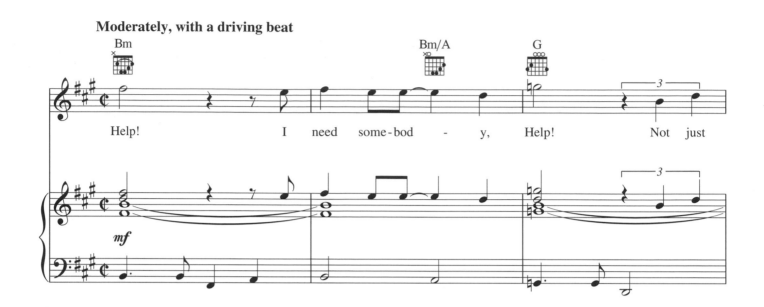

Help!   I need some-bod—y, Help!   Not just

an-y-bod—y, Help!   You know I need some-one, ___

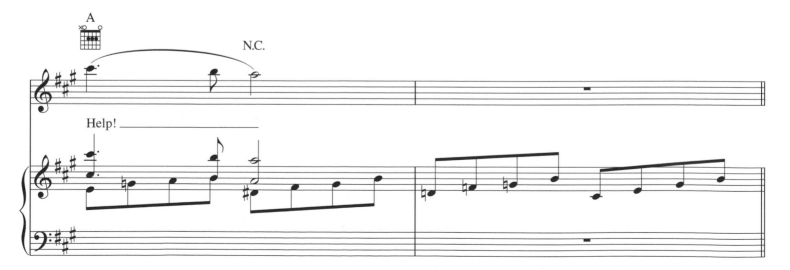

Help! _____

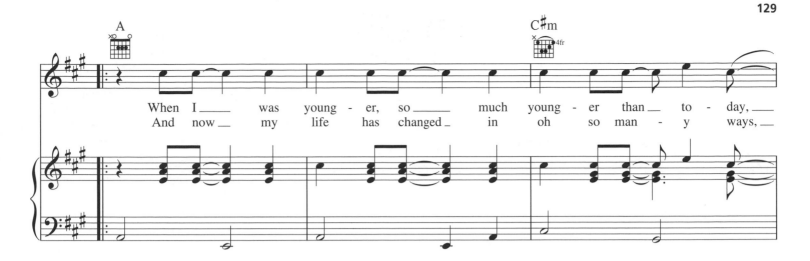

When I ___ was young-er, so ___ much young-er than ___ to-day, ___
And now ___ my life has changed ___ in oh so man-y ways, ___

I nev-er need-ed an-y-bod-y's
My in-de-pen-dence seems ___ to

help in an-y way. ___ But now these
van-ish in the haze. ___ But ev-'ry

days are gone, ___ I'm not so self-as-sured, ___
now and then ___ I feel so in-se-cure, ___

Now I find   I've changed my mind,   I've o - pened up   the doors._
I know that I   just need you like   I've nev - er   done be - fore._

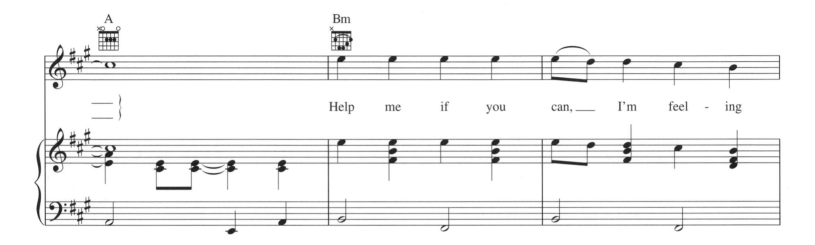

Help   me if   you   can, ___   I'm   feel - ing

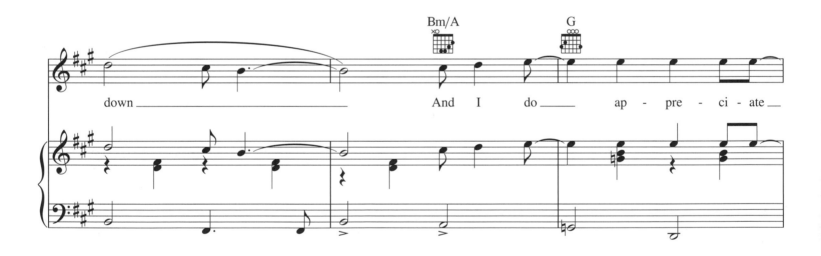

down _____   And   I   do ___   ap - pre - ci - ate ___

___   you   be - ing   'round, _____

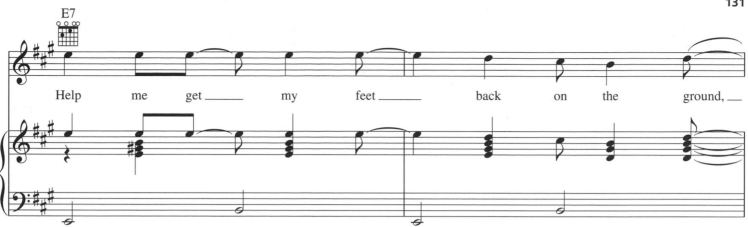

Help me get _____ my feet _____ back on the ground, _____

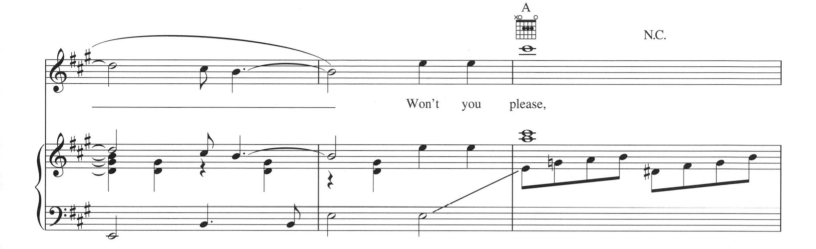

_____ Won't you please,

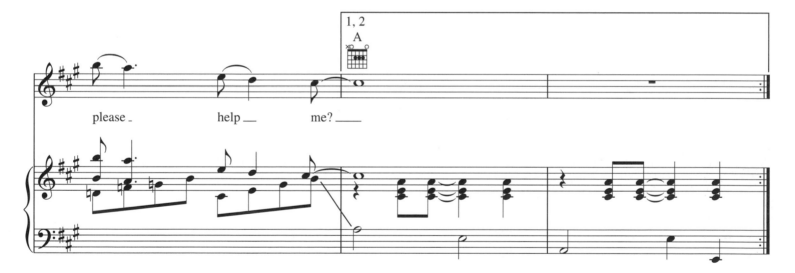

please _ help _ me? _____

_ Help me, help me _____ Ooh.

HIGH NOON
(Do Not Forsake Me)
from HIGH NOON

Words and Music by DIMITRI TIOMKIN
and NED WASHINGTON

or lie a cow - ard, a cra - ven cow - ard,

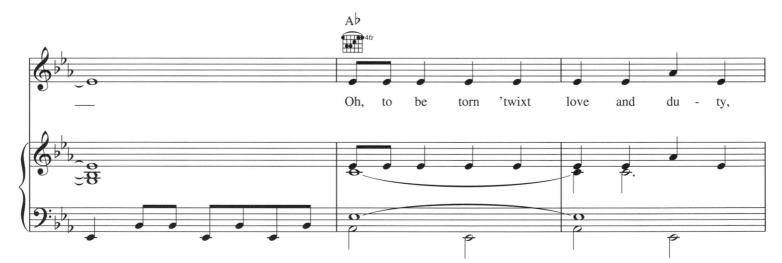

or lie a cow - ard in my grave! _____

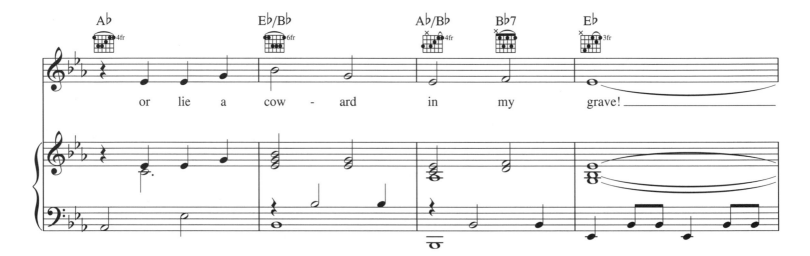

___ Oh, to be torn 'twixt love and du - ty,

s'pos - in' I lose my fair - haired beau - ty. Look at the big hand

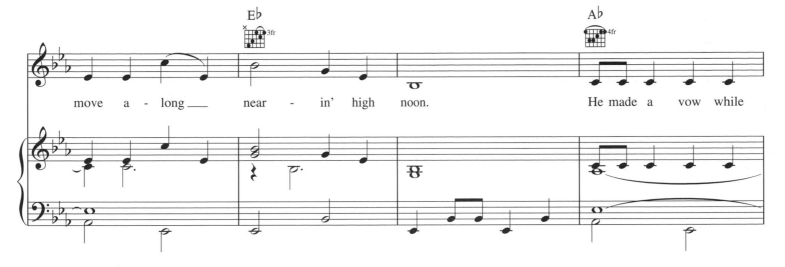

move a - long ___ near - in' high noon. He made a vow while

in state's pris - on, vowed it would be my life or his 'n. I'm not a - fraid of

death but, oh, ___ what will I do if you leave

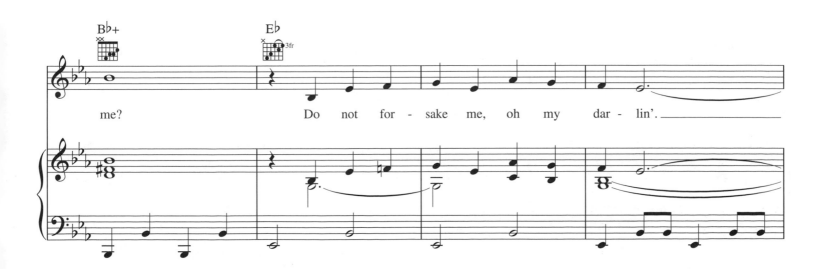

me? Do not for - sake me, oh my dar - lin'. ___

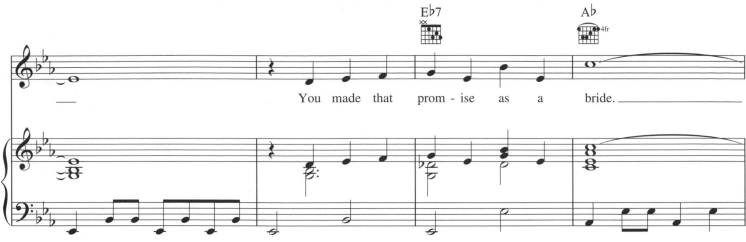

You made that prom-ise as a bride.

Do not for-sake me, oh my dar-lin'.

Al-though you're griev-in', don't think of

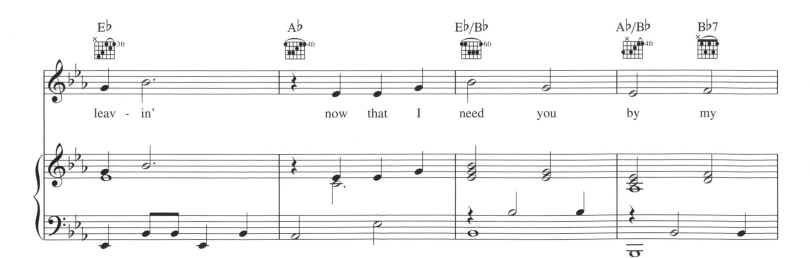

leav-in' now that I need you by my

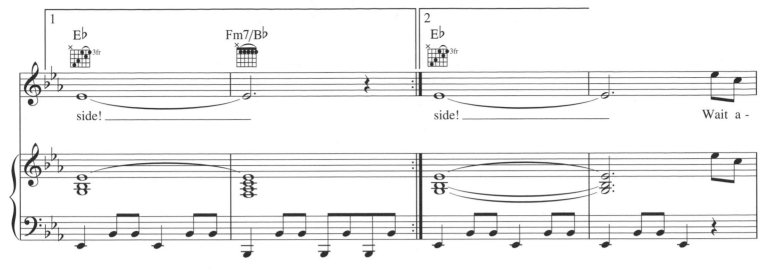

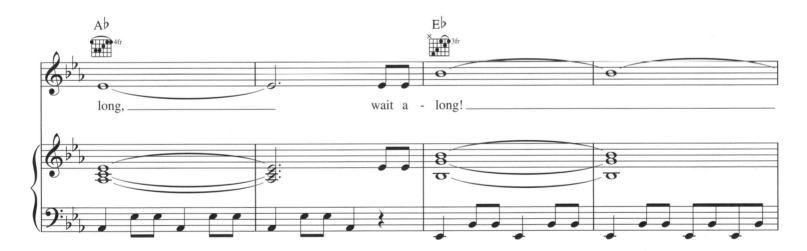

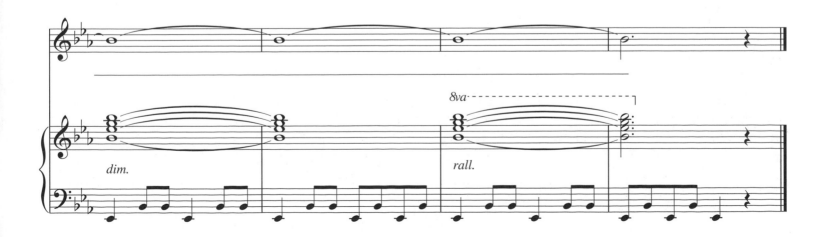

I AM A MAN OF CONSTANT SORROW

featured in O BROTHER, WHERE ART THOU?

Words and Music by
CARTER STANLEY

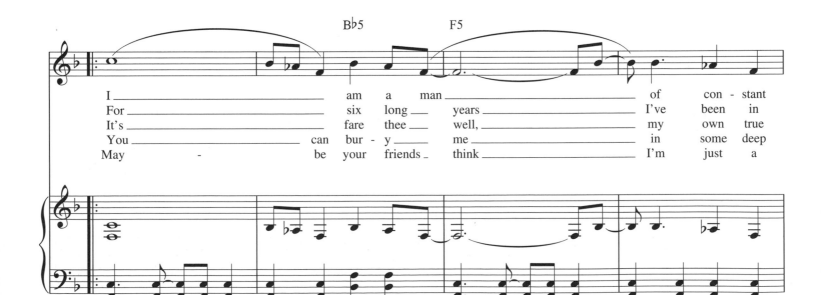

sor - row. _____ I've seen trou ble all __ my
trou - ble, _____ no pleas - ure here _____ on earth I've
lov - er, _____ I nev - er ex - pect _____ to see __ you a -
val - ley _____ for man - y years _____ where I __ may lay,
stran - ger; _____ my face __ you nev - er will see __ no

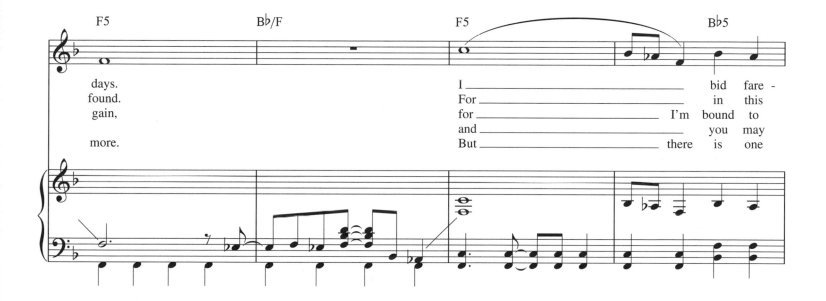

days. I _____ bid fare -
found. For _____ in this
gain, for _____ I'm bound to
more. and _____ you may
But _____ there is one

well _____ to old __ Ken - tuck - y, _____ the place __ where I _____
world _____ I'm bound __ to ram - ble; _____ I have __ no friends _____
ride _____ that North - ern rail - road; _____ per - haps __ I'll die _____
learn _____ to love __ an - oth - er _____ while I __ am sleep -
prom - ise that is giv - en: _____ I'll meet __ you on _____

was born and raised. The place where
to help me now. He has no
up - on this train. Per - haps he'll
ing in my grave. While he is
God's gold - en shore. He'll meet you

he _____ was born and raised.
friends _____ to help him now.
die _____ up - on this train.
sleep - ing in his grave.
on _____ God's gold - en

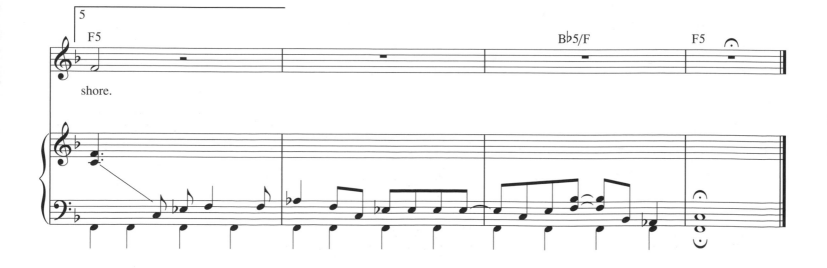

shore.

I COULD HAVE DANCED ALL NIGHT

from MY FAIR LADY

Words by ALAN JAY LERNER
Music by FREDERICK LOEWE

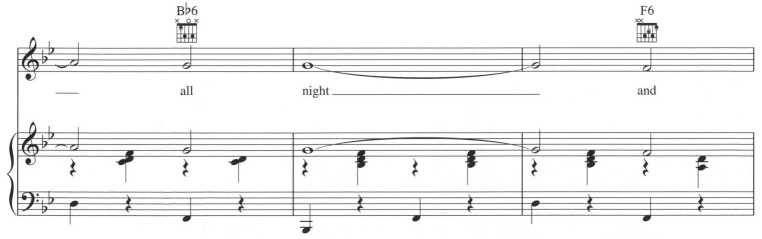

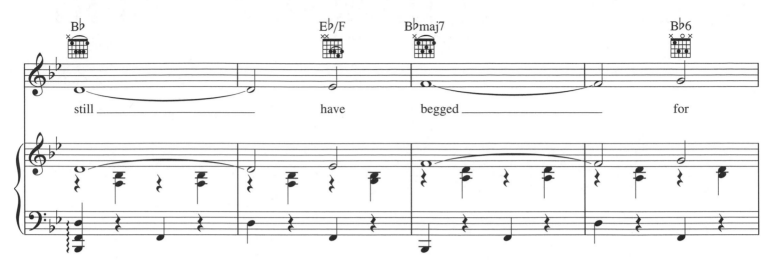

still _____ have begged _____ for

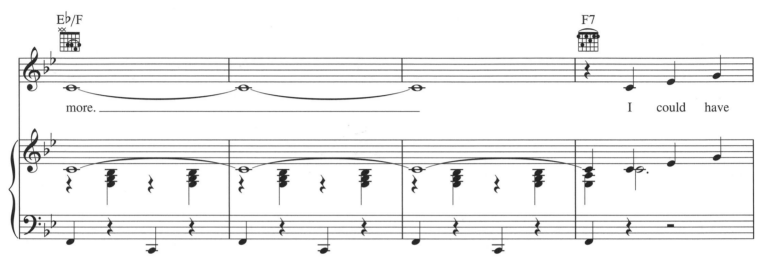

more. _____ I could have

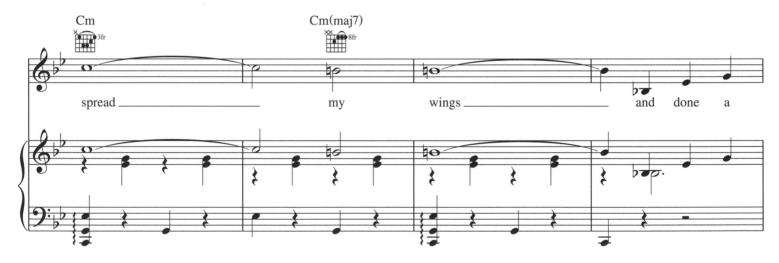

spread _____ my wings _____ and done a

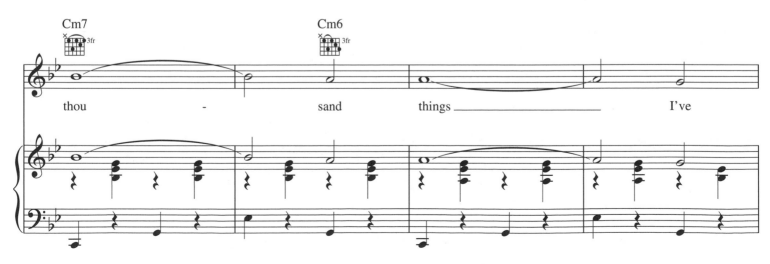

thou - sand things _____ I've

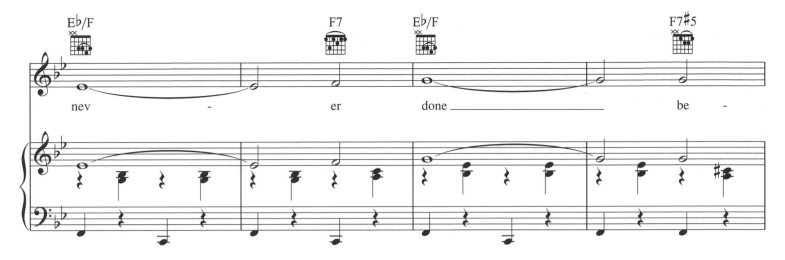

nev - er done _____ be -

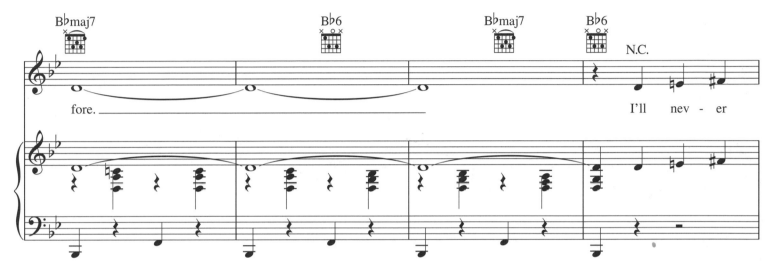

fore. _____ I'll nev - er

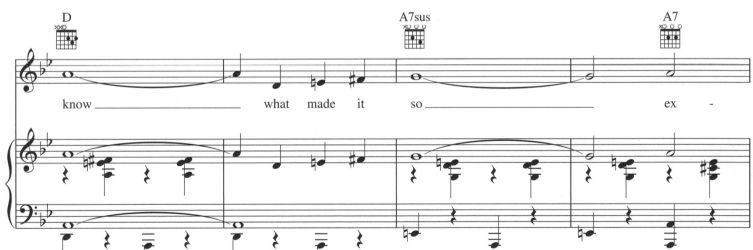

know _____ what made it so _____ ex -

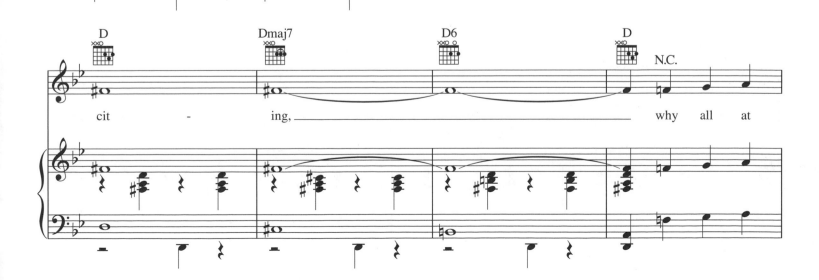

cit - ing, _____ why all at

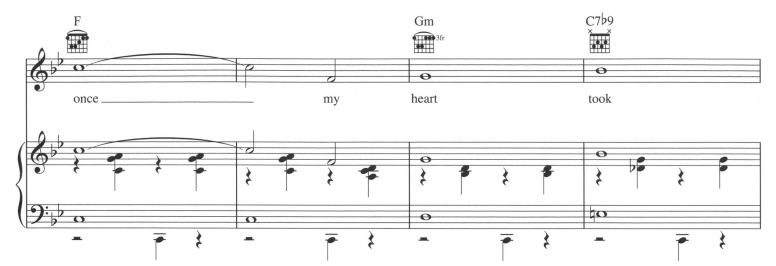

once _____ my heart took

flight. _____ I on - ly

know _____ when he _____ be - gan to

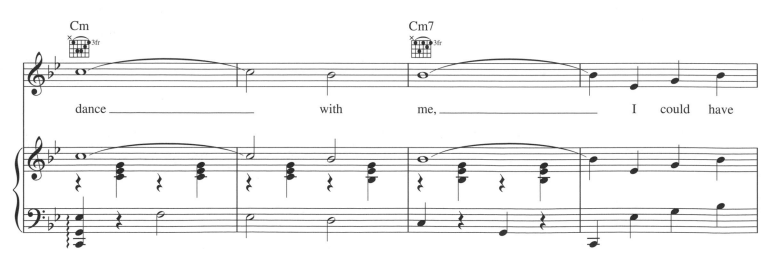

dance _____ with me, _____ I could have

danced,   danced,   danced _____

all   night!   I   could   have

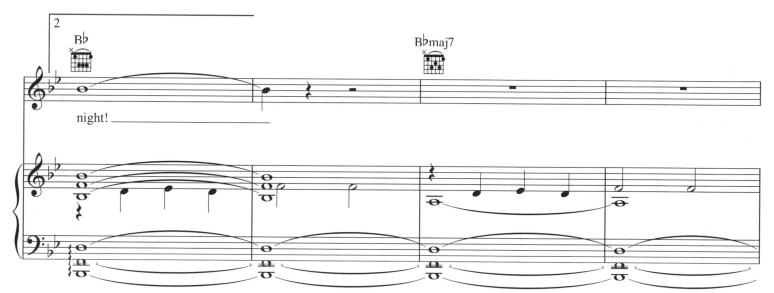

night! _____

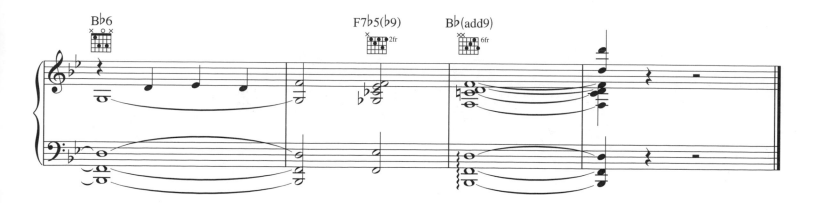

I FINALLY FOUND SOMEONE

from THE MIRROR HAS TWO FACES

Words and Music by BARBRA STREISAND,
MARVIN HAMLISCH, R.J. LANGE
and BRYAN ADAMS

Moderately slow

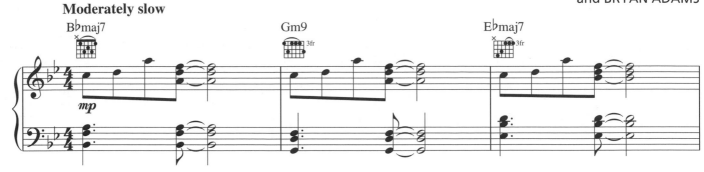

Male: I fi-n'lly found some-one who knocks me off my feet.

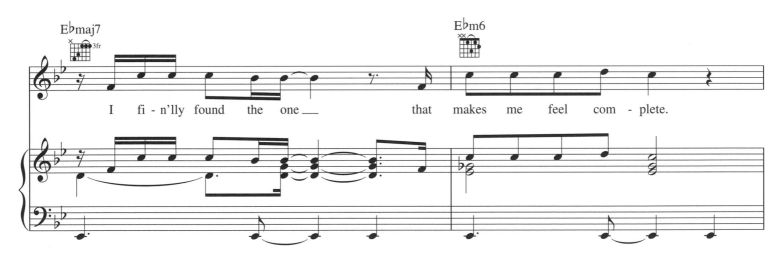

I fi-n'lly found the one ___ that makes me feel com-plete.

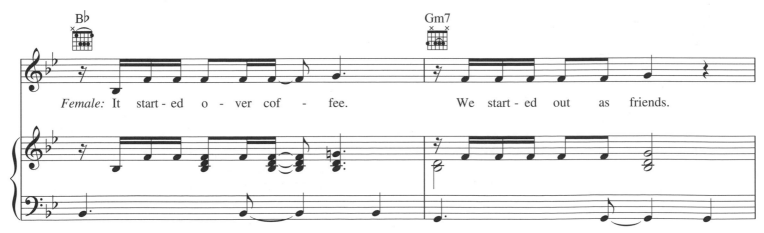

Female: It start-ed o-ver cof-fee. We start-ed out as friends.

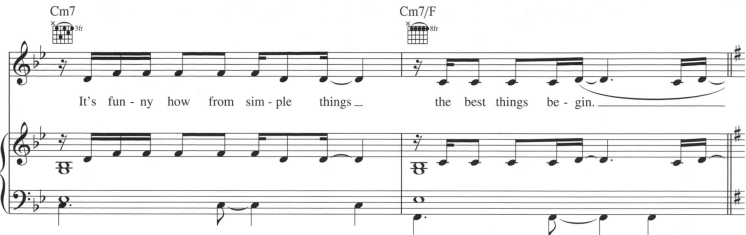

Cm7   Cm7/F

It's fun - ny how from sim - ple things ____ the best things be - gin. ____

G   Em7

____ *Male:* This time it's dif - f'rent.   It's all be - cause of you. __

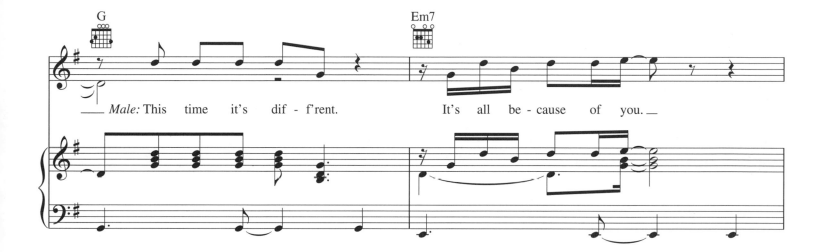

Cmaj7   Cm

It's bet - ter than it's ev - er been __ 'cause we can talk it through.

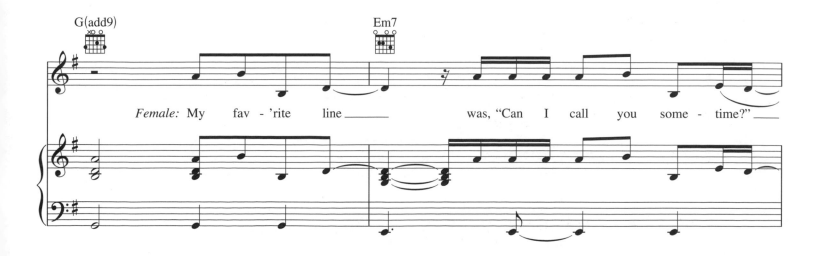

G(add9)   Em7

Female: My fav - 'rite line _____ was, "Can I call you some - time?" ____

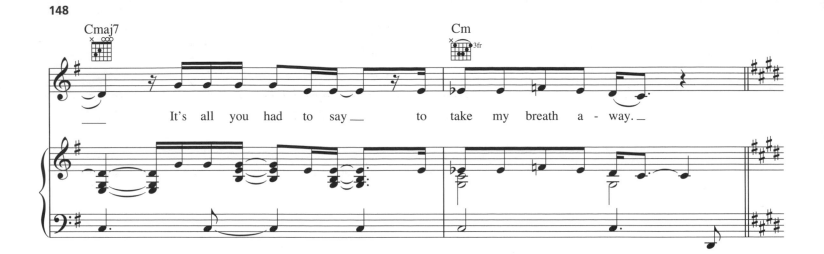

It's all you had to say ___ to take my breath a - way. ___

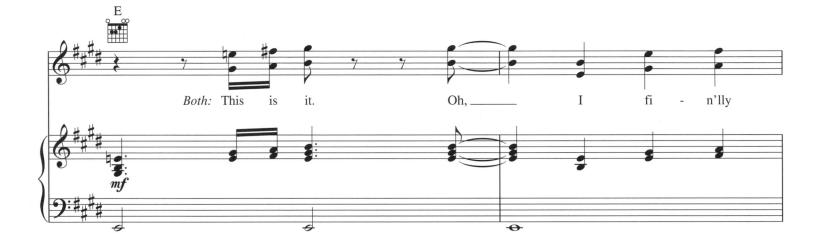

Both: This is it. Oh, _____ I fi - n'lly

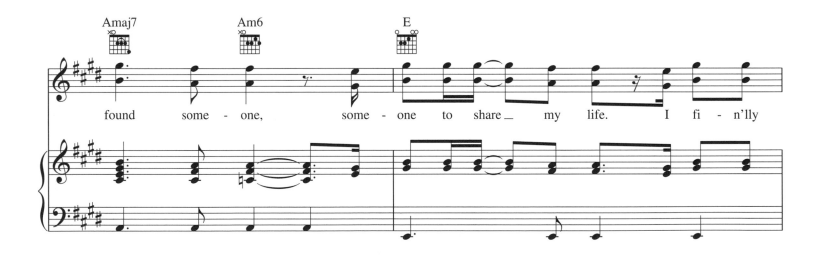

found some - one, some - one to share ___ my life. I fi - n'lly

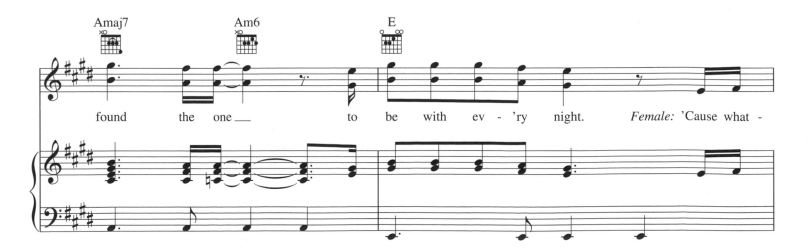

found the one ___ to be with ev - 'ry night. *Female:* 'Cause what -

ev - er I do, _____ *Male:* it's just got to be you. *Both:* My

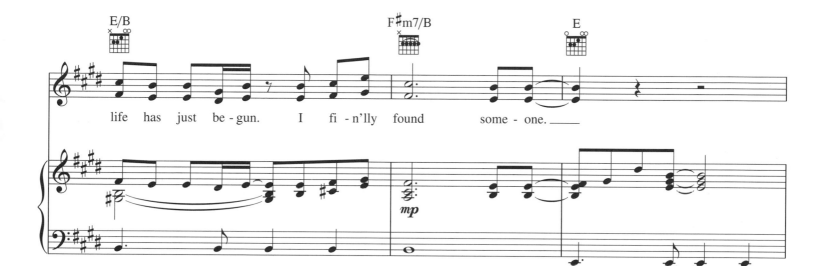

life has just be - gun. I fi - n'lly found some - one. _____

Male: Did I keep you wait - ing? I a - pol - o - gize. _____

Female: I did - n't mind. __ Ba - by, that's fine. __

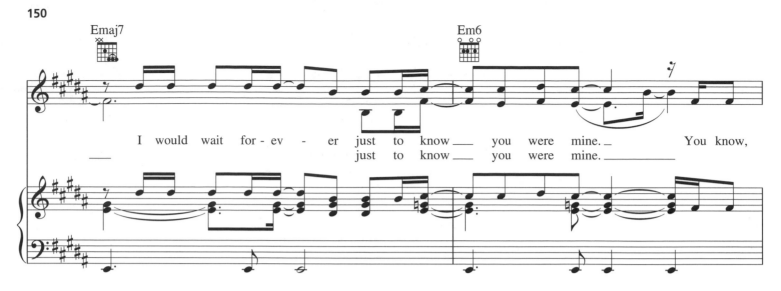

I would wait for - ev - er just to know___ you were mine.___ You know,
just to know___ you were mine.___

I love your hair.___ I love what you wear.
Are you sure it looks right?___ Is - n't it too tight?___

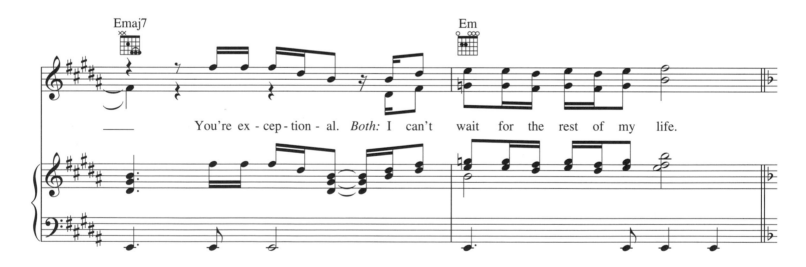

___ You're ex - cep - tion - al. *Both:* I can't wait for the rest of my life.

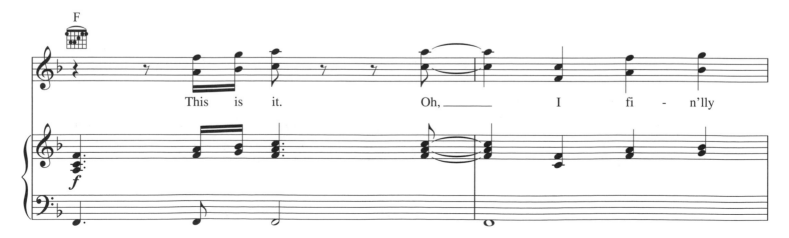

This is it. Oh,___ I fi - n'lly

found some-one, some-one to share __ my life. I fi-n'lly

found the one __ to be with ev-'ry night. *Female:* 'Cause what-

ev-er I do, _____ *Male:* it's just got to be you.

Both: My life has just __ be-gun. I fi-n'lly

found some - one. _____ *Female:* And what -

ev - er I do, _____ *Male:* it's just got to be _____ you. *Female:* My

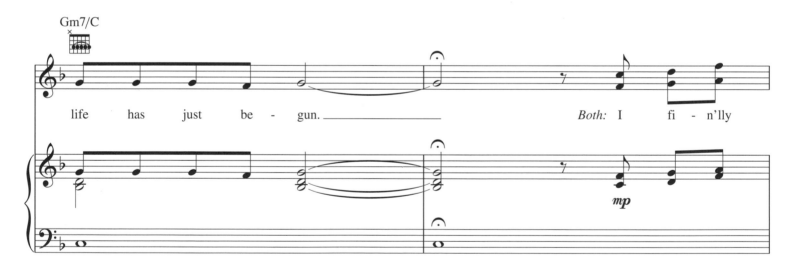

life has just be - gun. _____ *Both:* I fi - n'lly

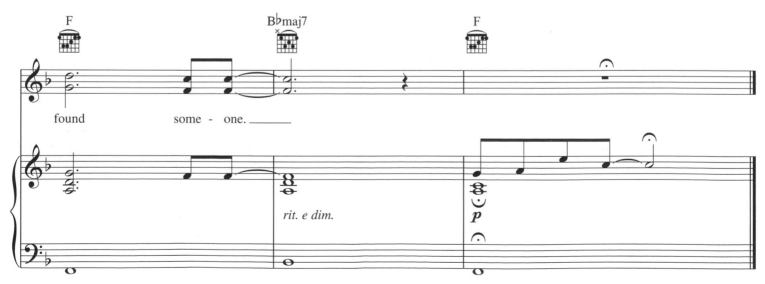

found some - one. _____

rit. e dim.

I WILL ALWAYS LOVE YOU
from THE BODYGUARD

Words and Music by
DOLLY PARTON

will _ al - ways _ love _ you. _____ I _

D.S.
(take 2nd ending)

_ will _ al - ways _ love _ you. _____

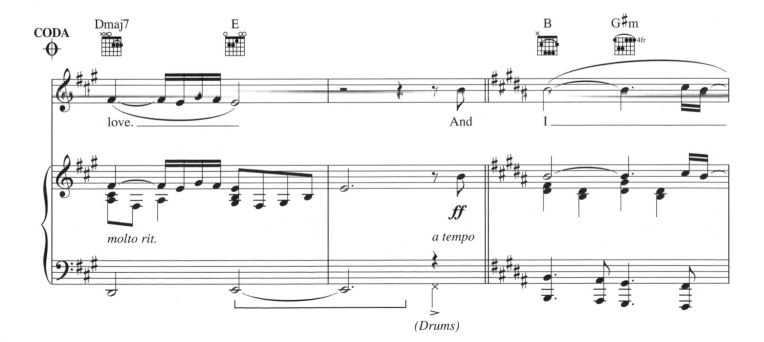

love. _____   And   I _____

molto rit.   *a tempo*   **ff**

(Drums)

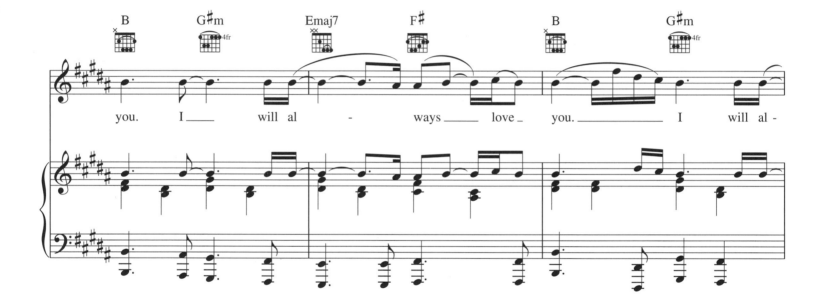

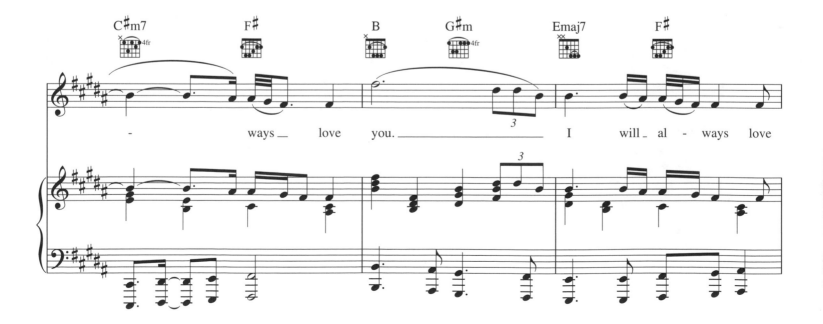

Additional Lyrics

3. I hope life treats you kind.
   And I hope you have all you've dreamed of.
   And I wish to you, joy and happiness.
   But above all this, I wish you love.

I WILL FOLLOW HIM

(I Will Follow You)

featured in the Motion Picture SISTER ACT

English Words by NORMAN GIMBEL and ARTHUR ALTMAN
French Words by JACQUES PLANTE
Music by J.W. STOLE and DEL ROMA

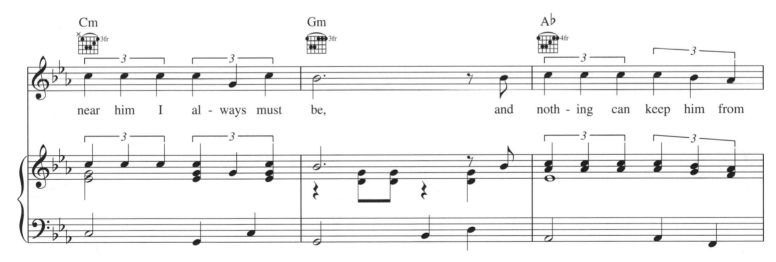

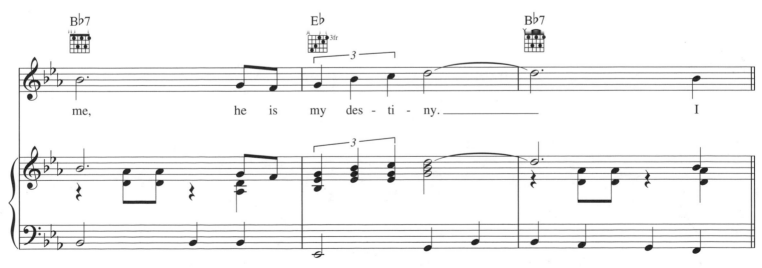

love him, I love him, I love him and where he goes I'll fol - low,
{ I'll fol - low, I'll
{ for - ev - er and

fol - low. He'll al - ways be my true love, my true love, my true love, from now un - til for -
ev - er and side by side to - geth - er I'll be with my true love, and share a thou - sand

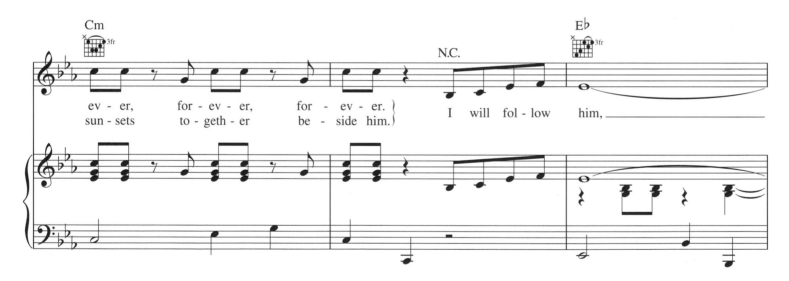

ev - er, for - ev - er, for - ev - er. }
sun - sets to - geth - er be - side him. }
I will fol - low him, _____

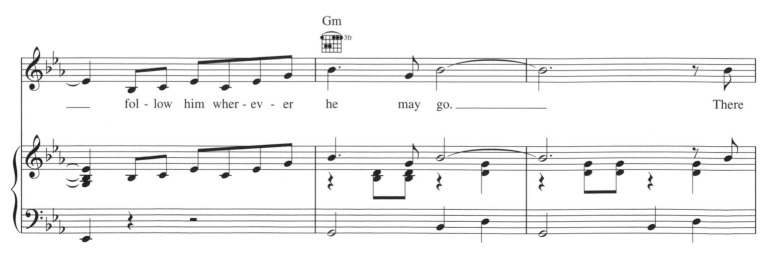

_____ fol - low him wher - ev - er he may go. _____ There

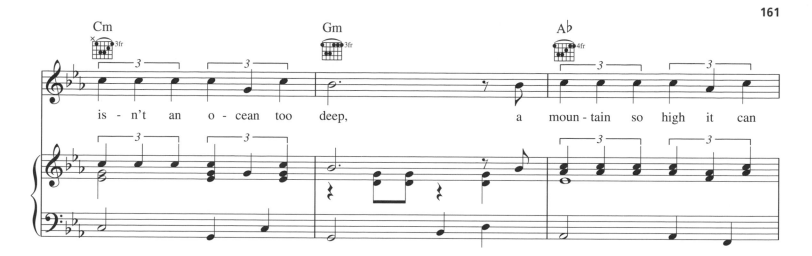

is - n't an o - cean too deep, a moun - tain so high it can

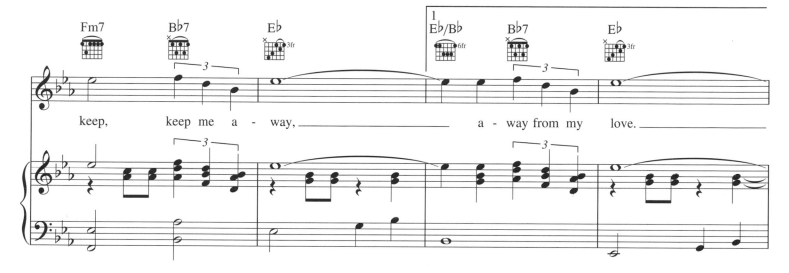

keep, keep me a - way, a - way from my love.

I a - way from my love. Ah.

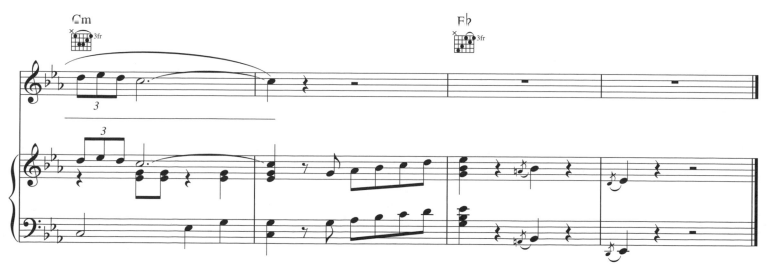

I'M A BELIEVER

featured in the DreamWorks Motion Picture SHREK

Words and Music by
NEIL DIAMOND

I thought love was on-ly true in
I thought love was more or less a

fair - y tales,
giv - in' thing;

meant for some-one else but not for
seems the more I gave the less I

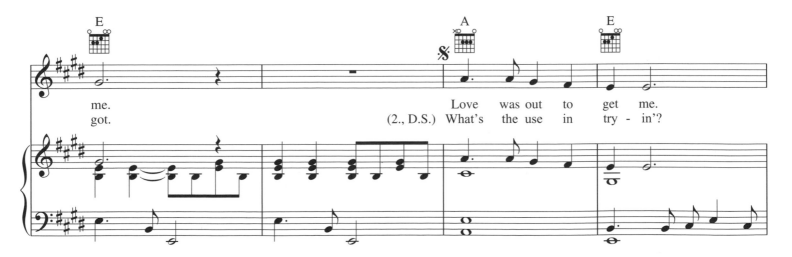

me.
got.

Love was out to get me.
(2., D.S.) What's the use in try - in'?

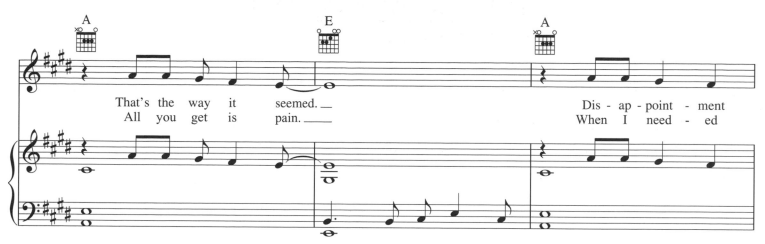

That's the way it seemed. ___
All you get is pain. ___

Dis - ap - point - ment
When I need - ed

haunt - ed all my dreams. }
sun - shine I got rain. }

Then I saw her face; ___

now I'm a be - liev - er!

Not a

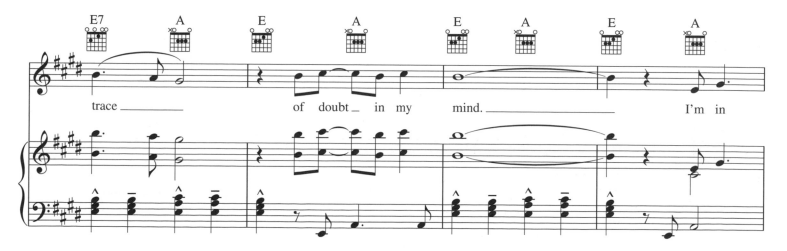

trace ___
of doubt __ in my mind. ___

I'm in

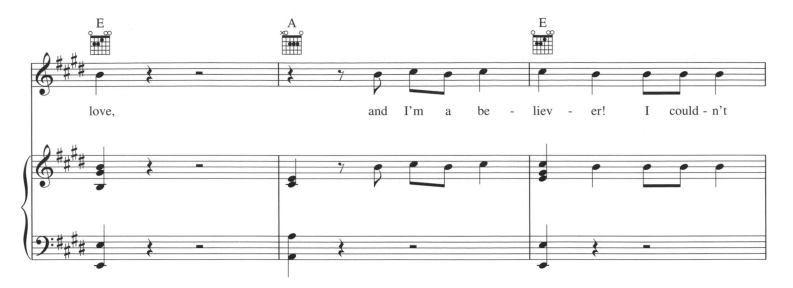

love,   and I'm a be - liev - er!   I could - n't

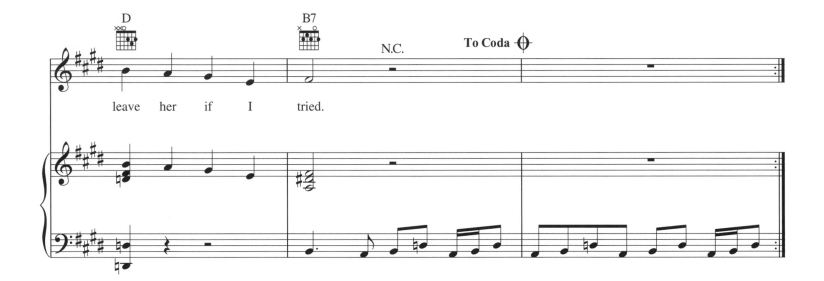

leave   her   if   I   tried.

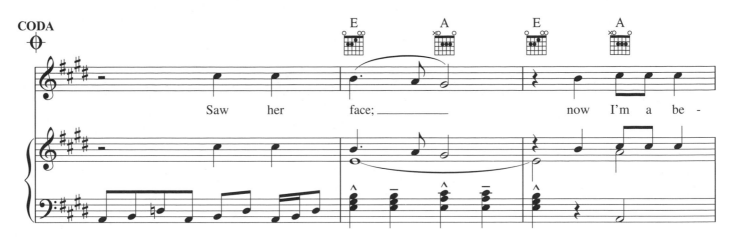

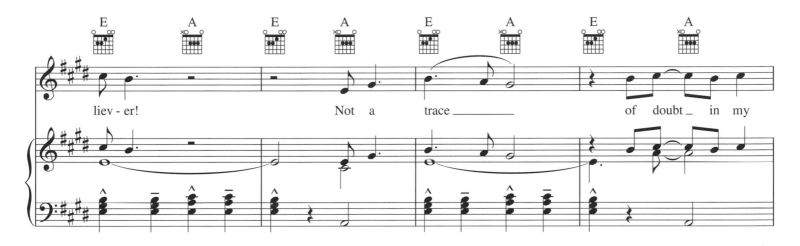

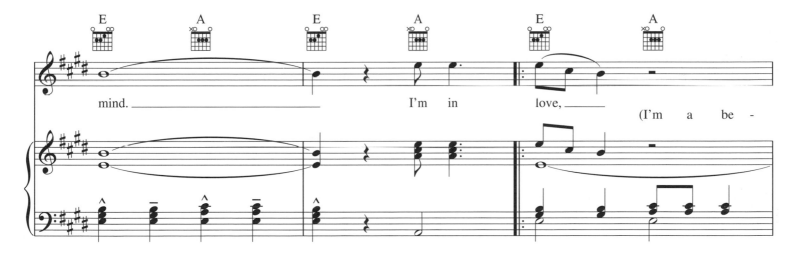

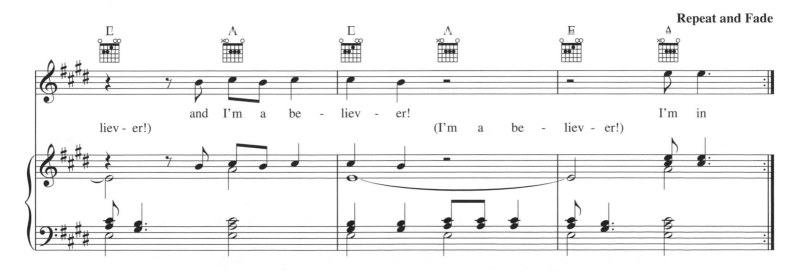

I'VE GOT MY EYES ON YOU

from BROADWAY MELODY OF 1940

Words and Music by
COLE PORTER

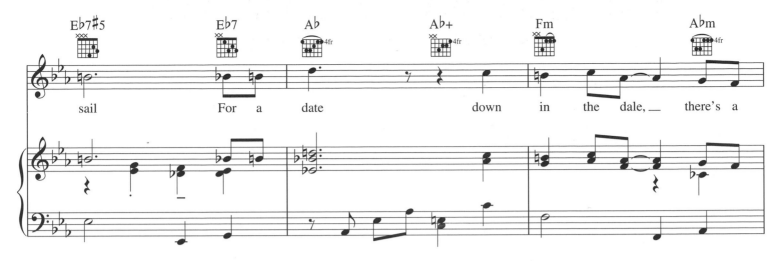

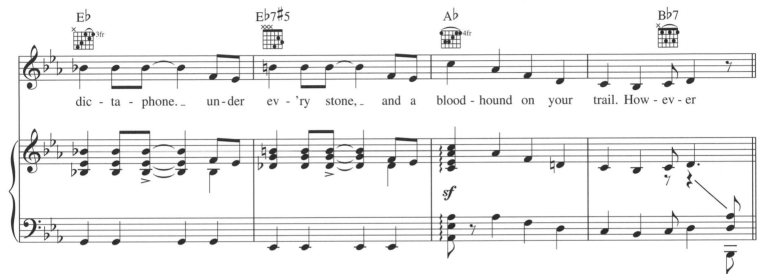

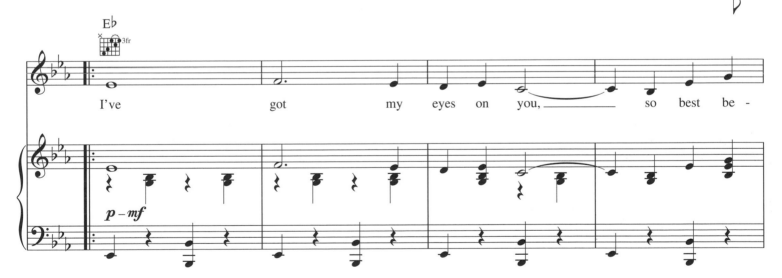

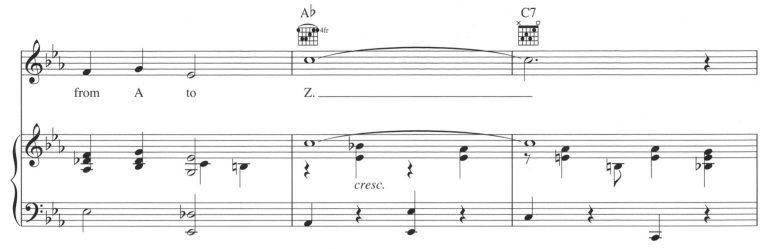

from A to Z.

So, dar - ling, just be wise,

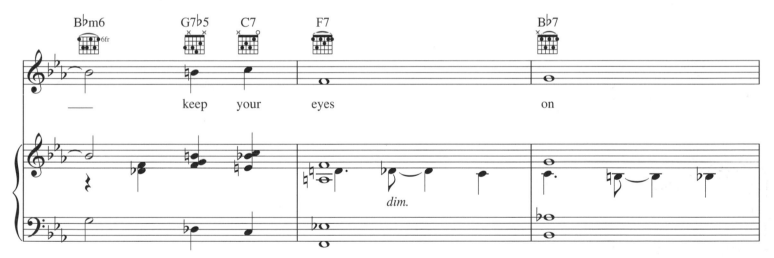

keep your eyes on

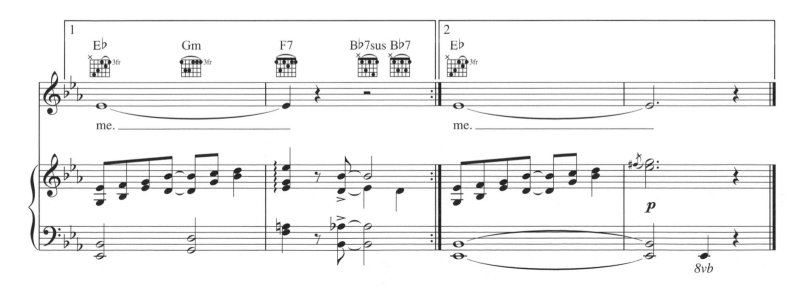

me.

me.

I'VE GOT MY LOVE TO KEEP ME WARM

from the 20th Century Fox Motion Picture ON THE AVENUE

Words and Music by
IRGIN BERLIN

Bright jump tempo

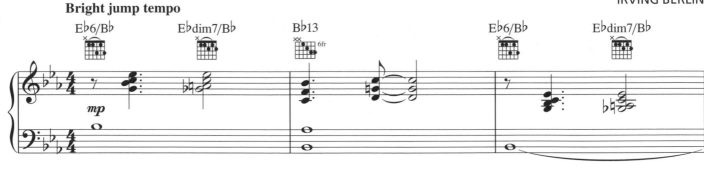

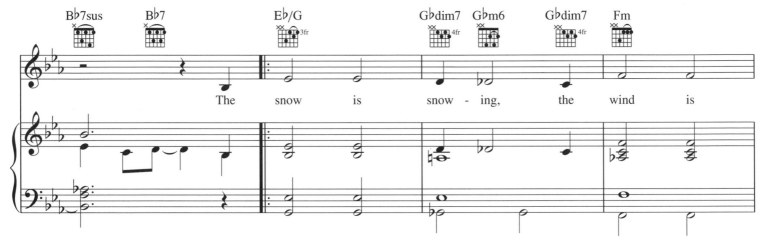

The snow is snow-ing, the wind is

blow-ing, but I can weath-er the storm. _____

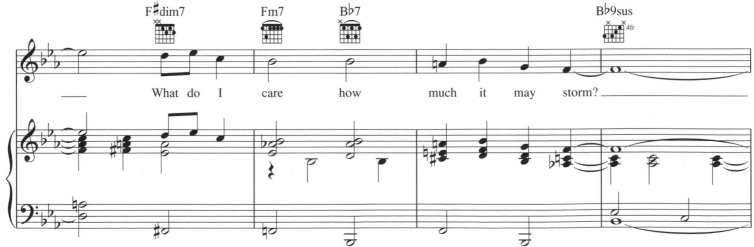

_____ What do I care how much it may storm? _____

I've got my love to keep me warm. _____

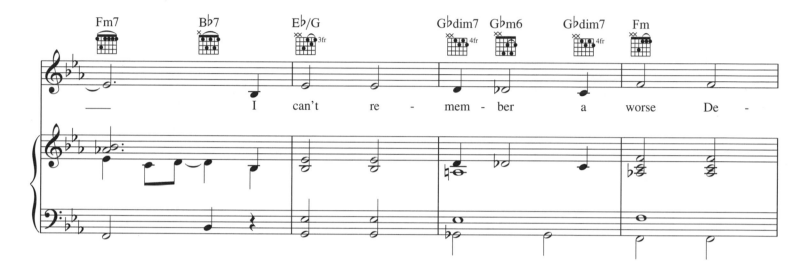

_____ I can't re - mem - ber a worse De -

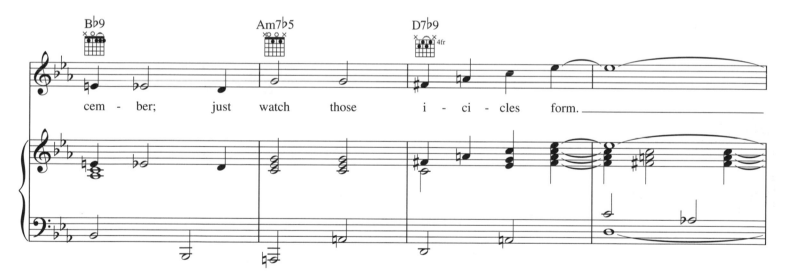

cem - ber; just watch those i - ci - cles form. _____

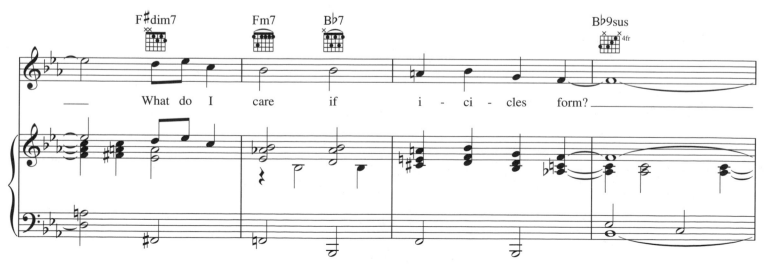

_____ What do I care if i - ci - cles form? _____

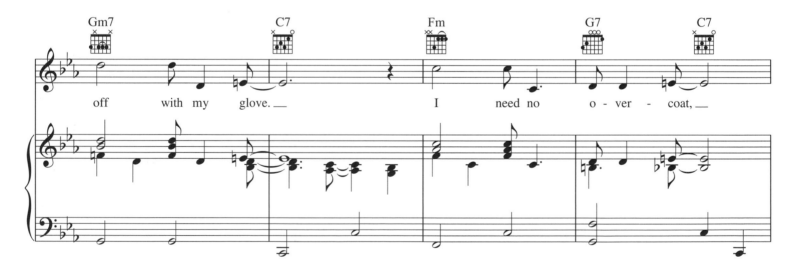

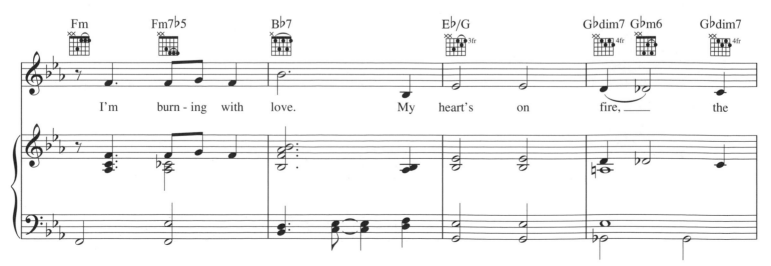

flame grows high - er, so I will weath - er the storm.

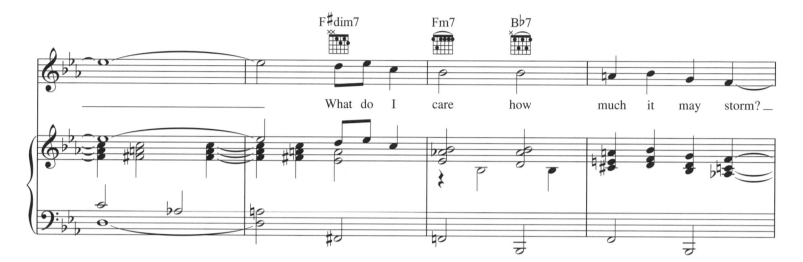

What do I care how much it may storm?

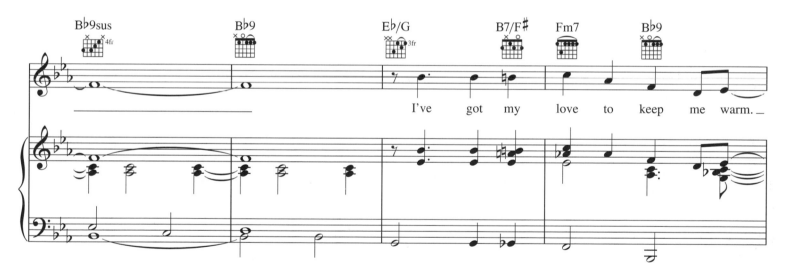

I've got my love to keep me warm.

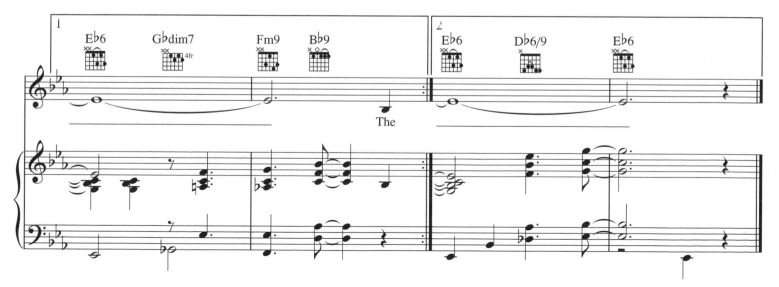

The

I'VE GOT YOU UNDER MY SKIN

from BORN TO DANCE

Words and Music by
COLE PORTER

you're real-ly a part of me. _____ I've

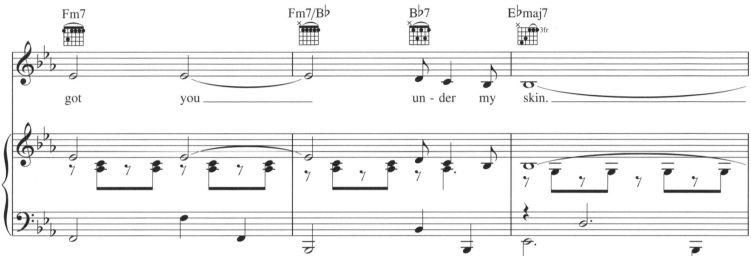

got you _____ un-der my skin. _____

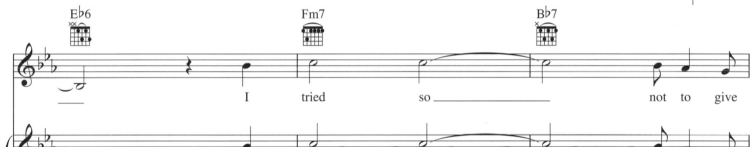

_____ I tried so _____ not to give

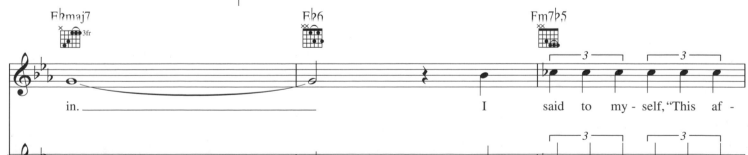

in. _____ I said to my-self, "This af -

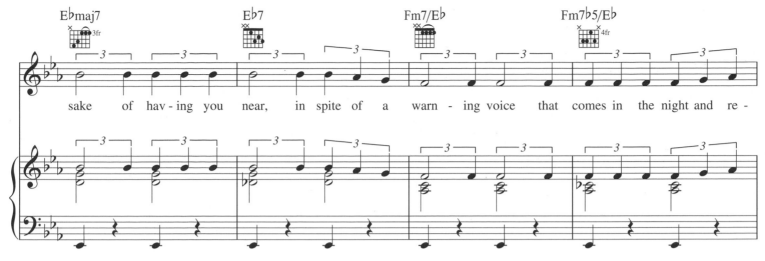

sake of hav-ing you near, in spite of a warn-ing voice that comes in the night and re-

peats and re-peats in my ear: ___ "Don't you know, lit-tle fool, ___

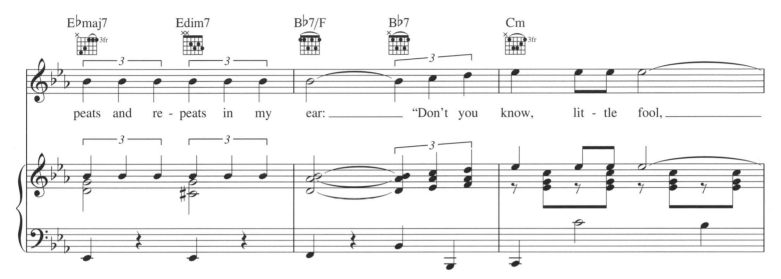

___ you nev-er can win. ___ Use your men-tal - i-ty, ___

___ wake up to re-al - i-ty." ___ But each

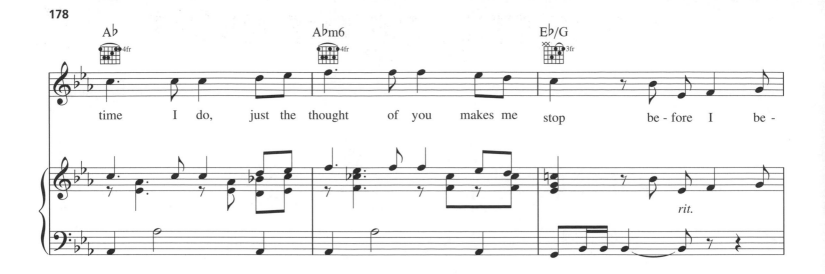

time I do, just the thought of you makes me stop be - fore I be -

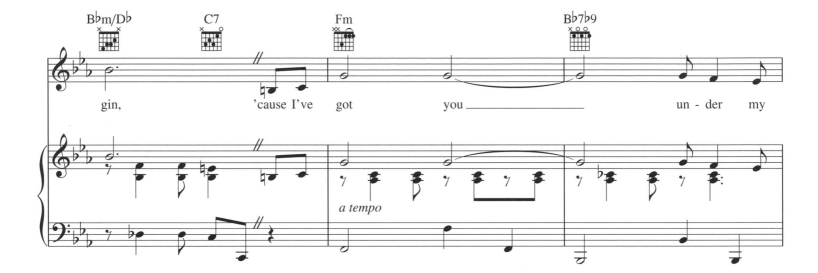

gin, 'cause I've got you _____ un - der my

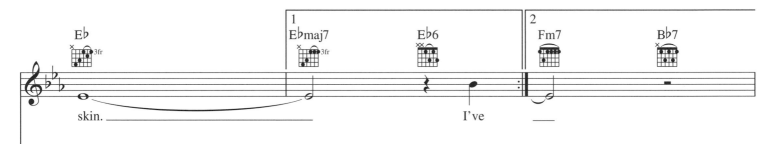

skin. _____ I've _____

IN THE STILL OF THE NIGHT
from ROSALIE

Words and Music by
COLE PORTER

Moderately, mysteriously

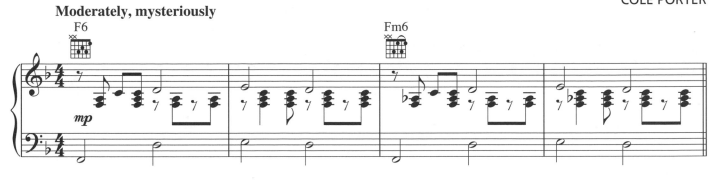

In the still of the night,

as I gaze from my win - dow

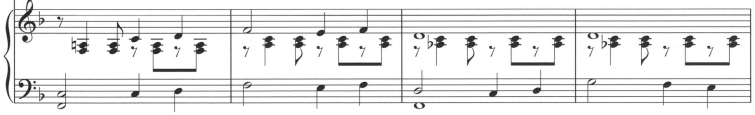

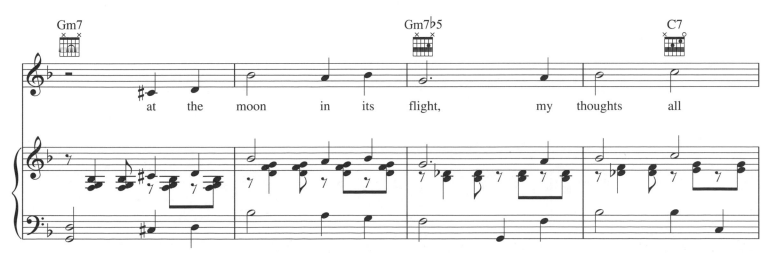

at the moon in its flight, my thoughts all

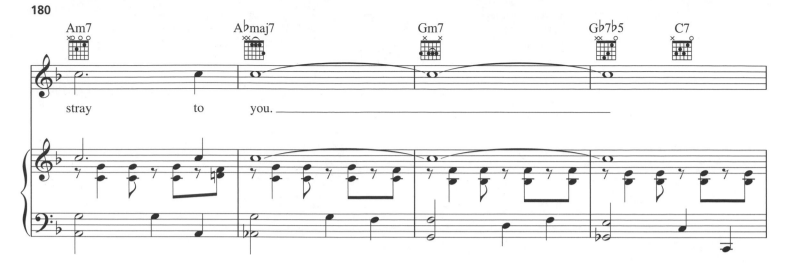

stray to you.

In the still of the night,

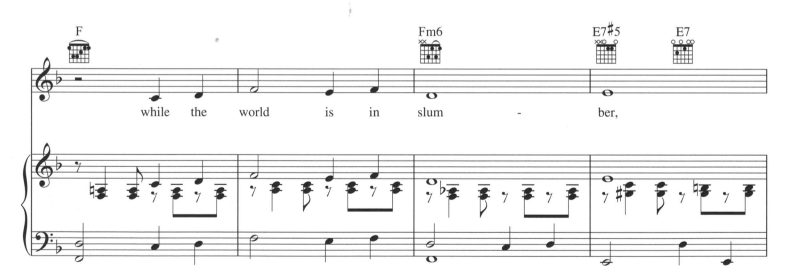

while the world is in slum - ber,

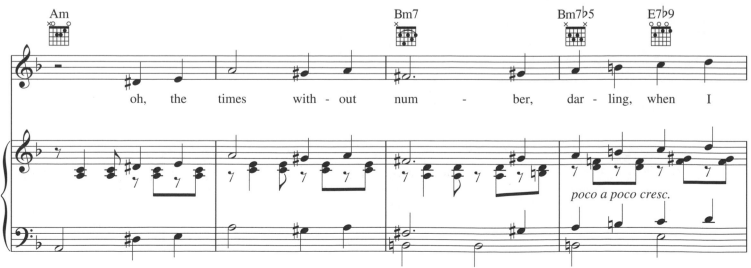

oh, the times with - out num - ber, dar - ling, when I

poco a poco cresc.

say   to   you: _____

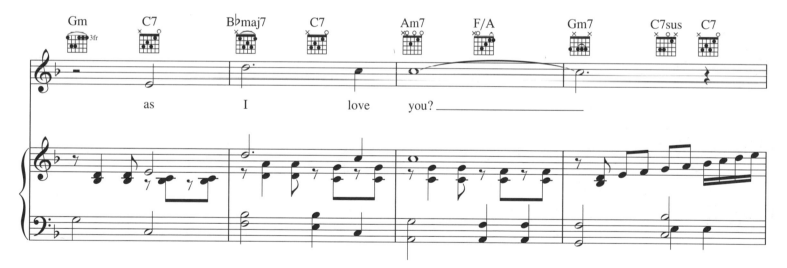

"Do _____   you   love   me

as   I   love   you? _____

Are   you   my   life   to   be,

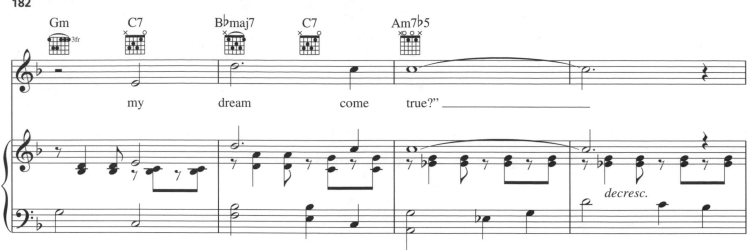

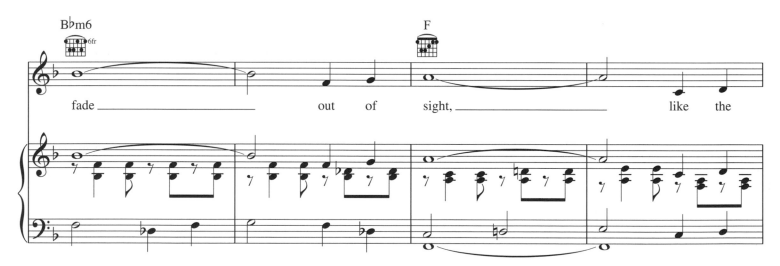

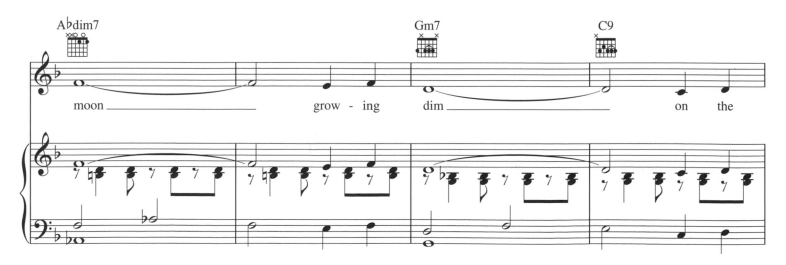

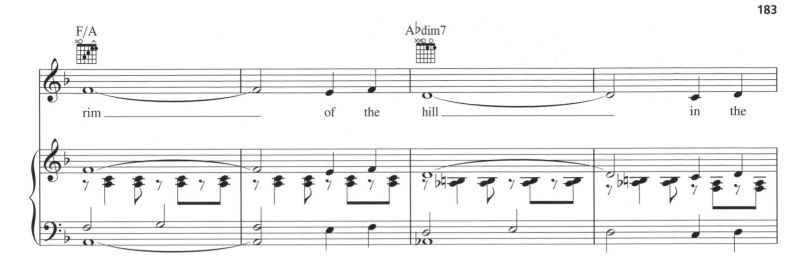

rim _____ of the hill _____ in the

chill, _____ still _____ of the

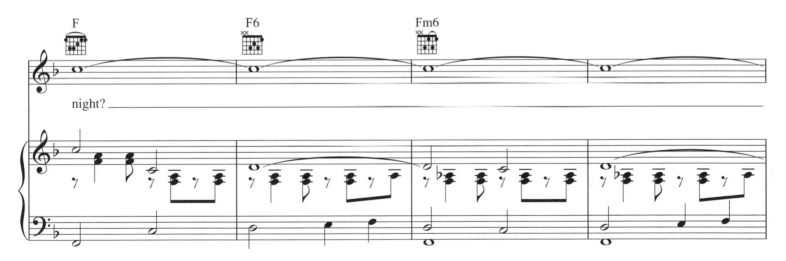

night? _____

IF I WERE A RICH MAN
from the Musical FIDDLER ON THE ROOF

Words by SHELDON HARNICK
Music by JERRY BOCK

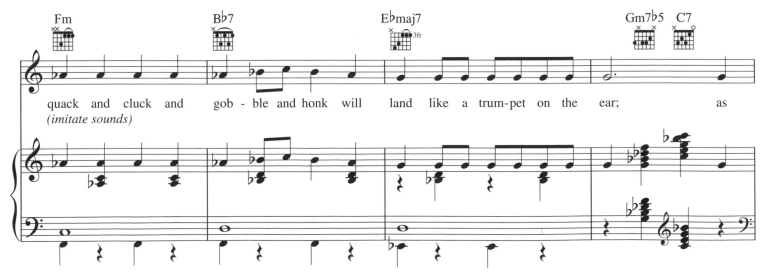

IT'S A GRAND NIGHT FOR SINGING

from STATE FAIR

Lyrics by OSCAR HAMMERSTEIN II
Music by RICHARD RODGERS

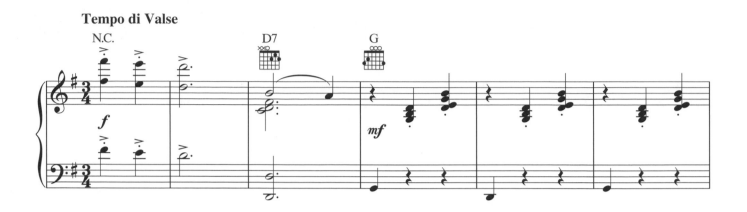

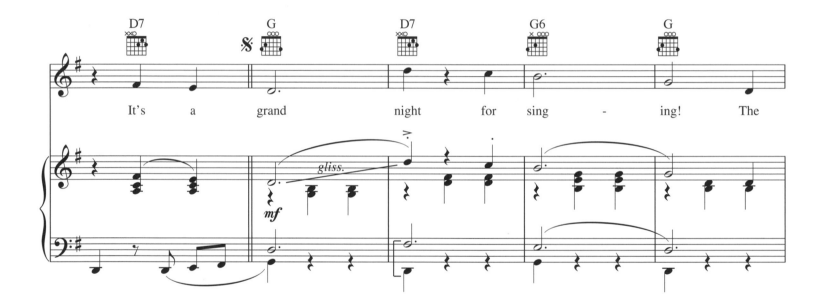

It's a grand night for sing - ing! The

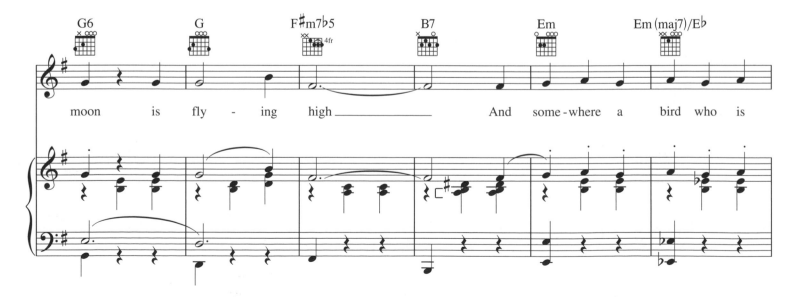

moon is fly - ing high ___ And some - where a bird who is

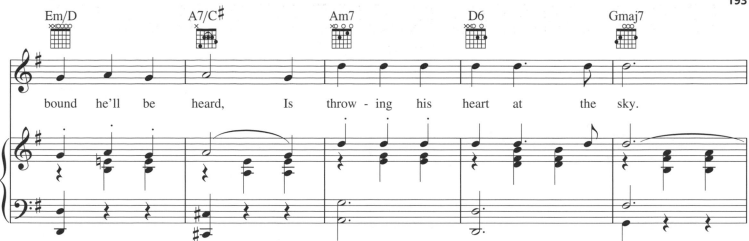

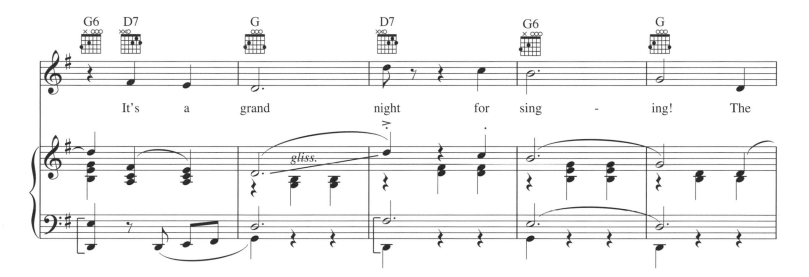

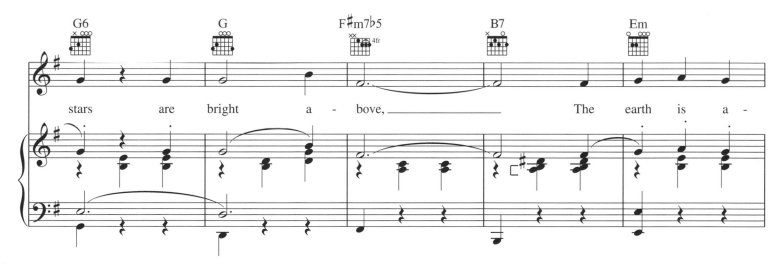

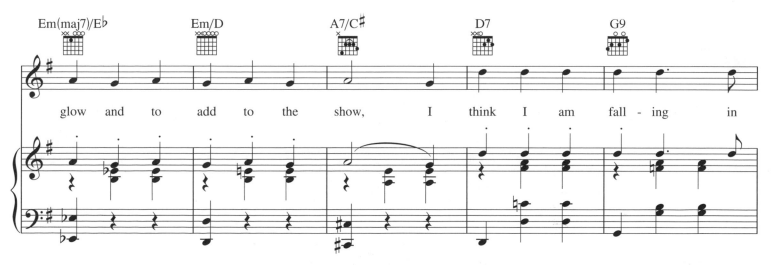

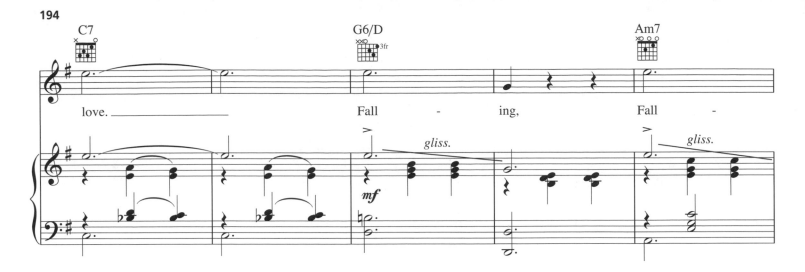

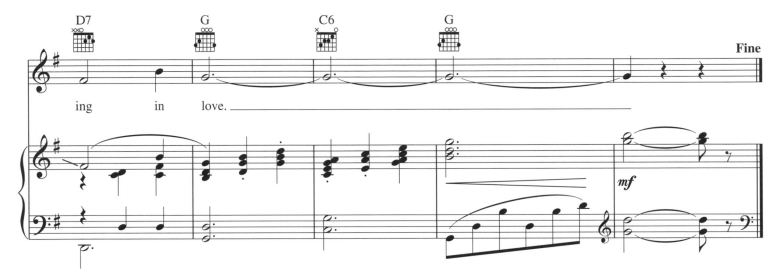

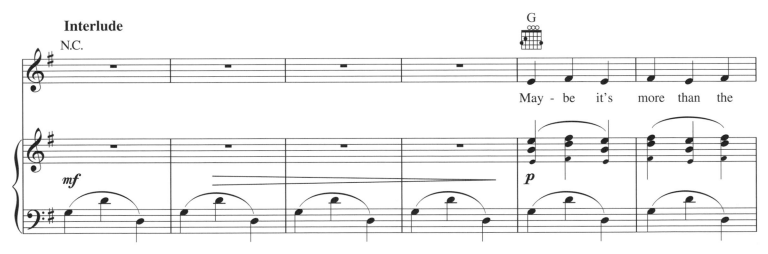

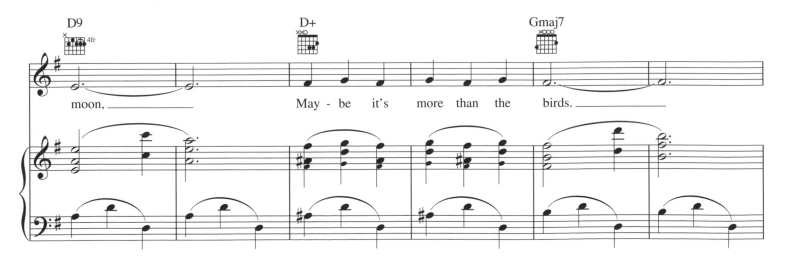

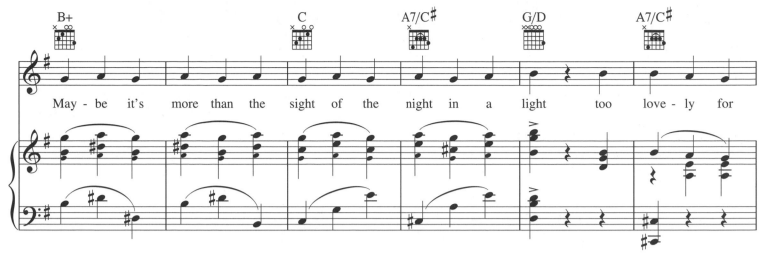

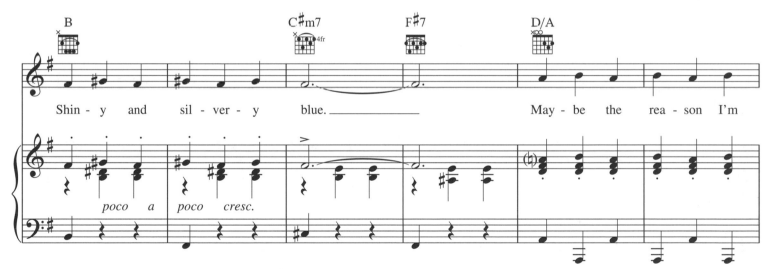

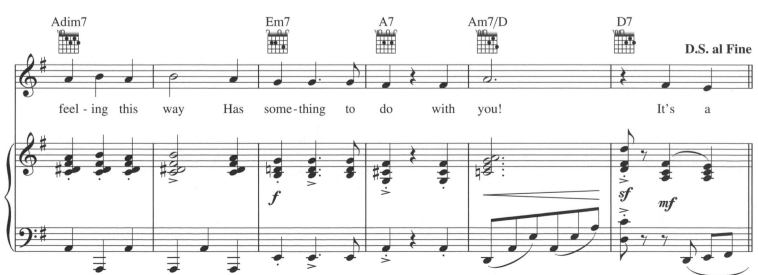

IT'S ONLY A PAPER MOON

featured in the Motion Picture TAKE A CHANCE

Lyric by BILLY ROSE and E.Y. "YIP" HARBURG
Music by HAROLD ARLEN

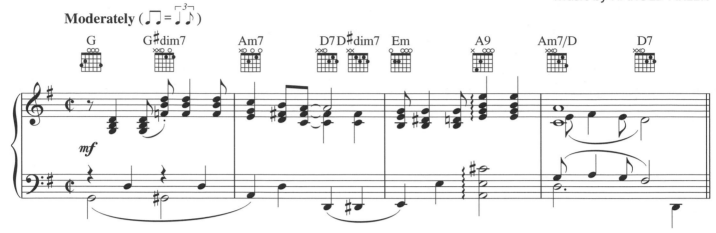

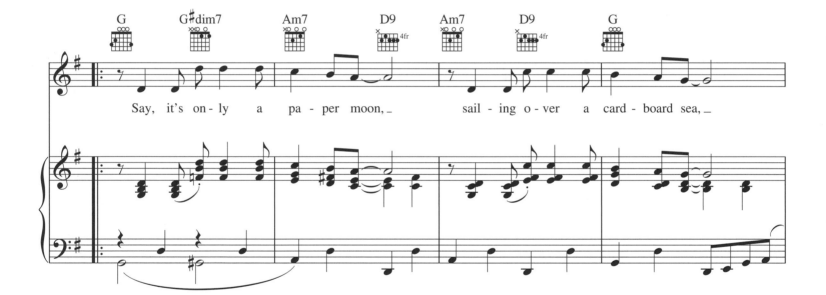

Say, it's on-ly a pa-per moon, __ sail-ing o-ver a card-board sea, __

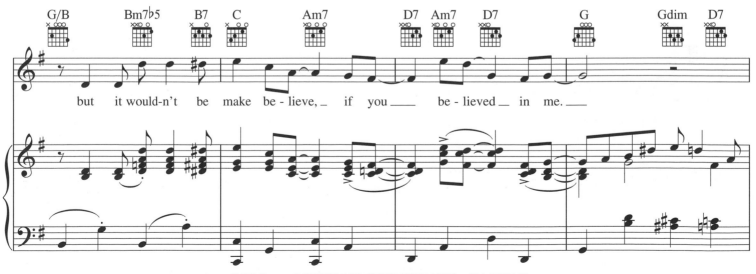

but it would-n't be make be-lieve, __ if you __ be-lieved __ in me. __

Yes, it's on-ly a can-vas sky, __ hang-ing o-ver a mus-lin tree, __

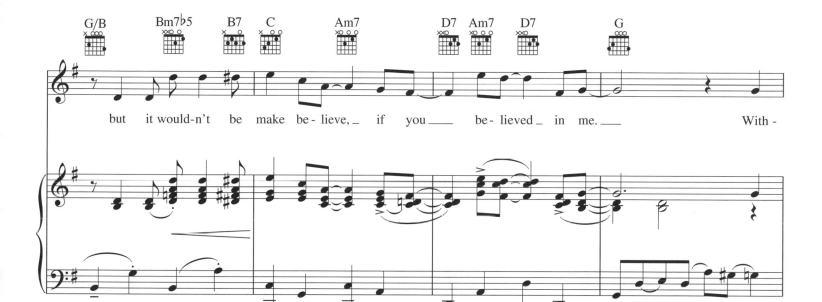

but it would-n't be make be-lieve, __ if you ___ be-lieved __ in me. ___ With-

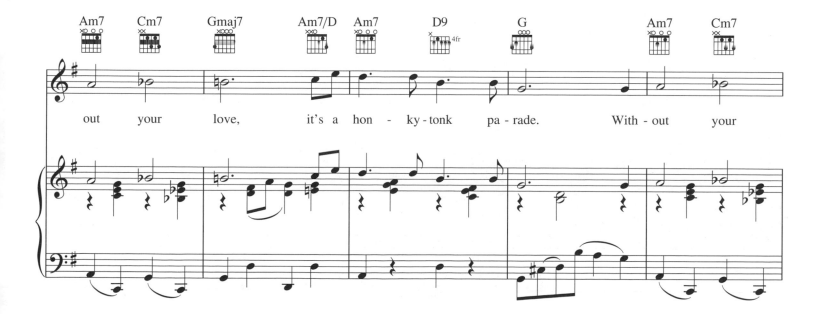

out your love, it's a hon-ky-tonk pa-rade. With-out your

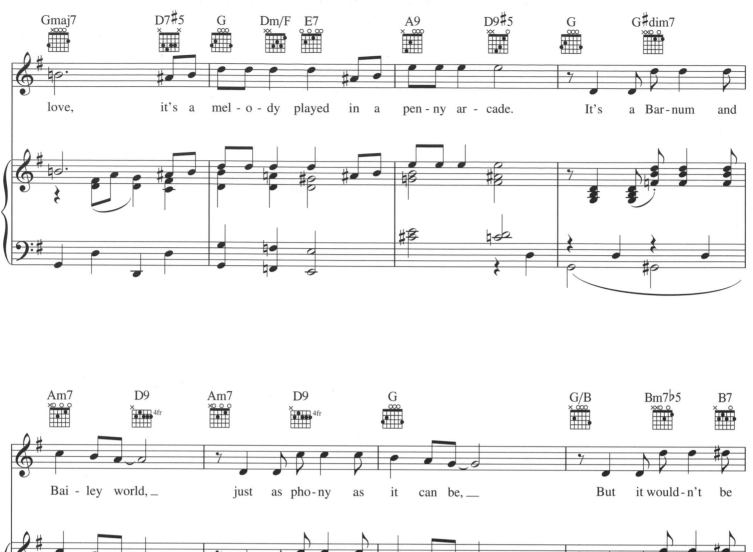

love, it's a mel-o-dy played in a pen-ny ar-cade. It's a Bar-num and

Bai-ley world, __ just as pho-ny as it can be, __ But it would-n't be

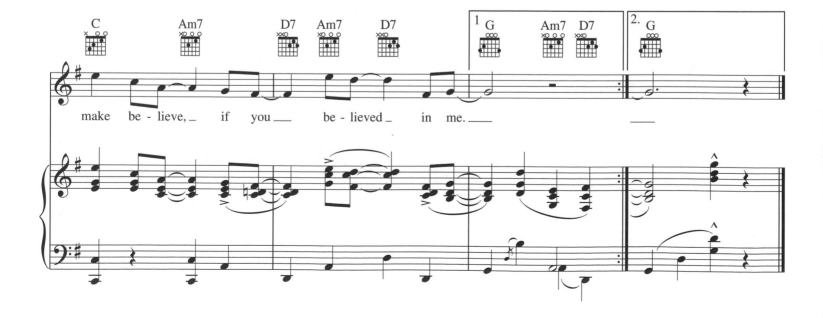

make be-lieve, __ if you __ be-lieved __ in me. __

THE LOOK OF LOVE

from CASINO ROYALE

Words by HAL DAVID
Music by BURT BACHARACH

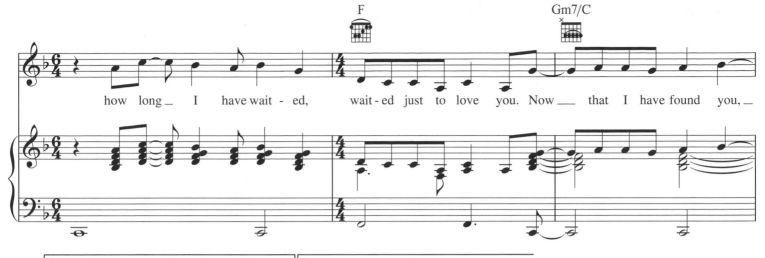

how long __ I have wait-ed, wait-ed just to love you. Now __ that I have found you, __

__ you've got the look __ don't ev-er go, _____

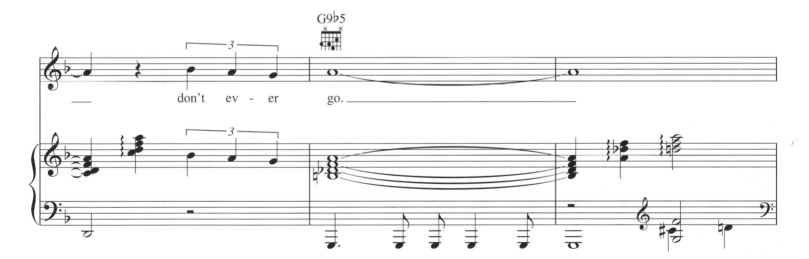

__ don't ev-er go. _____

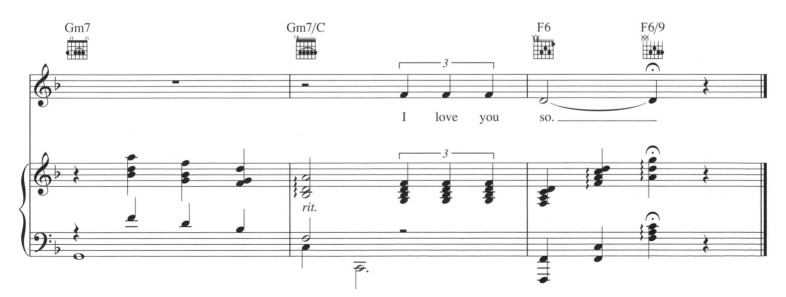

I love you so. _____

LAST DANCE
from THANK GOD IT'S FRIDAY

Words and Music by
PAUL JABARA

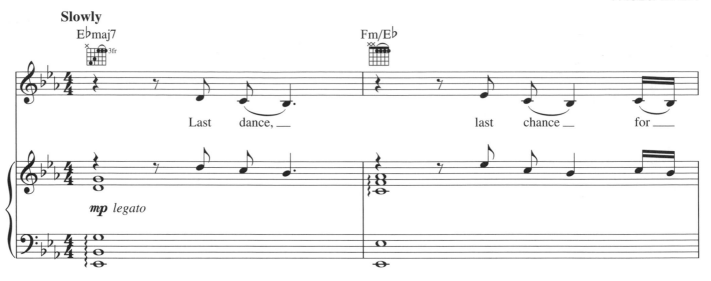

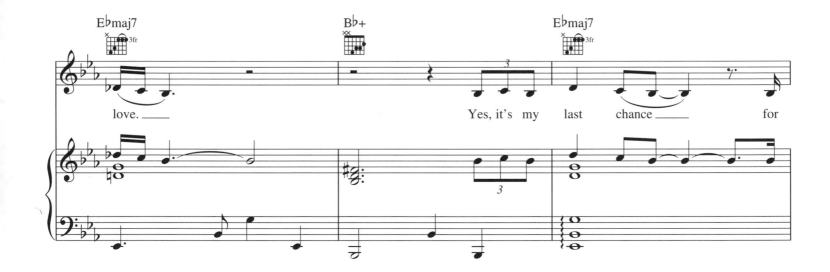

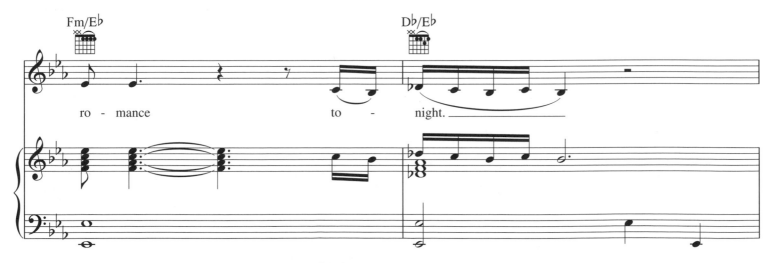

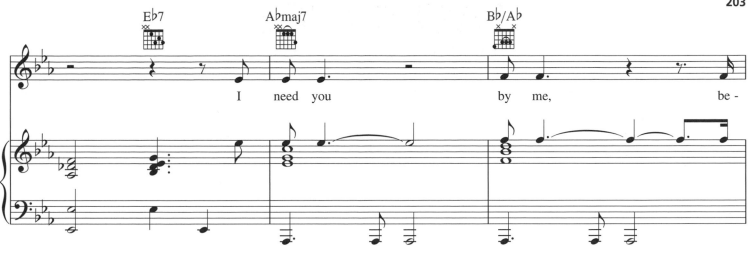

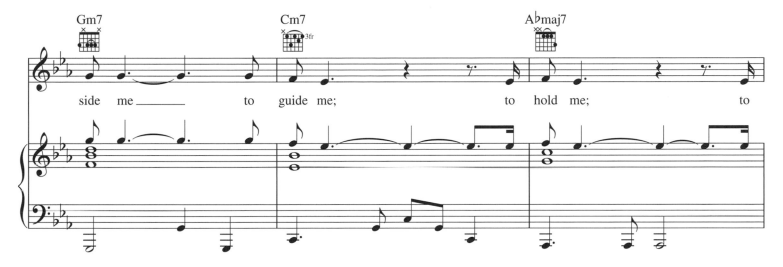

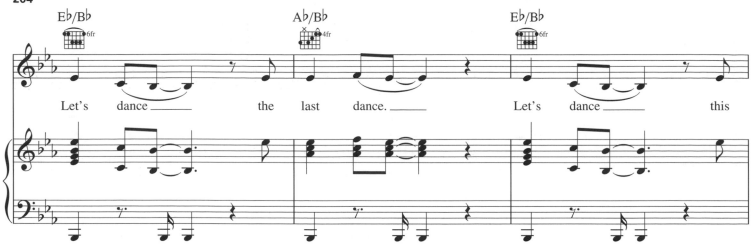

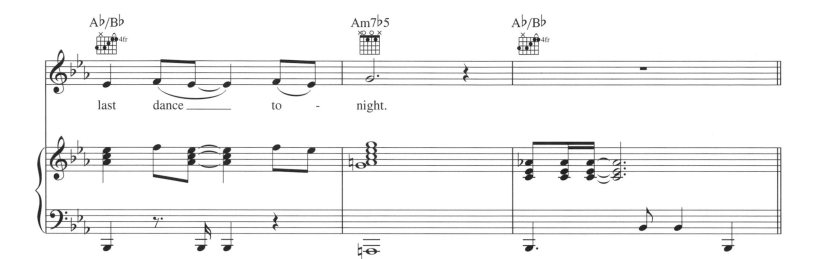

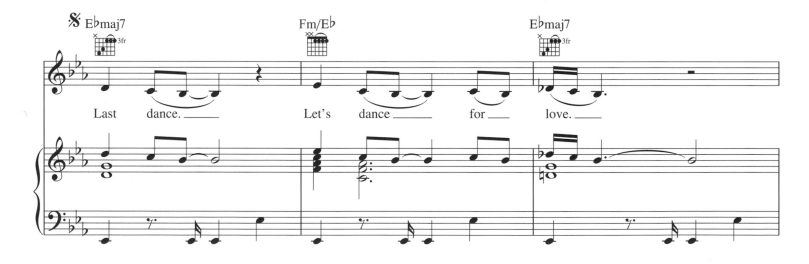

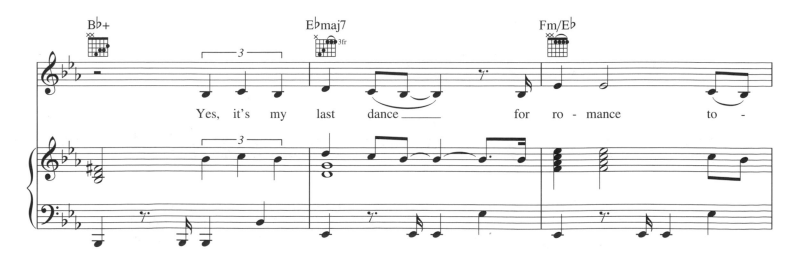

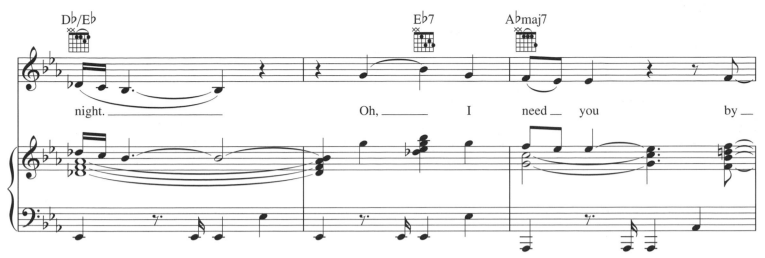

night. _____ Oh, _____ I need ___ you ____ by ___

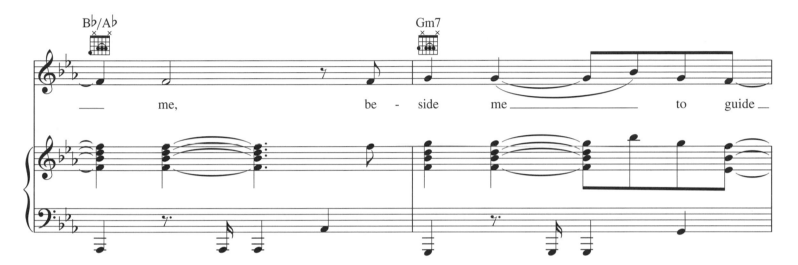

___ me, _____ be - side me _____ to guide ___

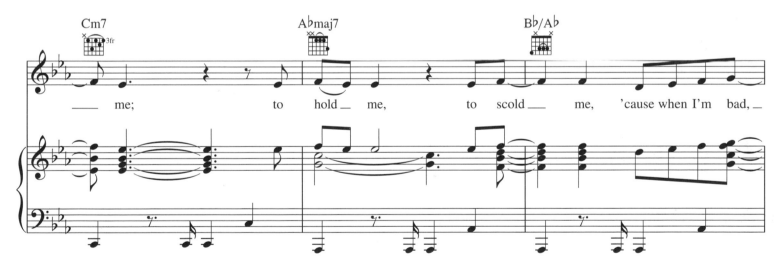

___ me; _____ to hold ___ me, to scold ___ me, 'cause when I'm bad, ___

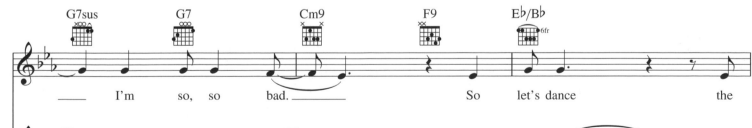

___ I'm so, so bad. _____ So ___ let's dance ___ the

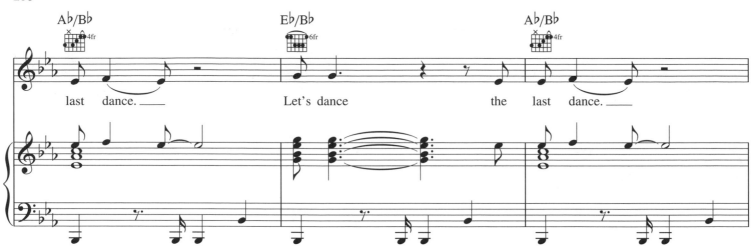

last dance. ___ Let's dance the last dance. ___

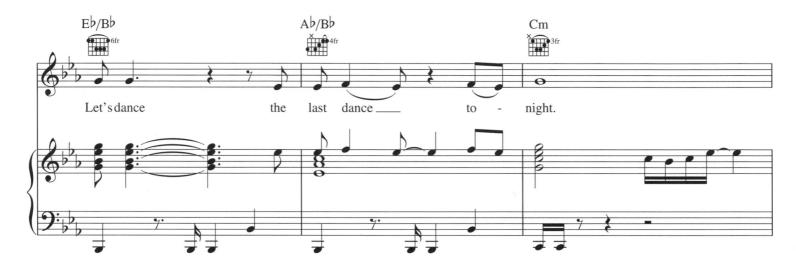

Let's dance the last dance ___ to - night.

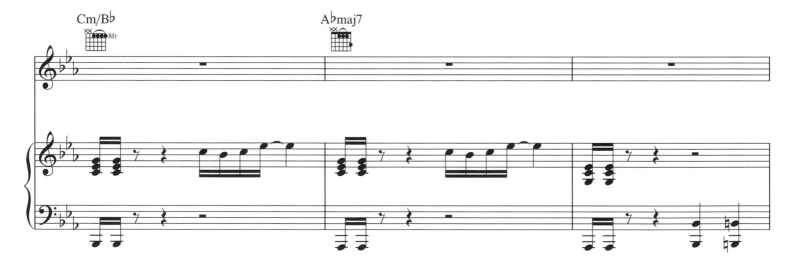

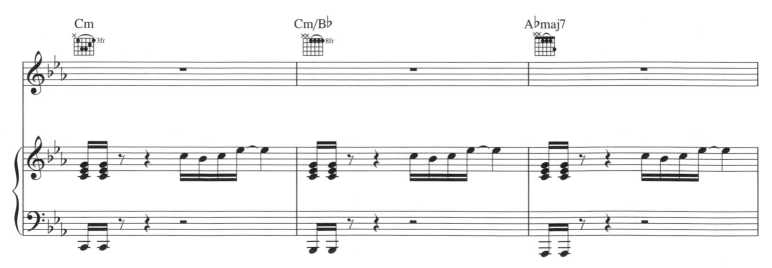

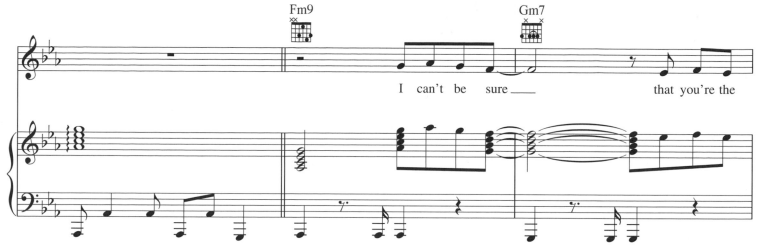

I can't be sure ___ that you're the

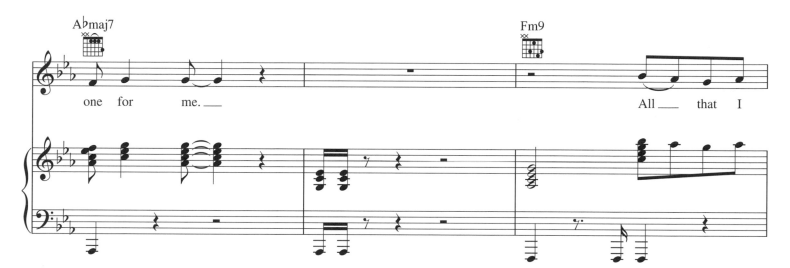

one for me. ___ All ___ that I

ask _____ is that you dance with ___ me. Dance with ___ me.

D.S. and Fade

Dance with me. Yeah. _____

THE LAST TIME I FELT LIKE THIS

from SAME TIME, NEXT YEAR

Words by ALAN BERGMAN and MARILYN BERGMAN
Music by MARVIN HAMLISCH

Slow Ballad tempo

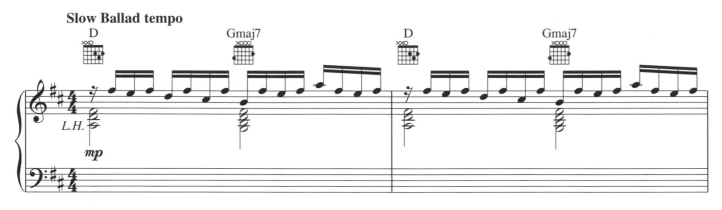

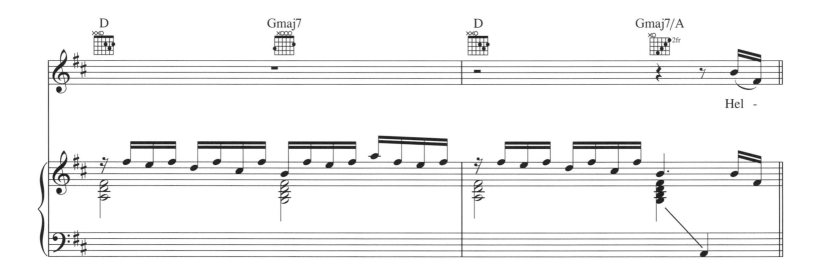

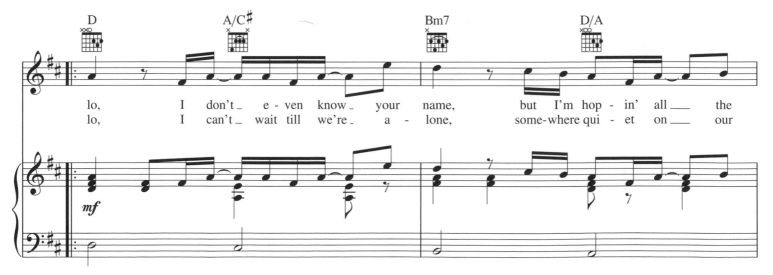

lo,   I don't e-ven know your name,   but I'm hop-in' all   the
lo,   I can't wait till we're a - lone,   some-where qui-et on   our

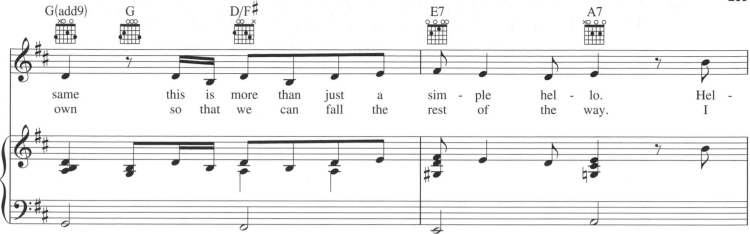

same this is more than just a sim - ple hel - lo. Hel -
own so that we can just fall the rest of the way. I

lo, do I smile and walk _ a - way? No, I think I'll smile _ and
know that be - fore the night _ is through, I'll be talk - ing love _ to

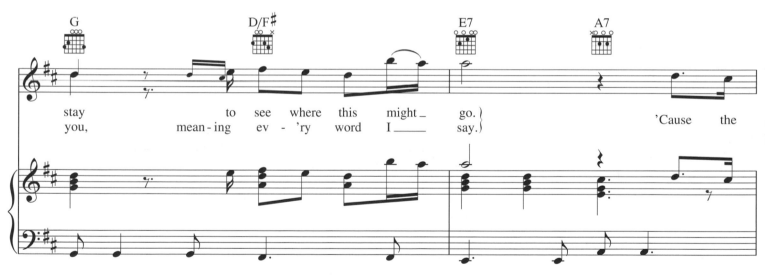

stay to see where this might _ go.}
you, mean - ing ev - 'ry word I ____ say.} 'Cause the

last time I felt like this I was fall - ing in love,

falling and feel - ing ___ I'd nev - er fall in love a - gain. Yes, the

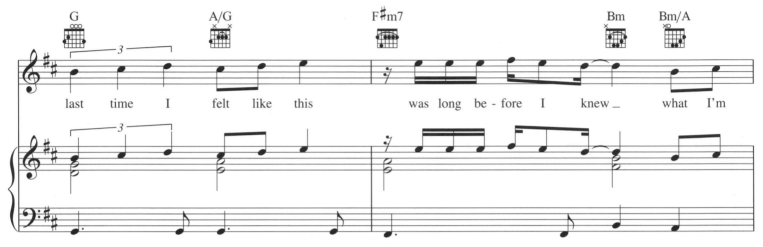

last time I felt like this was long be - fore I knew ___ what I'm

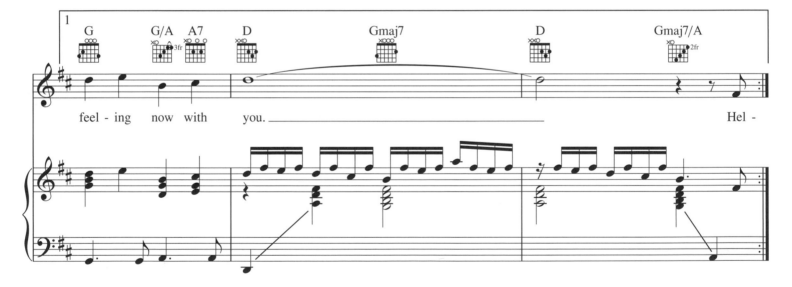

feel - ing now with you. ___ Hel -

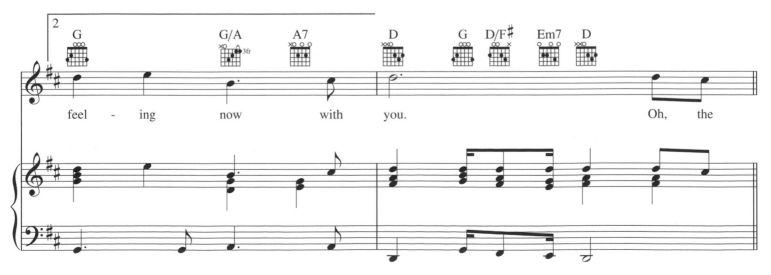

feel - ing now with you. Oh, the

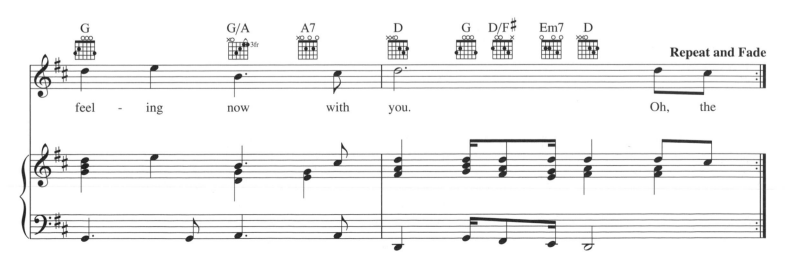

LOVE ME OR LEAVE ME

from LOVE ME OR LEAVE ME

Words by GUS KAHN
Music by WALTER DONALDSON

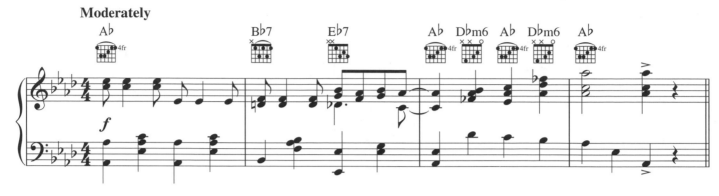

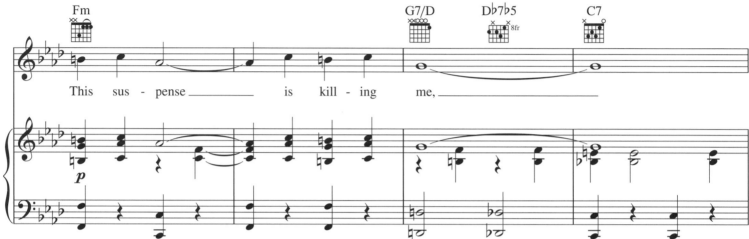

This sus-pense _____ is kill-ing me, _____

I can't stand _____ un-cer-tain-ty. _____

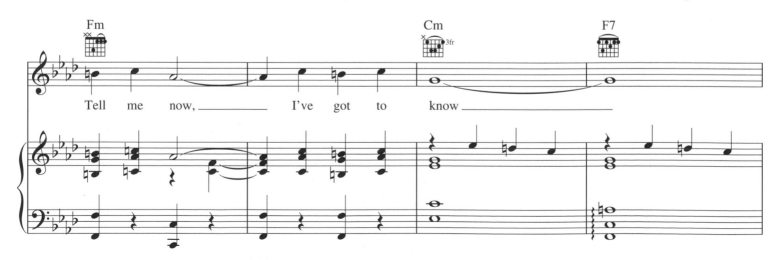

Tell me now, _____ I've got to know _____

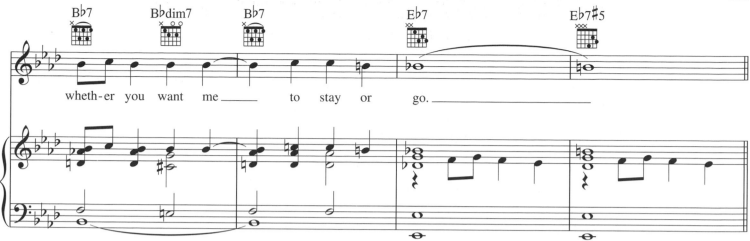

wheth-er you want me ___ to stay or go. ___

Love me or leave me and let me be lone-ly. You won't be-lieve me, and

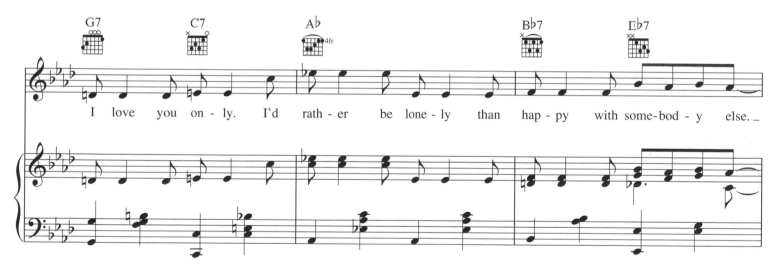

I love you on-ly. I'd rath-er be lone-ly than hap-py with some-bod-y else. _

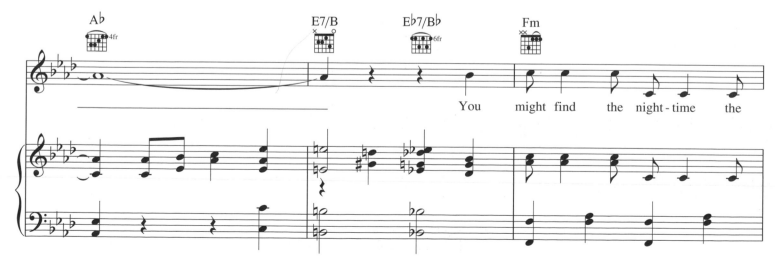

___ You might find the night-time the

right time for kiss - ing. But night-time is my time for just rem - i - nisc - ing. Re -

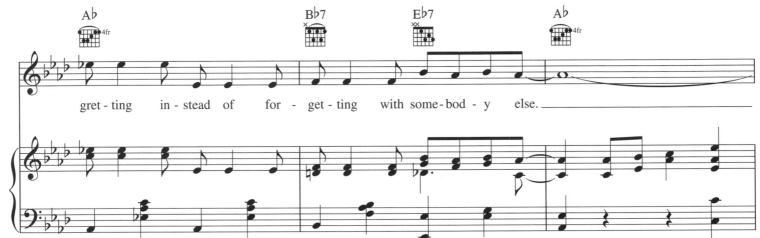

gret - ting in - stead of for - get - ting with some - bod - y else. _____

_____ There'll be no ___ one un - less that some - one is

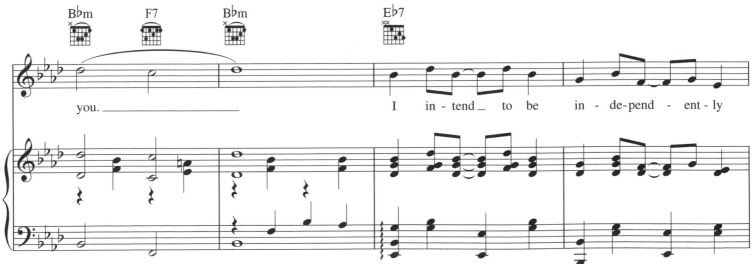

you. _____ I in - tend ___ to be in - de - pend - ent - ly

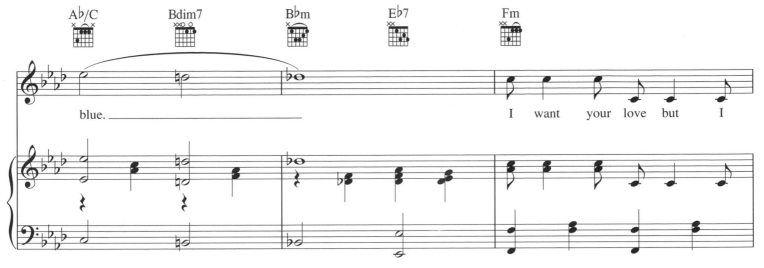

blue. _____

I want your love but I

don't want to bor - row to have it to - day and to give back to - mor - row, for

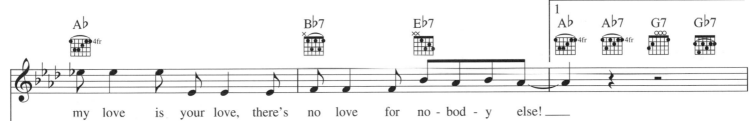

my love is your love, there's no love for no - bod - y else! ___

LOVE STORY
Theme from the Paramount Picture LOVE STORY

Music by FRANCIS LAI

Slowly, expressively

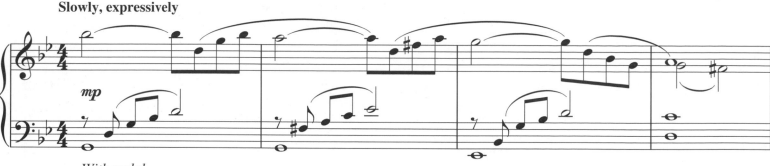

With pedal

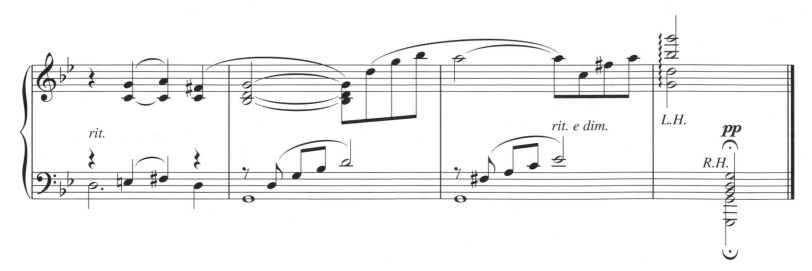

MAKE SOMEONE HAPPY

from DO RE MI

Words by BETTY COMDEN and ADOLPH GREEN
Music by JULE STYNE

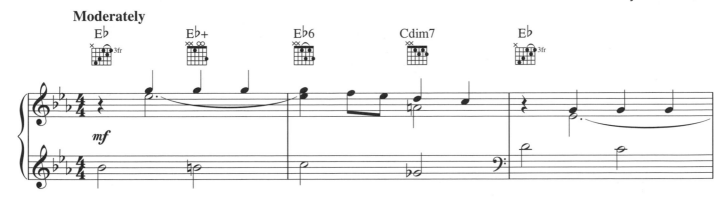

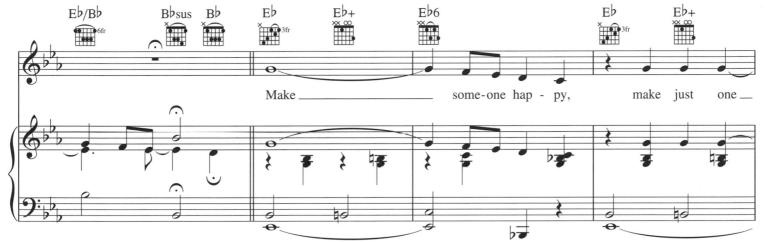

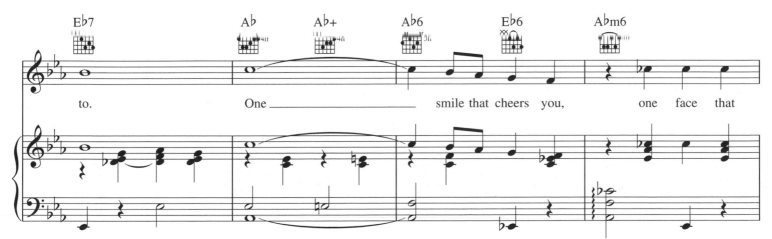

lights when it nears you, one {man/girl} you're ev - 'ry - thing

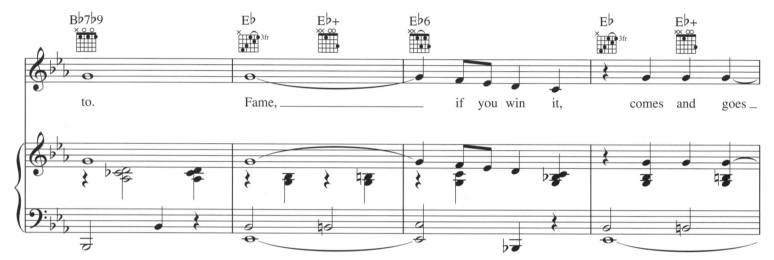

to. Fame, _____ if you win it, comes and goes _

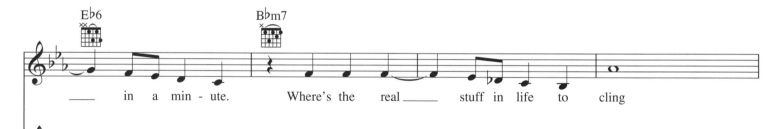

_ in a min - ute. Where's the real _ stuff in life to cling

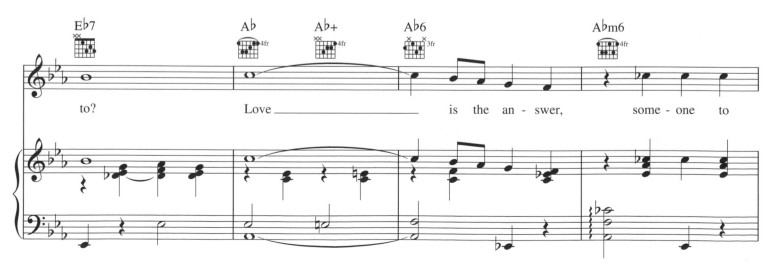

to? Love _____ is the an - swer, some - one to

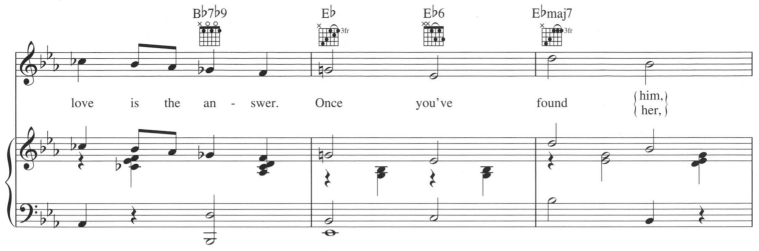

love is the an - swer. Once you've found (him,) (her,)

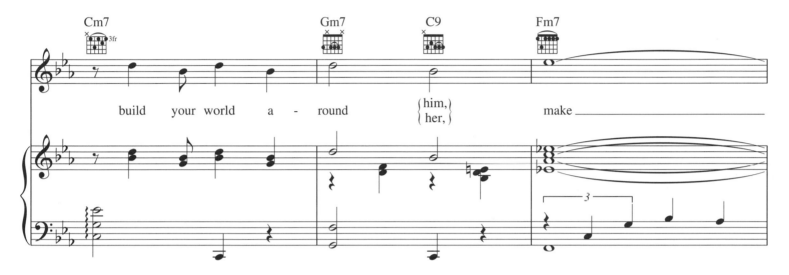

build your world a - round (him,) (her,) make _____

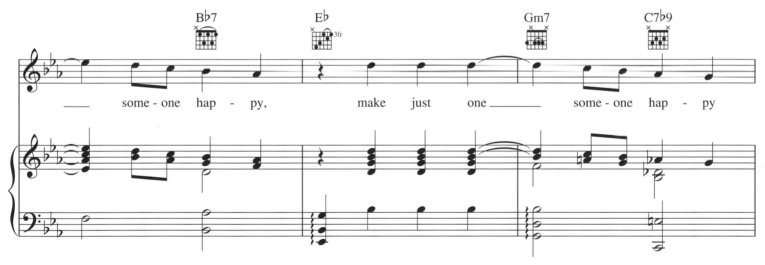

___ some - one hap - py, make just one _____ some - one hap - py

and you _____ will be hap - py, too. _____

THE MAN FROM SNOWY RIVER

(Main Title Theme)
from THE MAN FROM SNOWY RIVER

By BRUCE ROWLAND

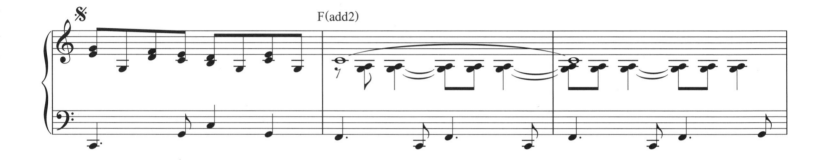

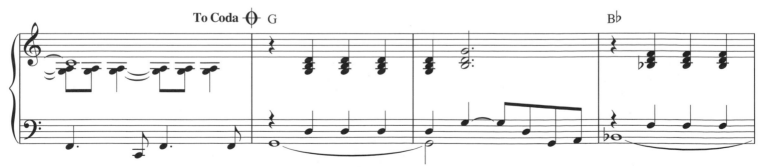

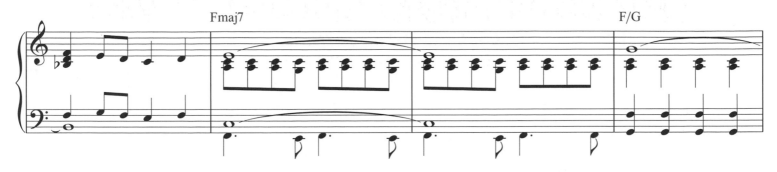

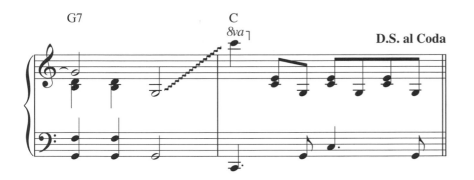
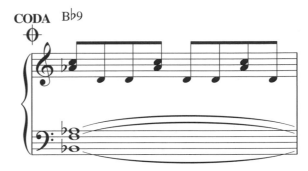

MISSION: IMPOSSIBLE THEME

from the Paramount Motion Picture MISSION: IMPOSSIBLE

By LALO SCHIFRIN

Moderately, with drive

MY OLD FLAME

from the Paramount Picture BELLE OF THE NINETIES

Words and Music by ARTHUR JOHNSTON
and SAM COSLOW

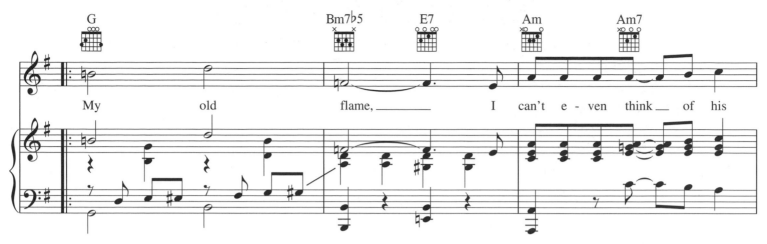

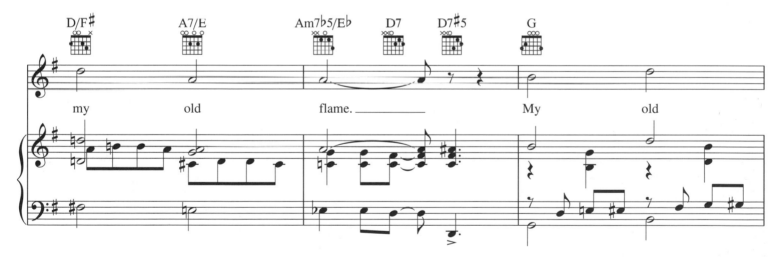

have-n't met a gent so mag - nif - i - cent or el - e - gant___ as my old

flame.___ I've met so man - y who had fas - ci - nat - in' ways, ___ a

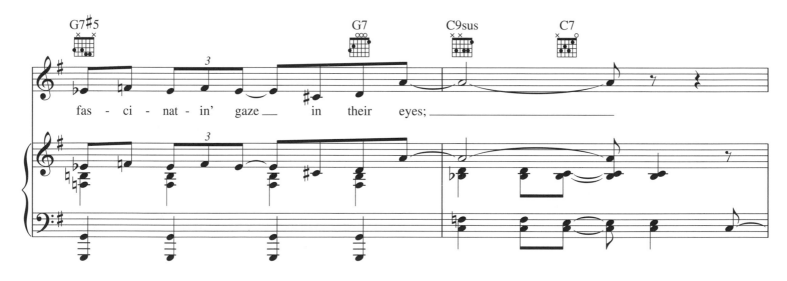

fas - ci - nat - in' gaze ___ in their eyes; ___

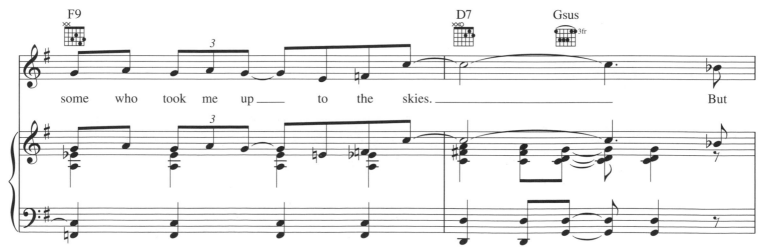

some who took me up ___ to the skies. ___ But

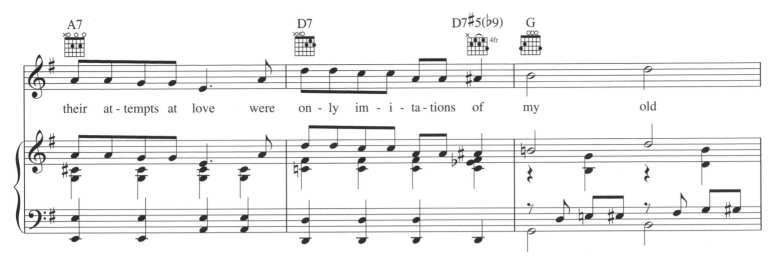

their at-tempts at love were on-ly im-i-ta-tions of my old

flame. _____ I can't e-ven think __ of his name, but I'll

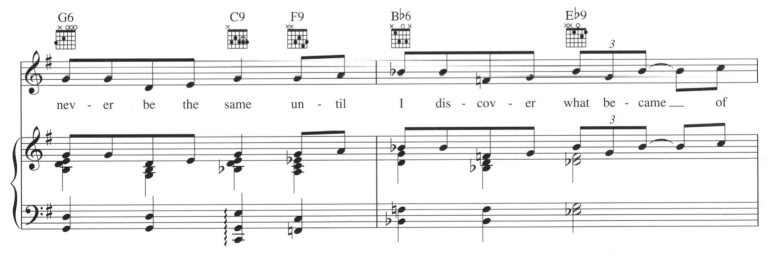

nev-er be the same un-til I dis-cov-er what be-came __ of

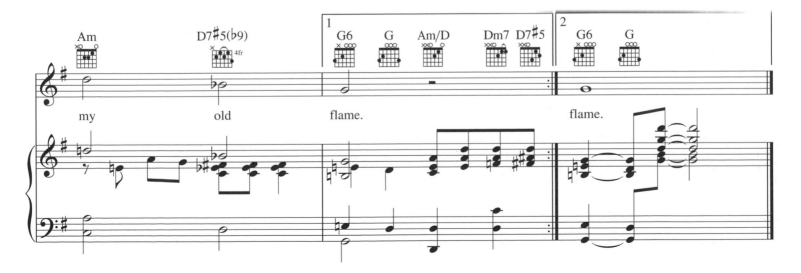

my old flame. flame.

NIGHT FEVER

from SATURDAY NIGHT FEVER

Words and Music by BARRY GIBB,
ROBIN GIBB and MAURICE GIBB

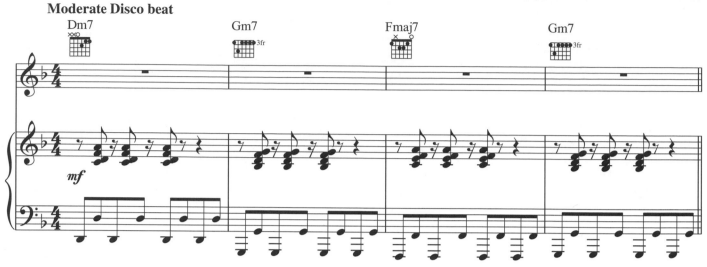

Lis-ten to __ the ground, __ there is move-ment all __ a-round. __ There is
heat of our ___ love, __ don't need no help for us __ to make __ it. Gim-me

some-thing go-in' down, __ and I can feel it. On the
just e-nough to take ___ us to the morn-in.' I got

waves of ___ the air, ___ there is danc - in' out ___ there. ___ If it's
fire in ___ my mind. ___ I got high - er in ___ my walk - in'. And I'm

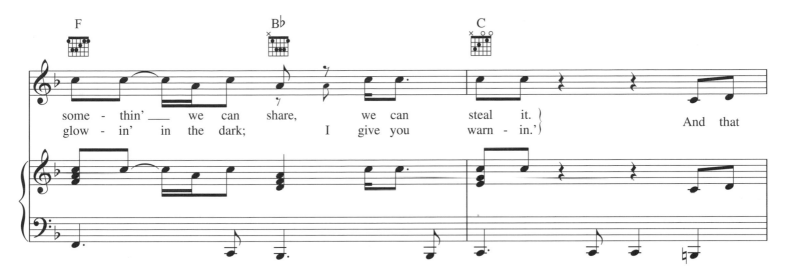

some - thin' ___ we can share, we can steal it.
glow - in' in the dark; I give you warn - in.' } And that

sweet cit - y wom - an, she moves through the light, _____ con -

trol - ling my mind ___ and my soul. _____ When you

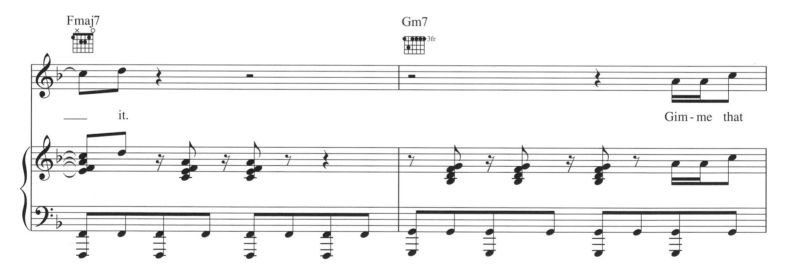

Here I am, prayin' for this mo-ment to last, _____

liv - in' on the mu - sic so fine, ____ borne on the wind, __

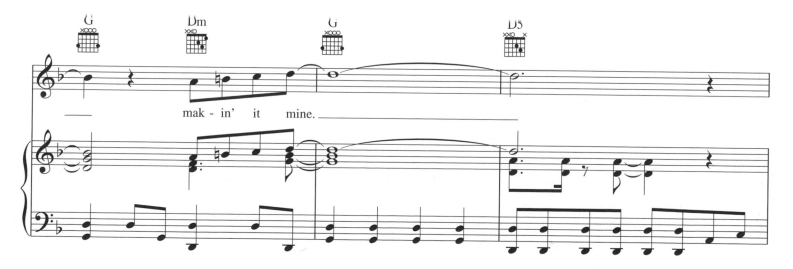

mak - in' it mine. _____

Night fe - ver, night fe - ver. ___
(D.S.) night fe - ver, night fe - ver. ___
We know how to do ___

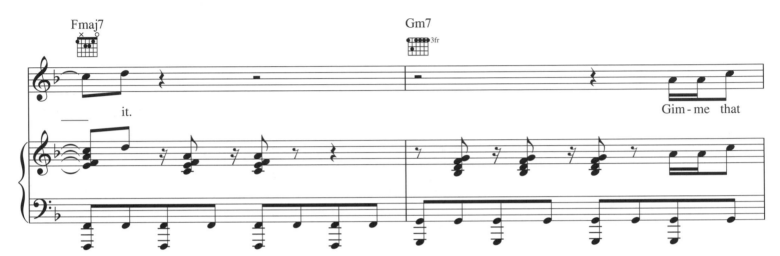

___ it.
Gim - me that

night fe - ver, night fe - ver. ___
We know how to show ___ it.

In the
D.S. and Fade
Gim - me that

NO TWO PEOPLE

from the Motion Picture HANS CHRISTIAN ANDERSEN

By FRANK LOESSER

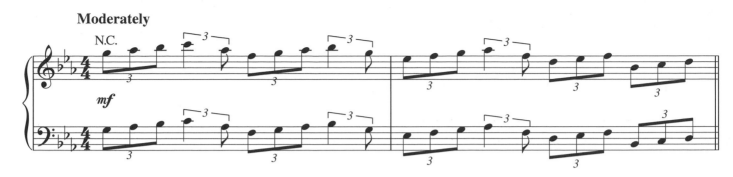

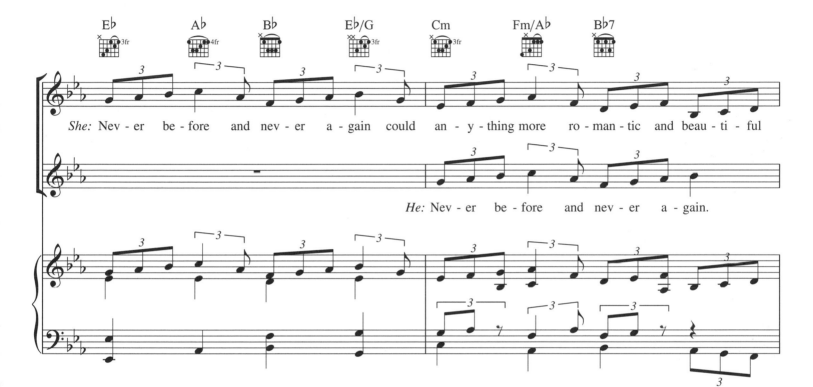

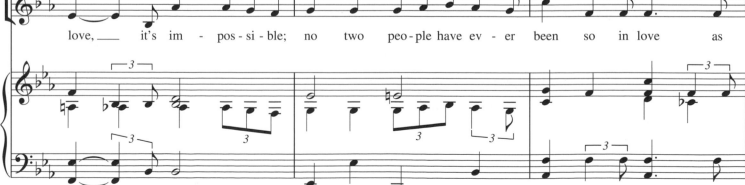

ON GOLDEN POND

Main Theme from ON GOLDEN POND

Music by DAVE GRUSIN

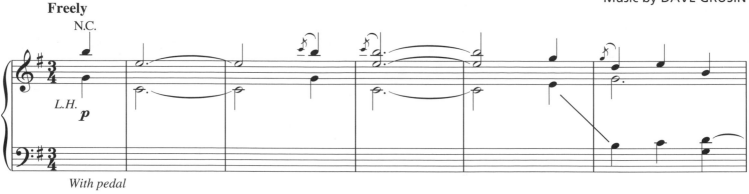

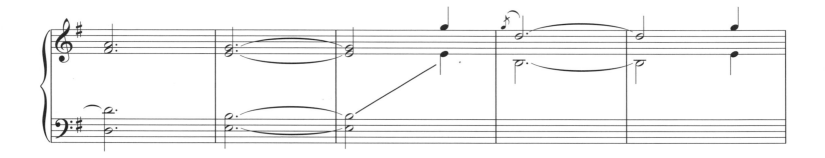

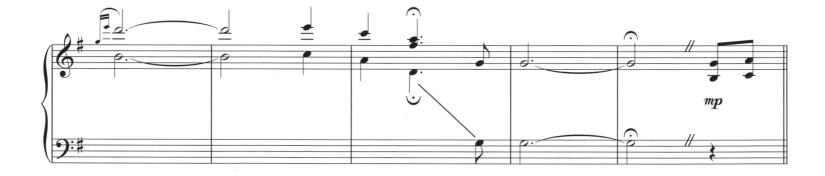

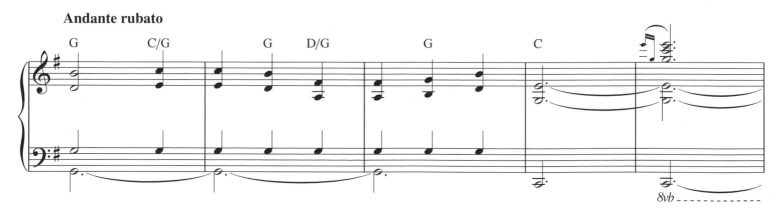

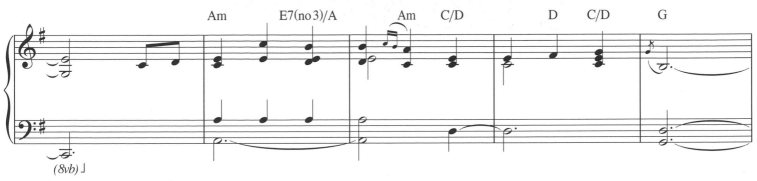

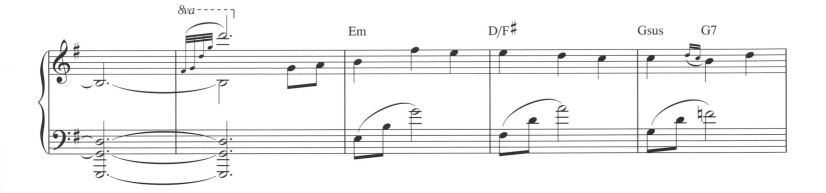

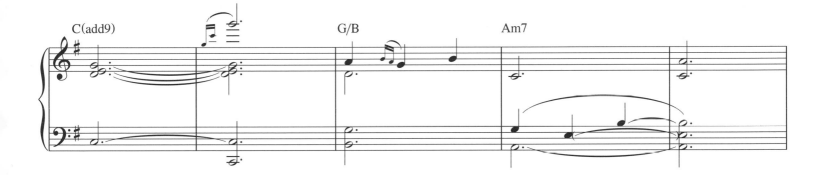

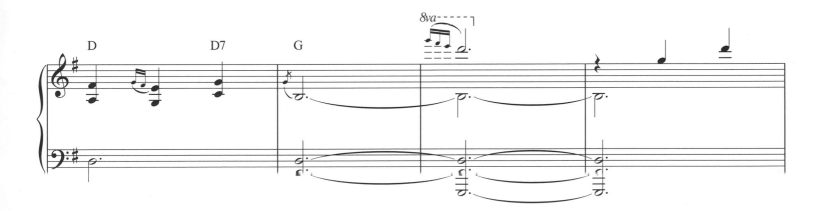

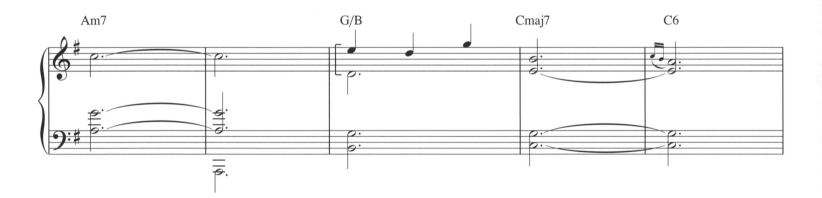

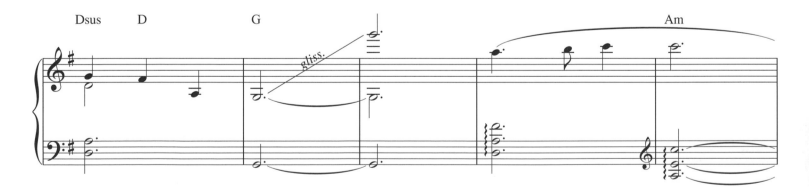

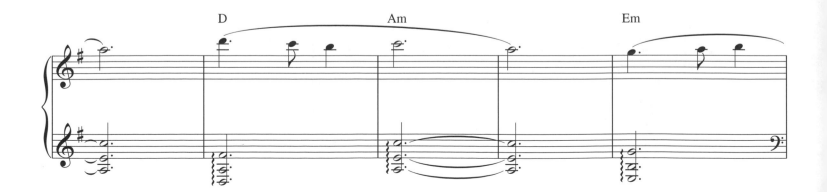

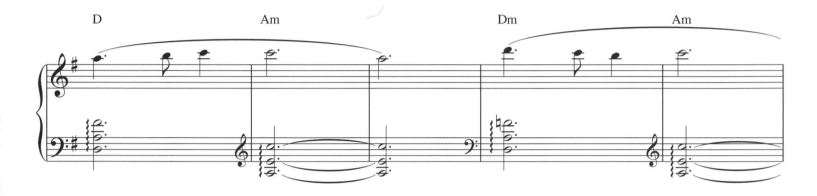

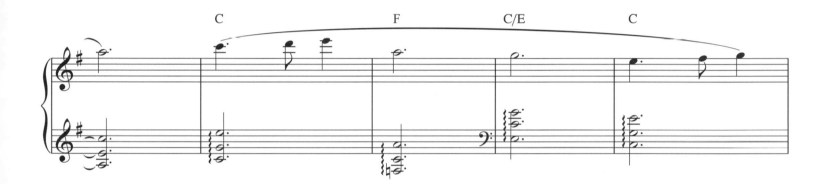

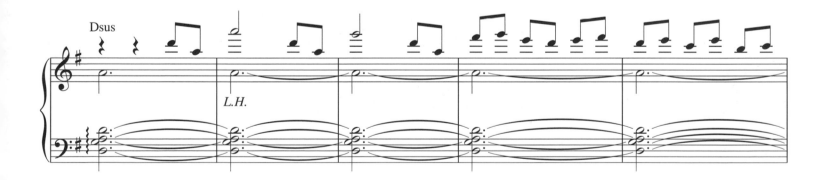

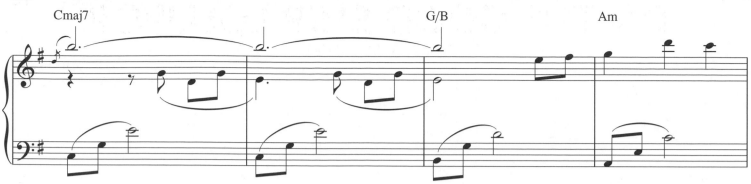

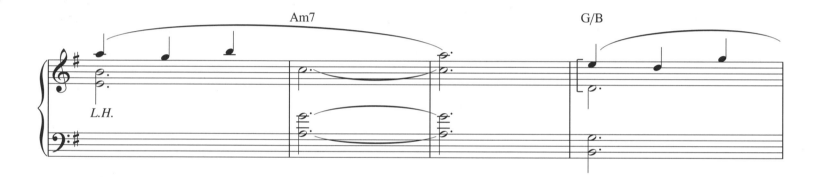

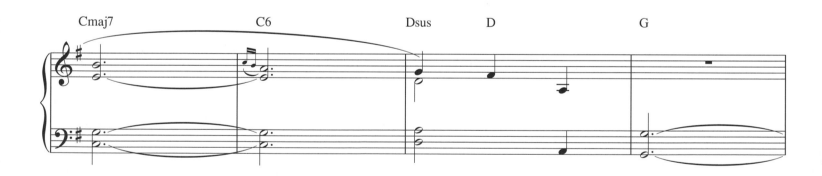

ON THE GOOD SHIP LOLLIPOP

from BRIGHT EYES

Words and Music by SIDNEY CLARE
and RICHARD A. WHITING

Lightly

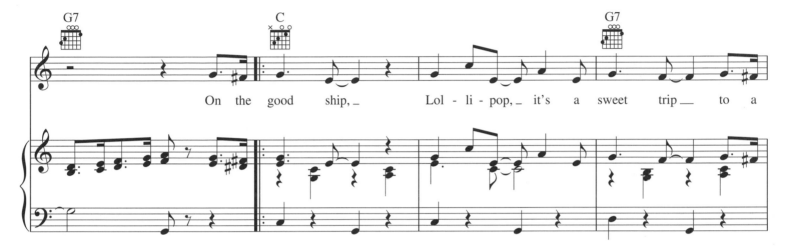

On the good ship, _ Lol - li - pop, _ it's a sweet trip _ to a

can - dy shop, _ where bon - bons play _____ on the sun - ny beach of

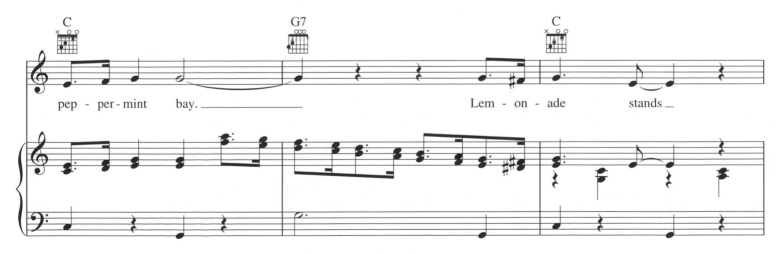

pep - per - mint bay. _____ Lem - on - ade stands _

ev - 'ry - where, __ crack - er - jack bands __ fill the air, __ and

there you are _____ hap - py land - ing on a choc - o - late bar. __

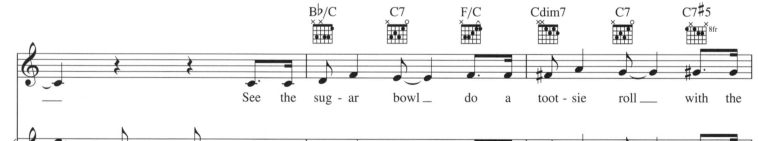

__ See the sug - ar bowl __ do a toot - sie roll __ with the

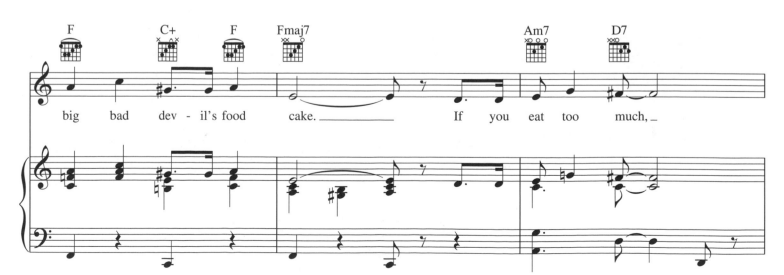

big bad dev - il's food cake. _____ If you eat too much, __

ONE

from A CHORUS LINE

Music by MARVIN HAMLISCH
Lyric by EDWARD KLEBAN

One

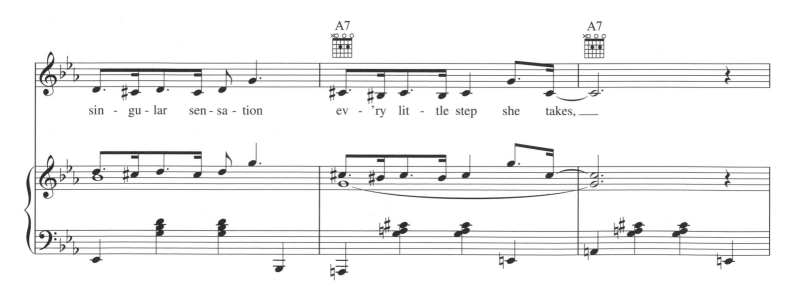

sin - gu - lar sen - sa - tion ev - 'ry lit - tle step she takes, ___

One mo - ment in her pres - ence and you can for - get the rest, —

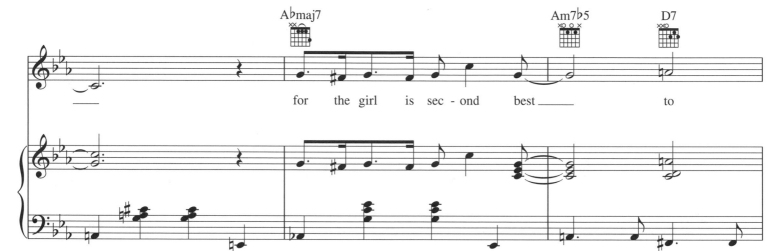

— for the girl is sec - ond best _____ to

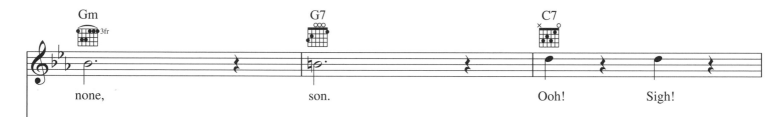

none, son. Ooh! Sigh!

Give her your at - ten - tion, do I real - ly have to men - tion

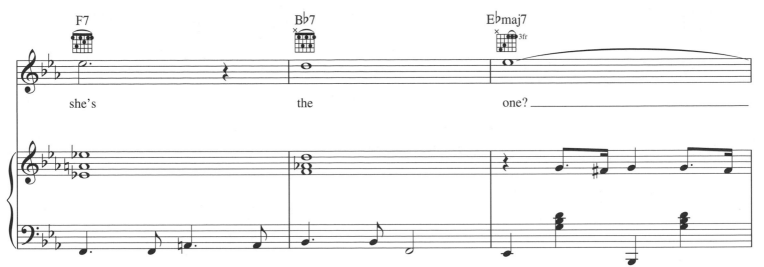

she's the one? _____

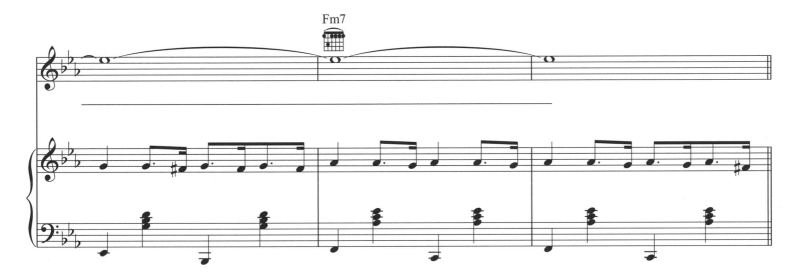

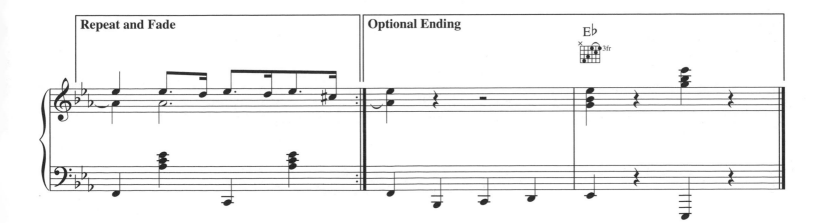

Repeat and Fade

Optional Ending

THEME FROM "ORDINARY PEOPLE"

from ORDINARY PEOPLE

Arranged by MARVIN HAMLISCH

Sostenuto (♪ = ca. 100)

Peo - ple. _____

PICNIC
from the Columbia Technicolor Picture PICNIC

Words by STEVE ALLEN
Music by GEORGE W. DUNING

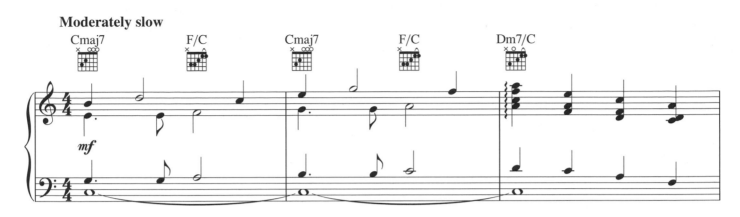

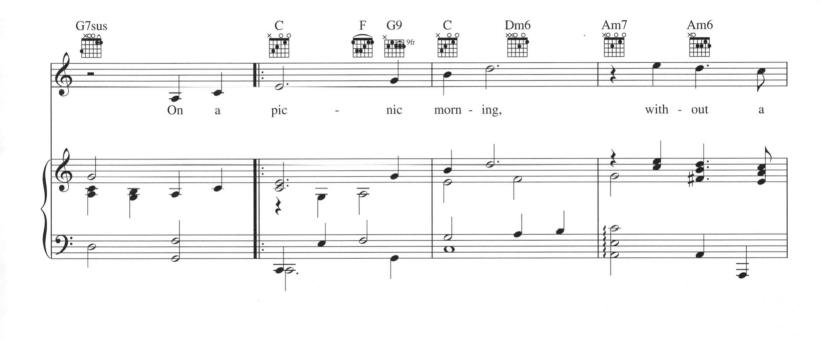

On a pic - nic morn - ing, with - out a

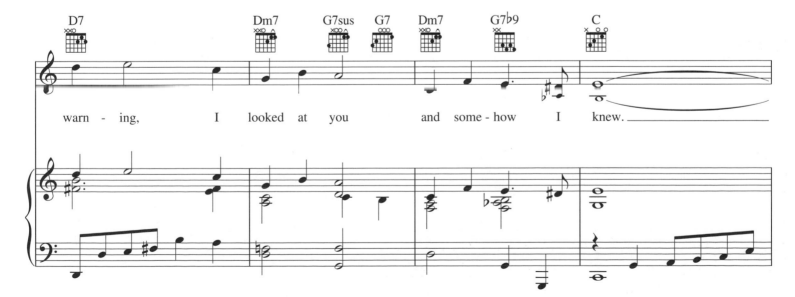

warn - ing, I looked at you and some - how I knew. _____

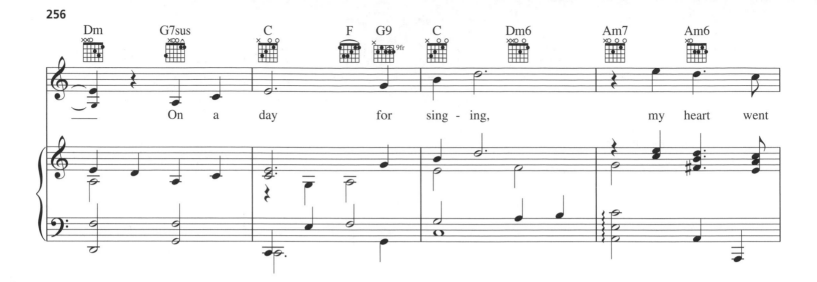

On a day for sing - ing, my heart went

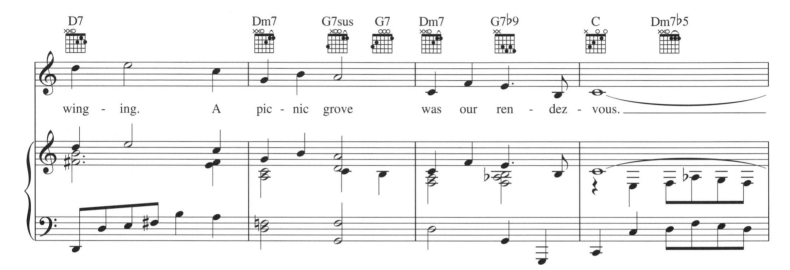

wing - ing. A pic - nic grove was our ren - dez - vous. ___

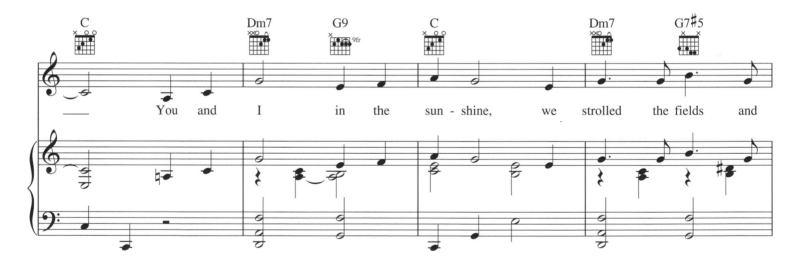

___ You and I in the sun - shine, we strolled the fields and

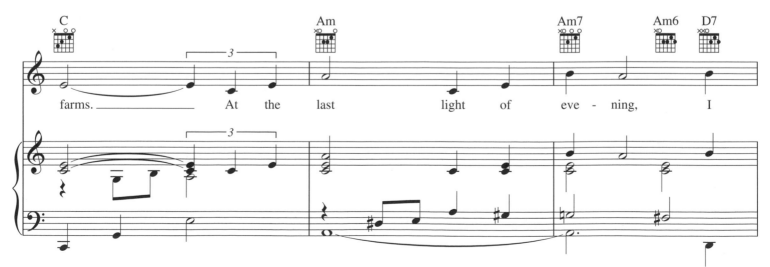

farms. ___ At the last light of eve - ning, I

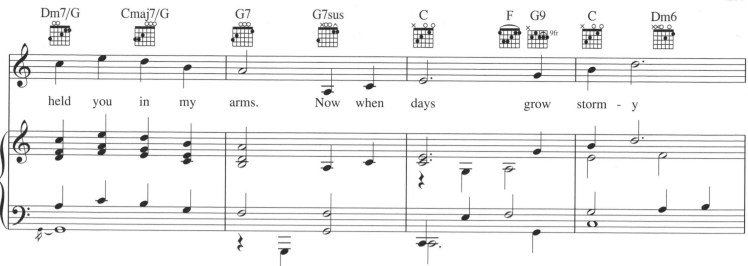

held you in my arms. Now when days grow storm-y

and lone-ly for me, I just re-call

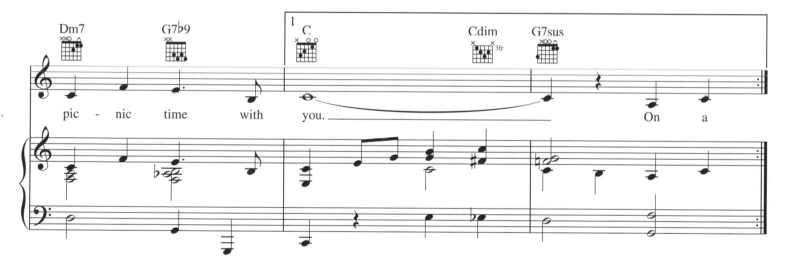

pic-nic time with you. _____ On a

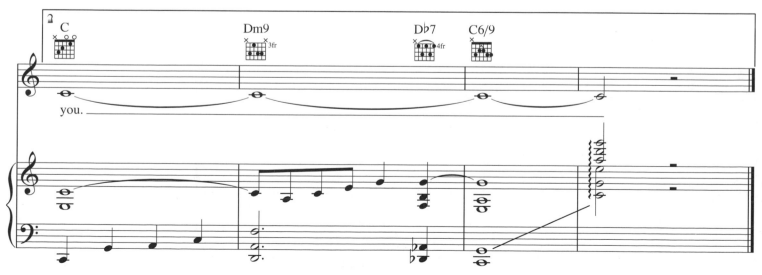

you. _____

PEOPLE
from FUNNY GIRL

Words by BOB MERRILL
Music by JULE STYNE

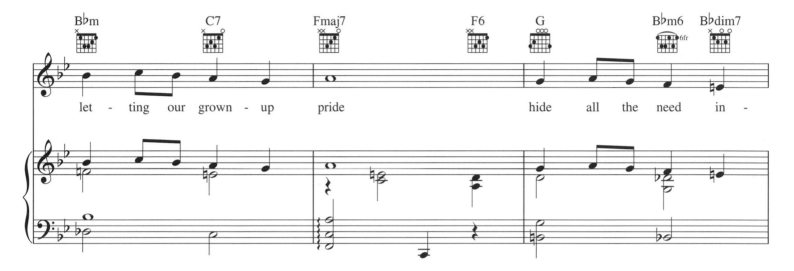

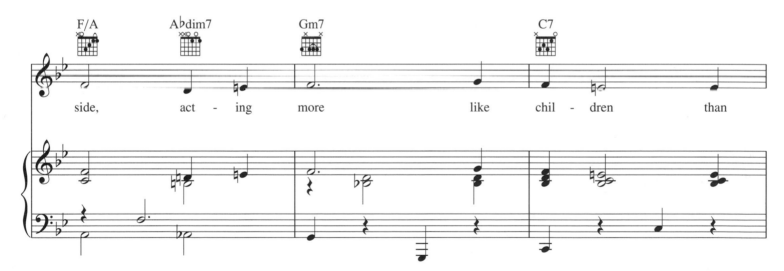

RING OF FIRE
from I WALK THE LINE

Words and Music by MERLE KILGORE
and JUNE CARTER

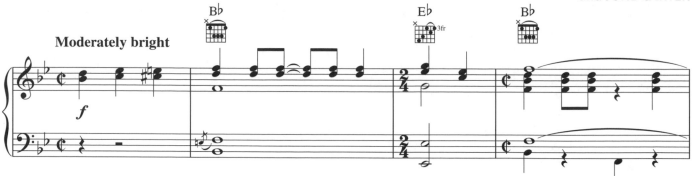

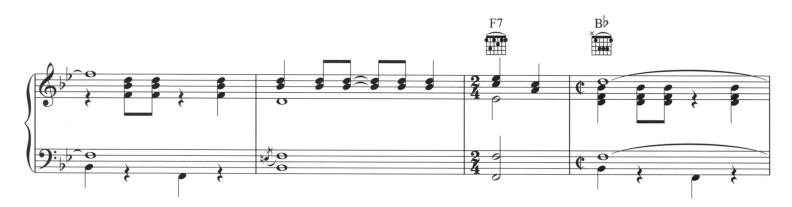

Love _____ is a burn-ing
taste _____ of love is

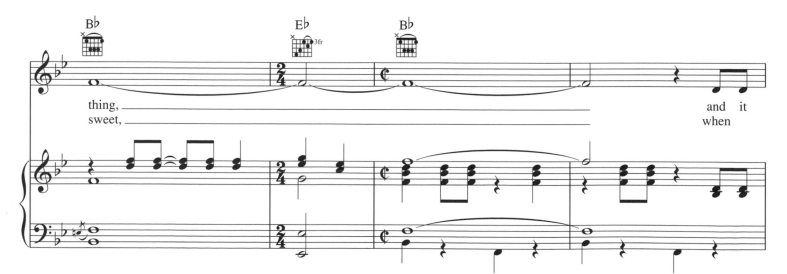

thing, _____ and it
sweet, _____ when

makes _____ a fi - er - y ring.
hearts _____ like ours ____ beat.

Bound _____
I fell

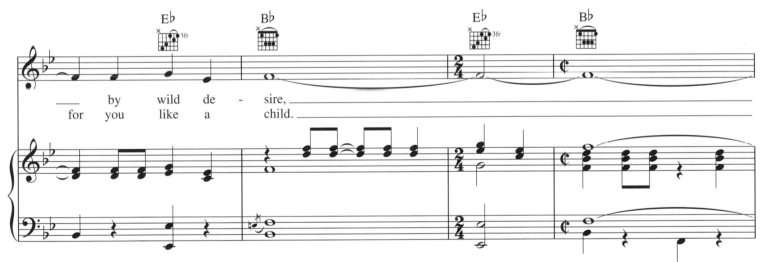

____ by wild de - sire, _____
for you like a child. _____

____ I fell in - to a ring of fire. _____
____ Oh, ____ but the fire went wild. _____

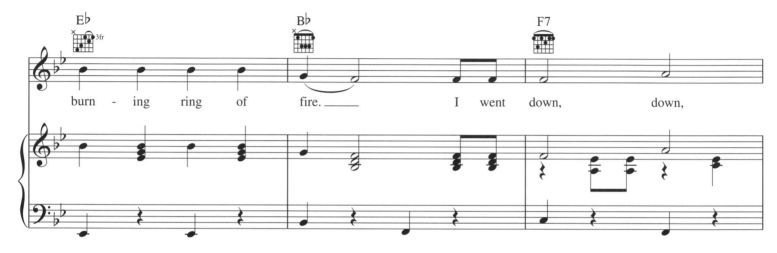

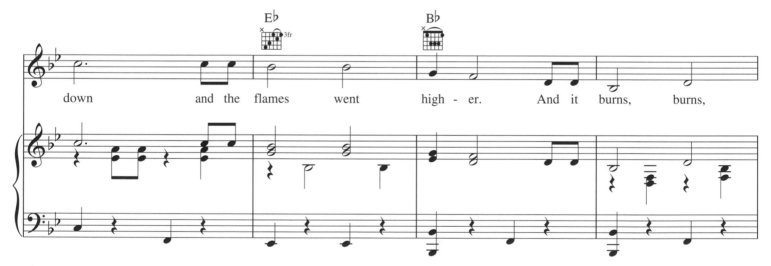

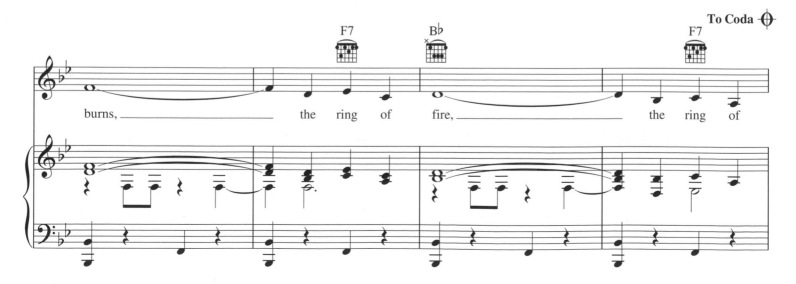

ROMEO AND JULIET
(Love Theme)
from the Paramount Picture ROMEO AND JULIET

By NINO ROTA

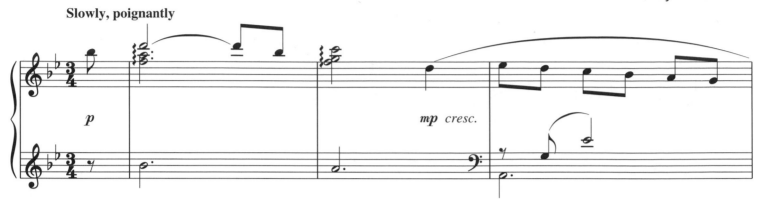

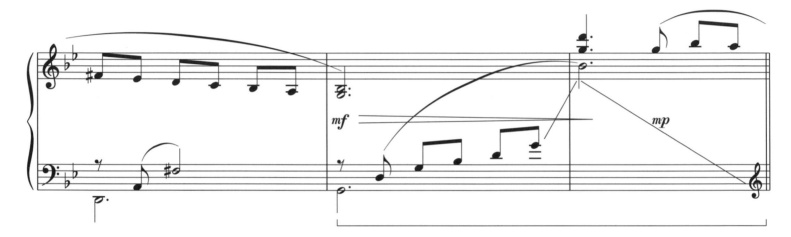

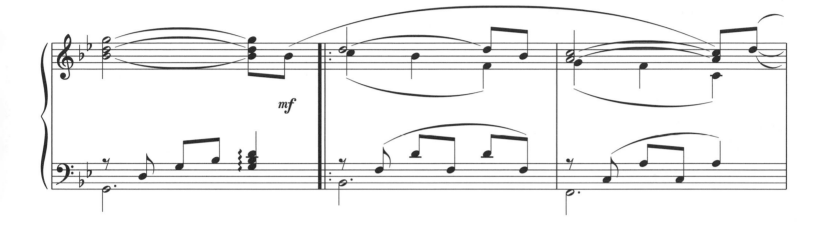

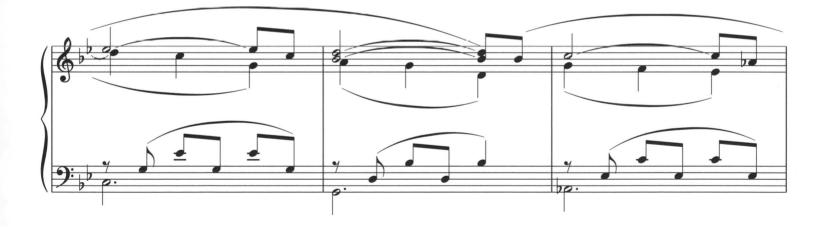

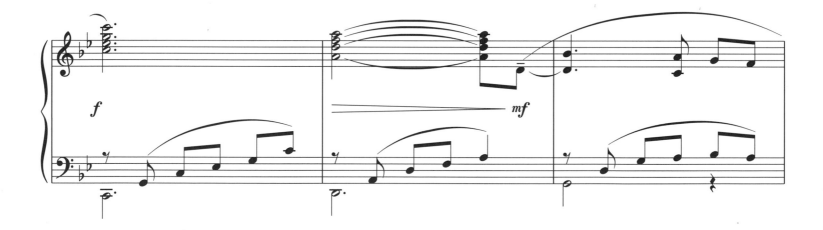

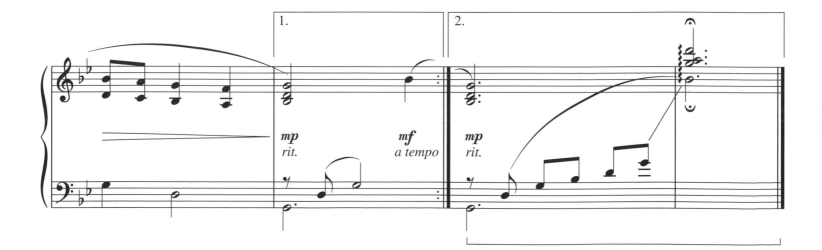

SEPARATE LIVES
Love Theme from WHITE NIGHTS

Words and Music by
STEPHEN BISHOP

and that you miss me some-times when you're a-

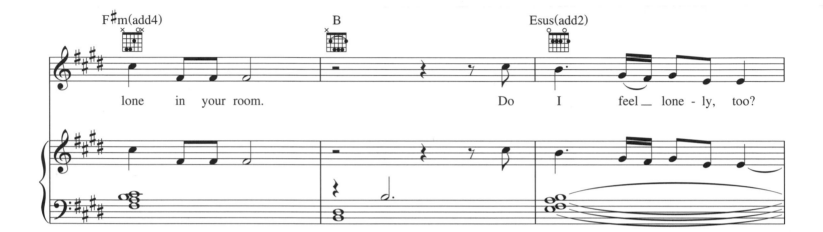

lone in your room. Do I feel __ lone - ly, too?

Both: You have __ no right ___

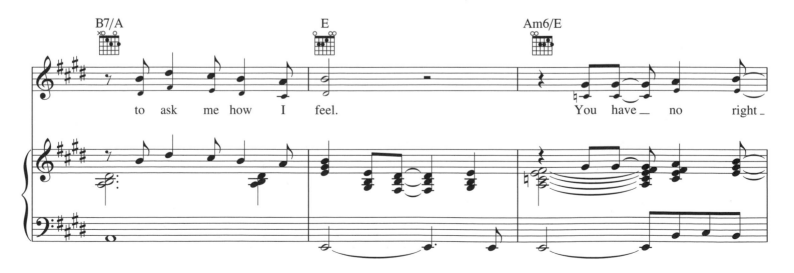

to ask me how I feel. You have __ no right __

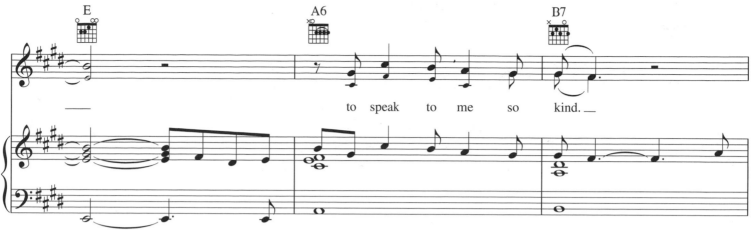

to speak to me so kind.

I can't go on ___ just hold-ing on ___ to ties, ___

Male: now that we're liv-ing, *Female:* liv-ing ___

Both: sep - 'rate lives. ___

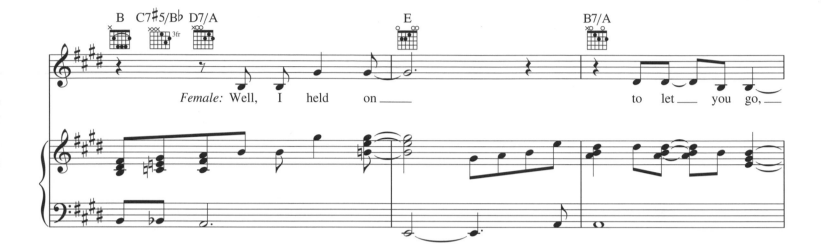

Female: Well, I held on _____ to let ___ you go, ___

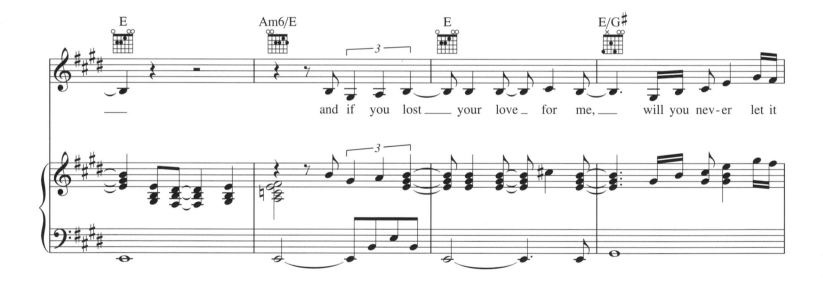

___ and if you lost ___ your love__ for me, ___ will you nev-er let it

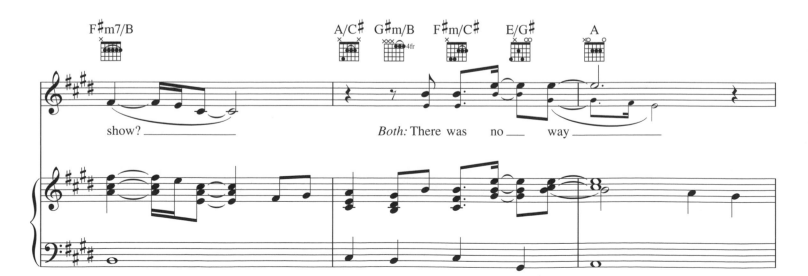

show? _____ *Both:* There was no ___ way _____

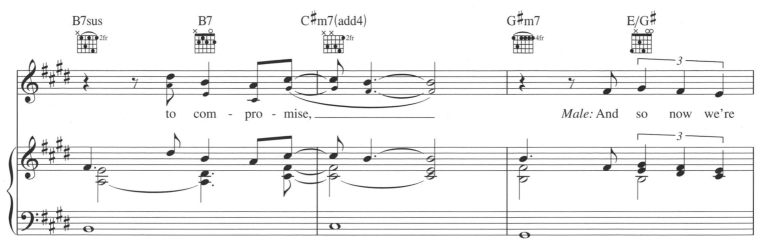

to com - pro - mise, _____ *Male:* And so now we're

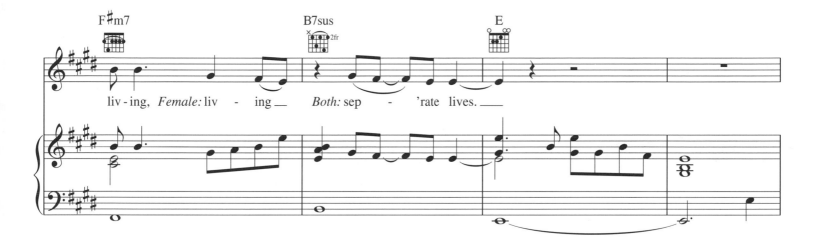

liv - ing, *Female:* liv - ing __ *Both:* sep - - 'rate lives. _____

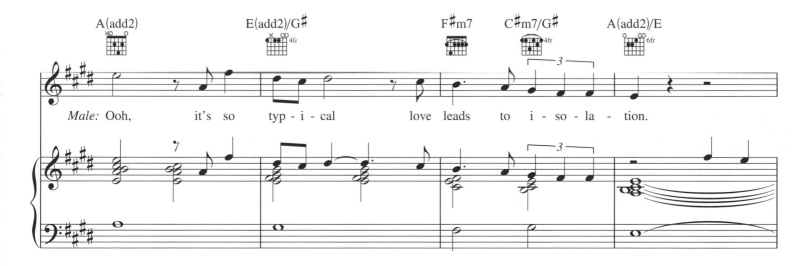

Male: Ooh, it's so typ - i - cal love leads to i - so - la - tion.

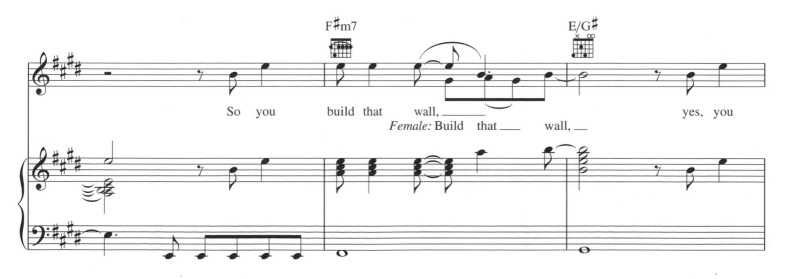

So you build that wall, _____ yes, you
Female: Build that __ wall, __

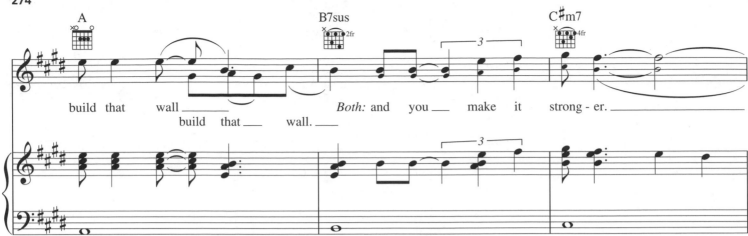

build that wall ____ *Both:* and you __ make it strong-er. ____
build that __ wall. __

__ Well, you have __ no right __ to ask me how I

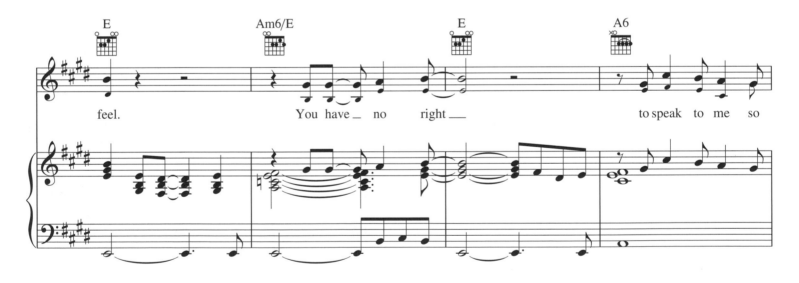

feel. You have __ no right __ to speak to me so

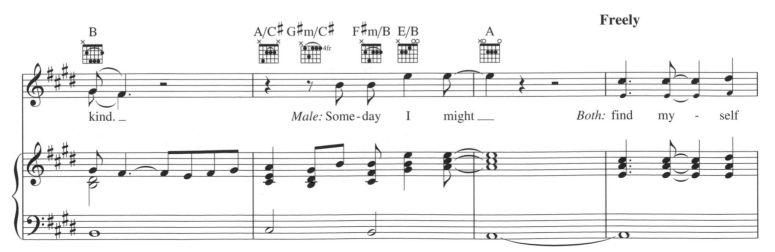

kind. __ *Male:* Some-day I might __ *Both:* find my-self

look - ing in ___ your eyes, *Male:* but for now we'll go on

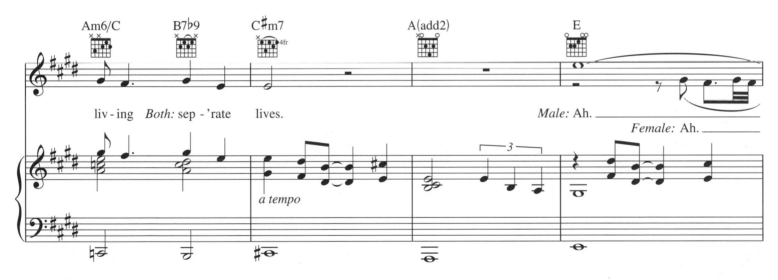

liv - ing sep - 'rate lives. *Female:* Yes, for now we'll go on

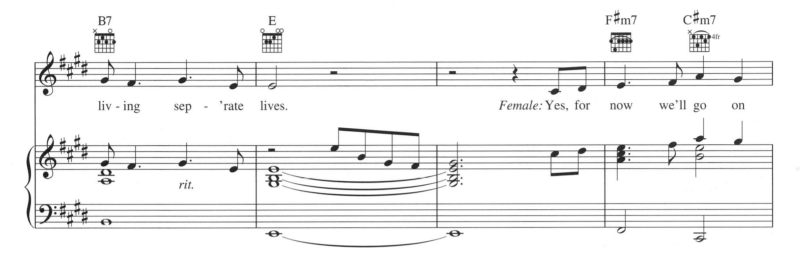

liv - ing *Both:* sep - 'rate lives. *Male:* Ah. ___ *Female:* Ah. ___

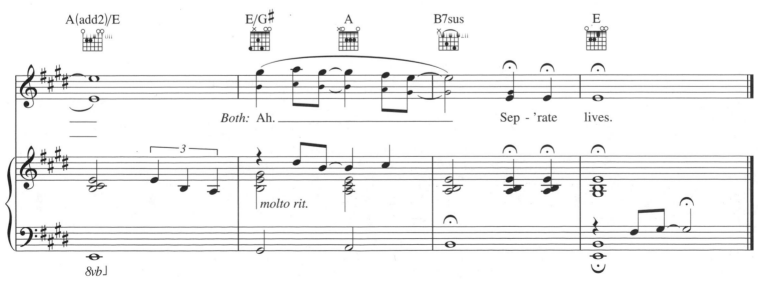

Both: Ah. ___ Sep - 'rate lives.

THEME FROM "SCHINDLER'S LIST"

from the Universal Motion Picture SCHINDLER'S LIST

Composed by
JOHN WILLIAMS

SHOUT
featured in the Walt Disney Movie SISTER ACT

Words and Music by O'KELLY ISLEY,
RONALD ISLEY and RUDOLPH ISLEY

say you will. _____ Don't for - get to

say yeah, yeah, ___ yeah, yeah, ___ yeah. Say _____

_____ you will. ___ Say it right now, ba - by. Say _____

_____ you will. ___ Come on, _____ come on. _____ Say _____

you will _____ hey, _____ hey, _____ hey. Say _____

_____ you will. _____ Come on _____ now. _____ (Say) Say that you
(Say) Say that you

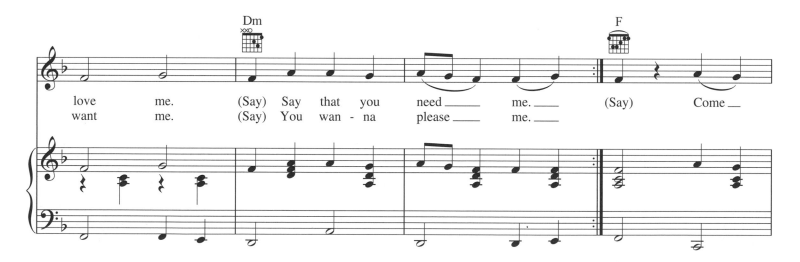

love me. (Say) Say that you need _____ me. _____ (Say) Come _____
want me. (Say) You wan-na need please _____ me. _____

on, now. _____ (Say) Come _____ on, now. _____ (Say) Come _____

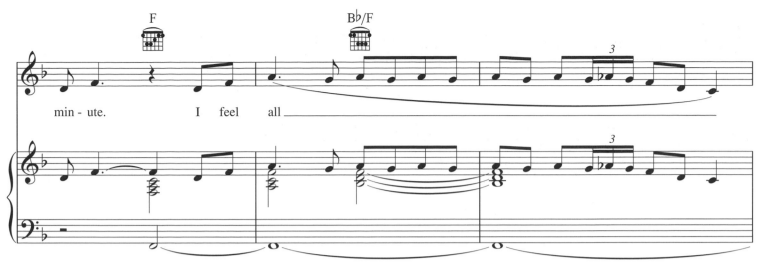

min - ute.   I feel all _____

right. _____ (Yeah, yeah, yeah, yeah, yeah, yeah.) Now that I've got my wom-an, I feel   all _____

right. _ (Yeah, yeah, yeah, yeah, yeah.) Ev -'ry time I think a - bout you.

Original tempo

You been so good   to me.   You know you   make me wan - na

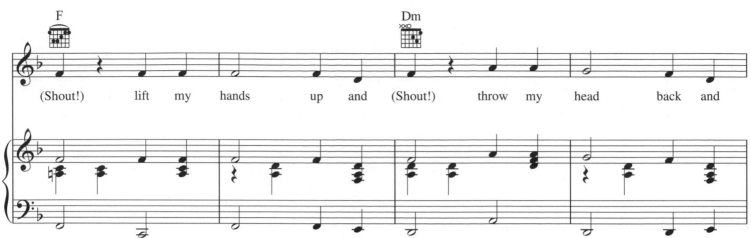

(Shout!) lift my hands up and (Shout!) throw my head back and

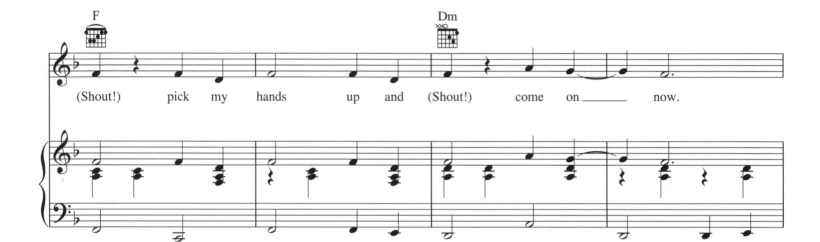

(Shout!) pick my hands up and (Shout!) come on _____ now.

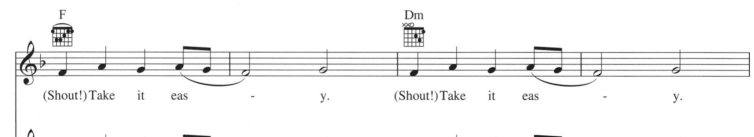

(Shout!) Take it eas - y. (Shout!) Take it eas - y.

(Shout!) Take it eas - y. (Shout!) A lit - tle bit

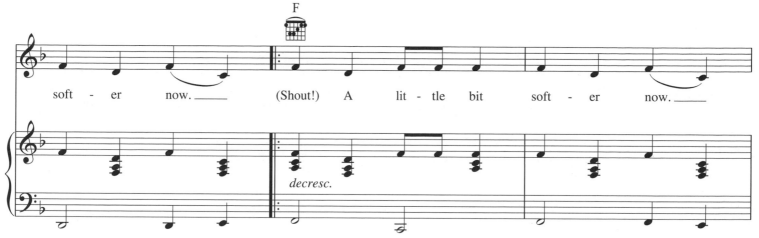

soft - er now. _____ (Shout!) A lit - tle bit soft - er now. _____

(Shout!) A lit - tle bit soft - er now. _____ (Shout!) A lit - tle bit

Play 8 times

loud - er now. _____ (Shout!) A lit - tle bit loud - er now. _____ (Shout!) Hey, _____

Play 6 times

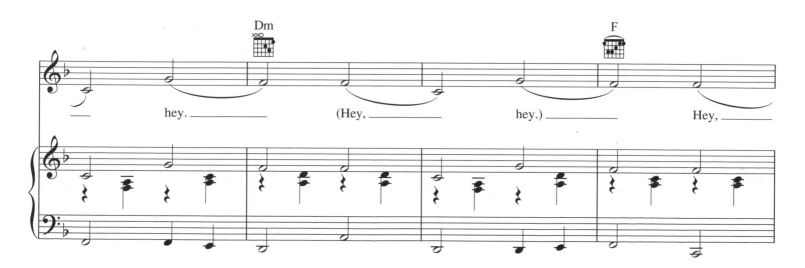

_____ hey. _____ (Hey, _____ hey.) _____ Hey, _____

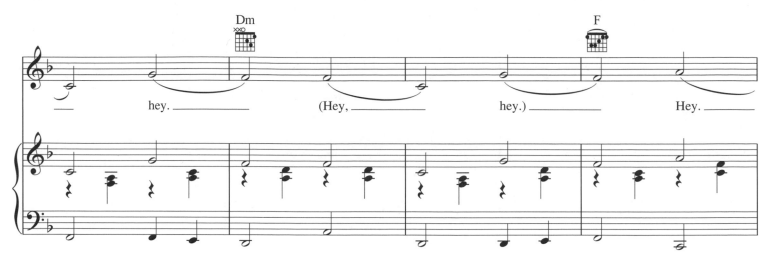

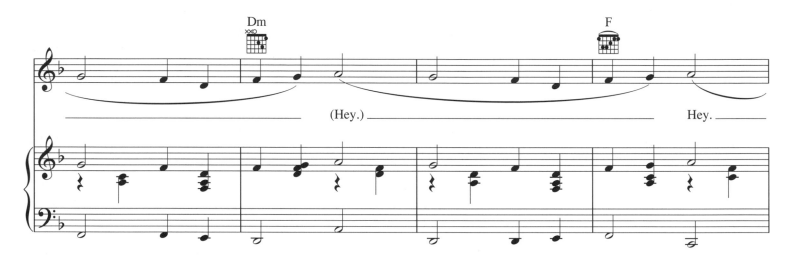

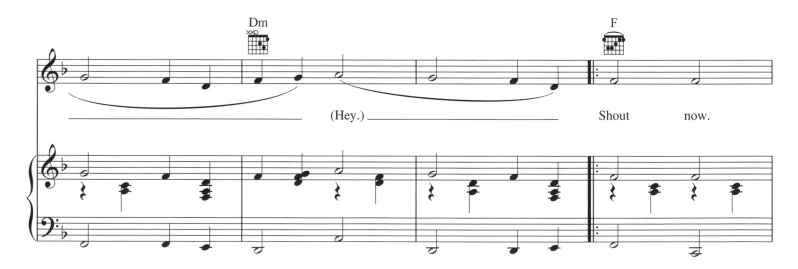

THEME FROM THE SIMPSONS™

from the Twentieth Century Fox Television Series THE SIMPSONS

Music by DANNY ELFMAN

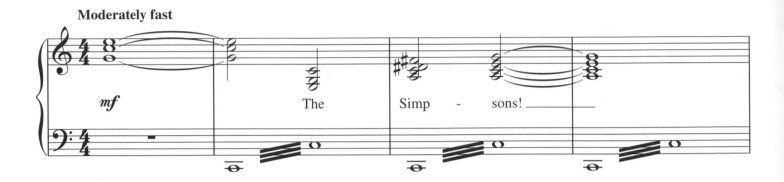

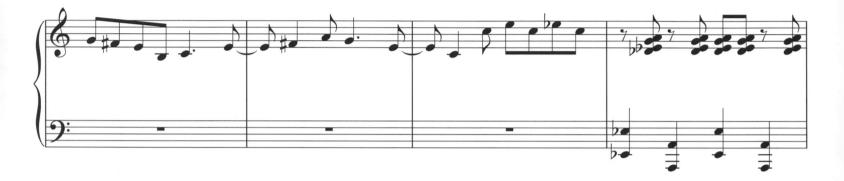

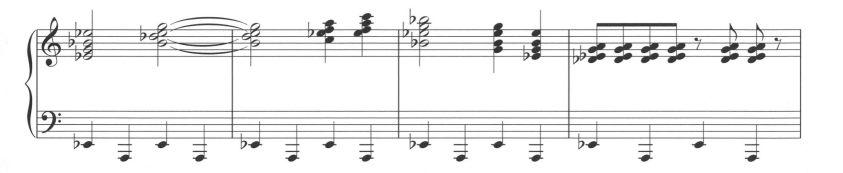

SOME DAY MY PRINCE WILL COME

from Walt Disney's SNOW WHITE AND THE SEVEN DWARFS

Words by LARRY MOREY
Music by FRANK CHURCHILL

Rather fast

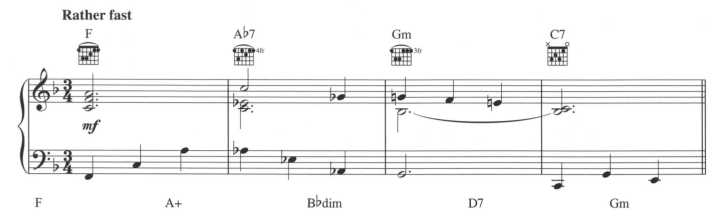

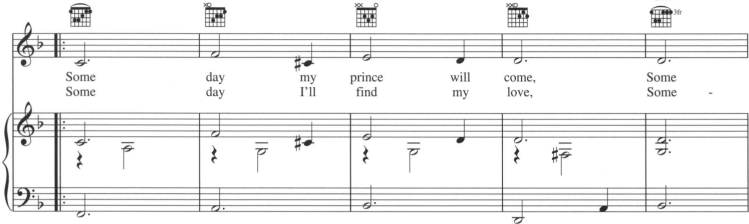

Some day my prince will come, Some

Some day I'll find my love, Some -

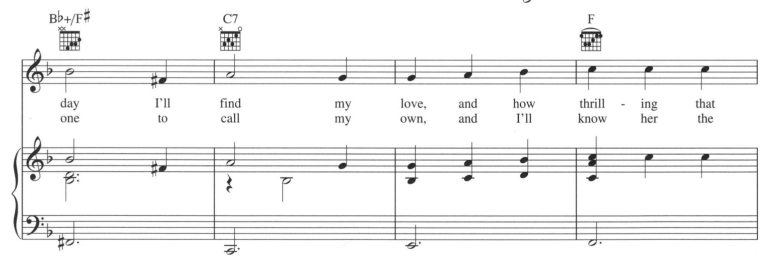

day I'll find my love, and how thrill - ing that

one to call my own, and I'll know her that the

mo - ment will be, _____ When the prince of my dreams comes to

mo - ment we meet, _____ For my heart will start skip - ping a

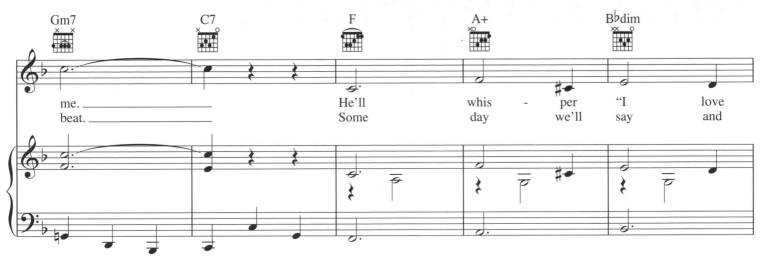

me. _____ He'll whis - per "I love
beat. _____ Some day we'll say and

you" And steal a kiss or two. Though he's
do things we've been long - ing to. Though she's

far a - way I'll find my love some day, some day when my

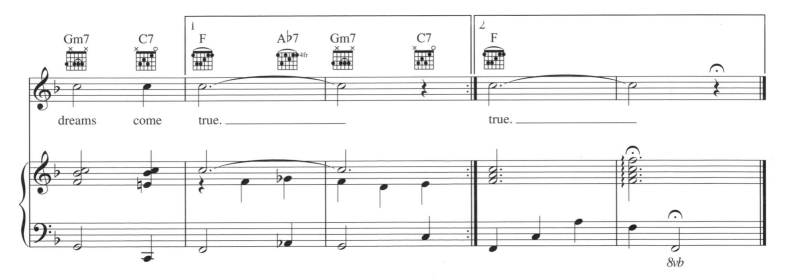

dreams come true. _____ true. _____

SOMEWHERE
from WEST SIDE STORY

Lyrics by STEPHEN SONDHEIM
Music by LEONARD BERNSTEIN

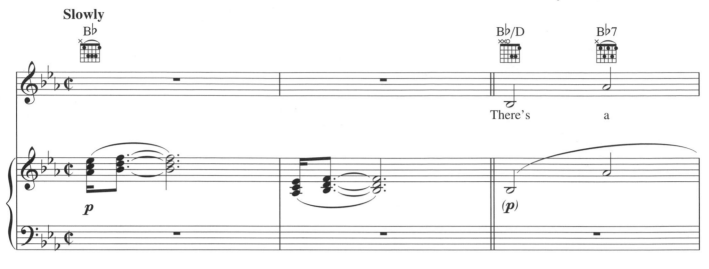

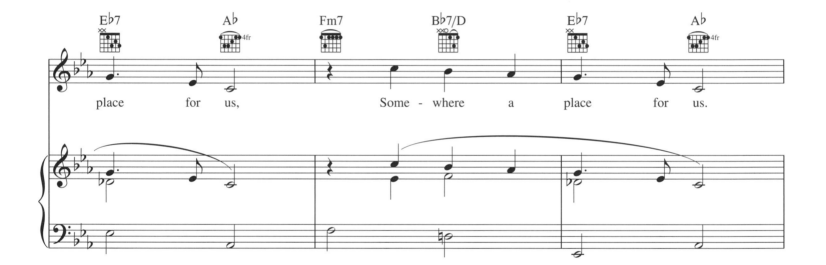

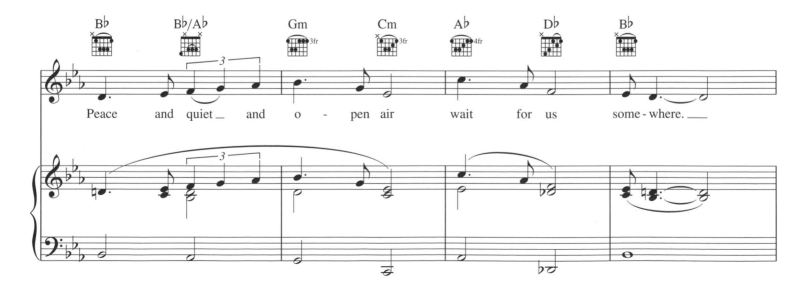

THE SOUND OF SILENCE
from THE GRADUATE

Words and Music by
PAUL SIMON

Hel - lo dark - ness, my old friend,

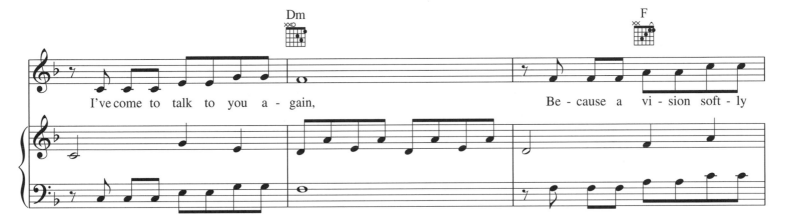

I've come to talk to you a - gain, Be - cause a vi - sion soft - ly

creep - ing, left it's seeds while I was sleep - ing,

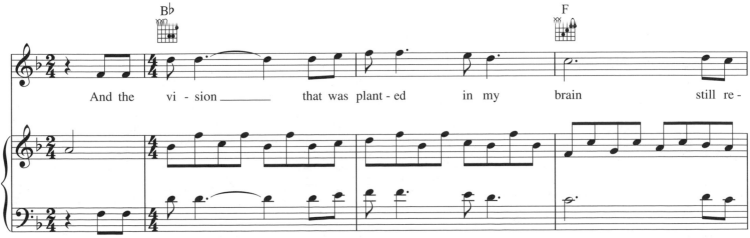

And the vi - sion ___ that was plant - ed in my brain still re -

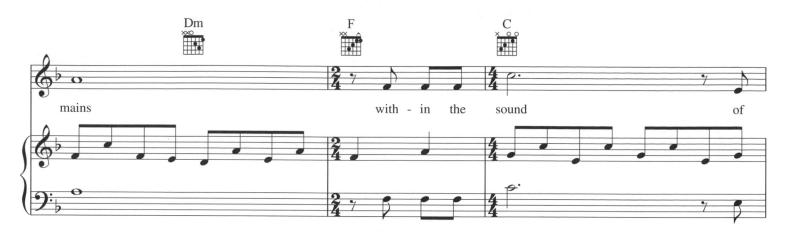

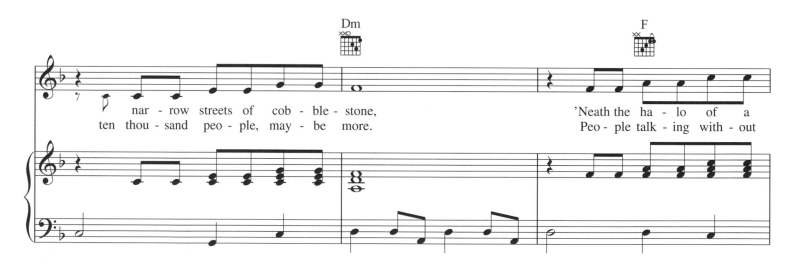

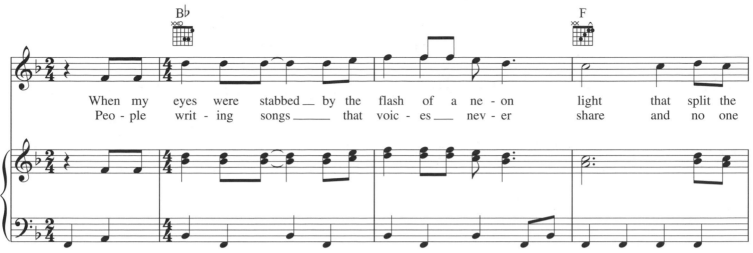

When my eyes were stabbed by the flash of a ne-on light that split the
Peo-ple writ-ing songs that voic-es nev-er share and no one

night and touched the sound of si-lence.
dare dis-turb the sound of si-lence.

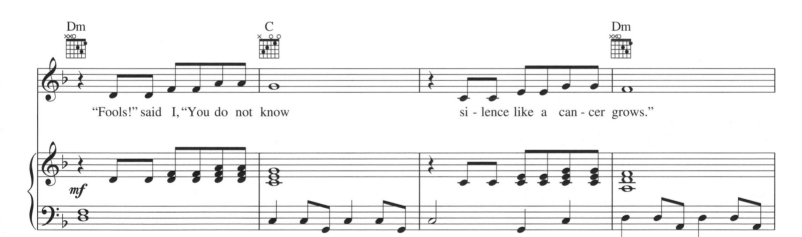

"Fools!" said I, "You do not know si-lence like a can-cer grows."

"Hear my words that I might teach you, Take my arms that I might

reach you." ___ But my words like si - lent rain - drops

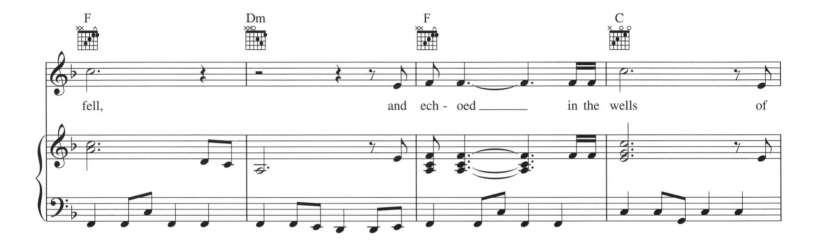

fell, and ech - oed ___ in the wells of

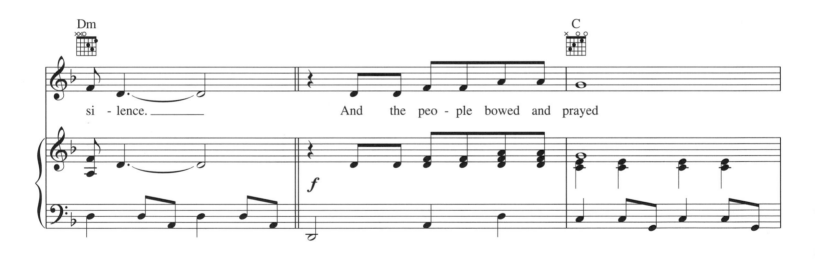

si - lence. ___ And the peo - ple bowed and prayed

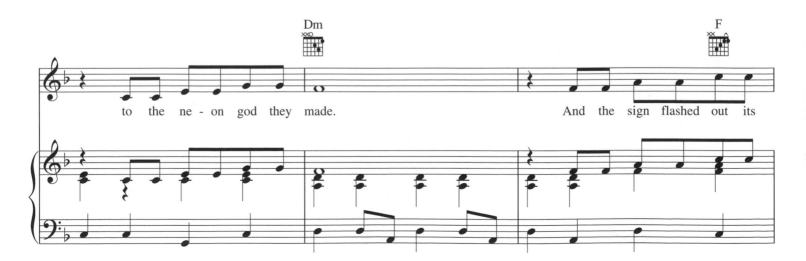

to the ne - on god they made. And the sign flashed out its

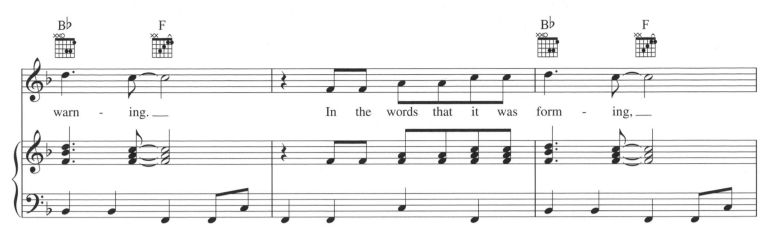

warn - ing. ___ In the words that it was form - ing, ___

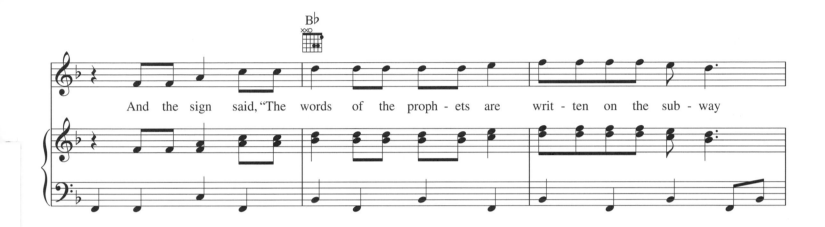

And the sign said, "The words of the proph - ets are writ - ten on the sub - way

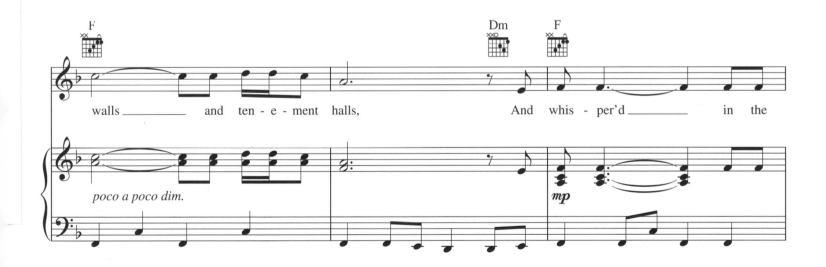

walls _____ and ten - e - ment halls, And whis - per'd _____ in the

poco a poco dim. *mp*

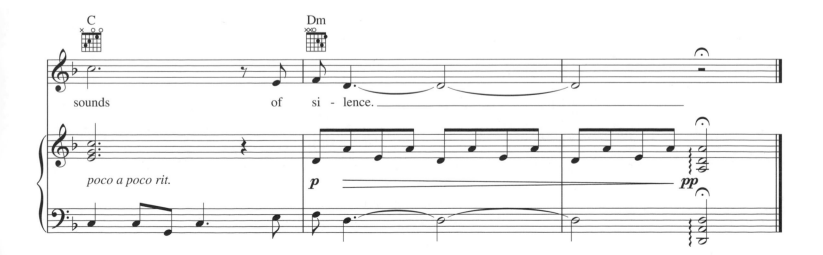

sounds of si - lence. _____

poco a poco rit. *p* _____ *pp*

SPARTACUS - LOVE THEME

from the Universal-International Picture Release SPARTACUS

By ALEX NORTH

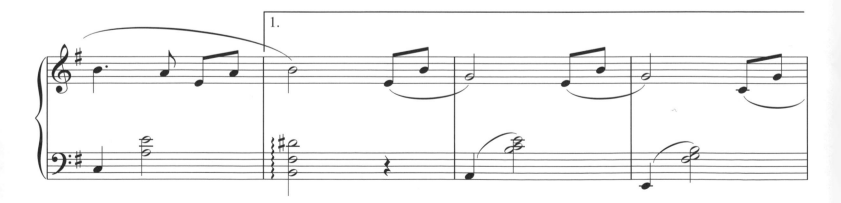

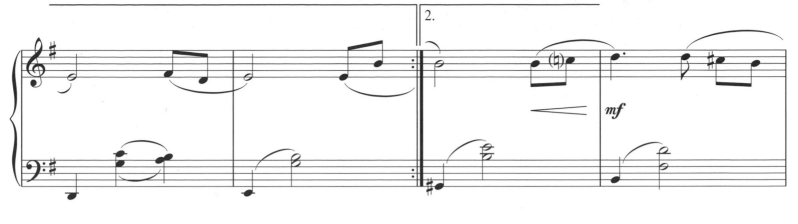

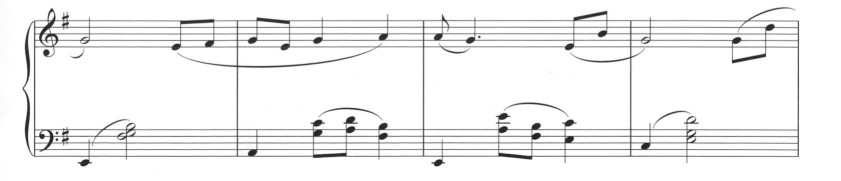

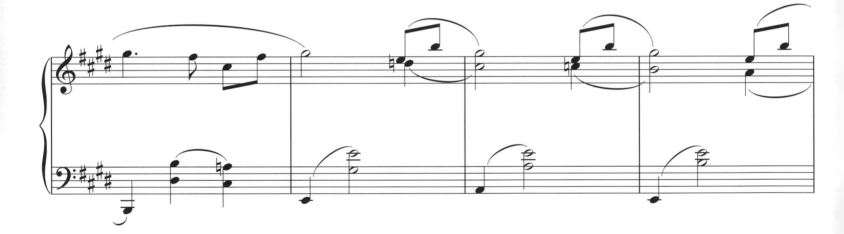

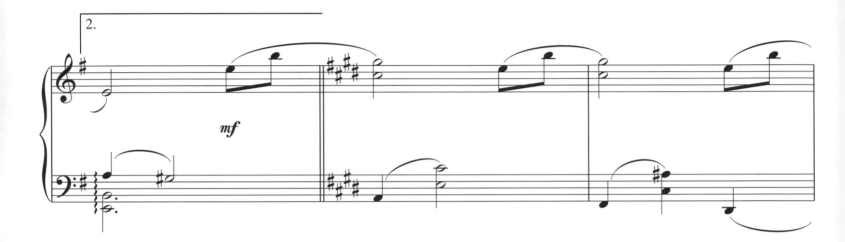

STARDUST
from STARDUST

Words by MITCHELL PARISH
Music by HOAGY CARMICHAEL

we're a - part. You wan - dered down the lane and far a - way, leav - ing me a song that will not

die. Love is now the star - dust of yes - ter - day,

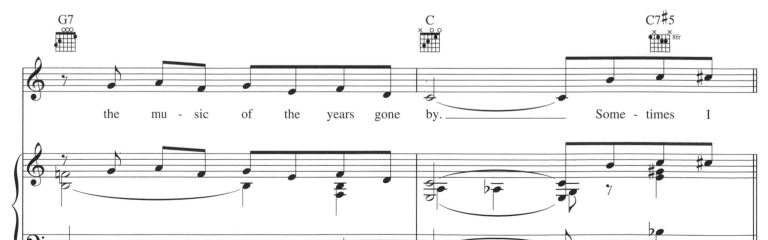

the mu - sic of the years gone by. _____ Some - times I

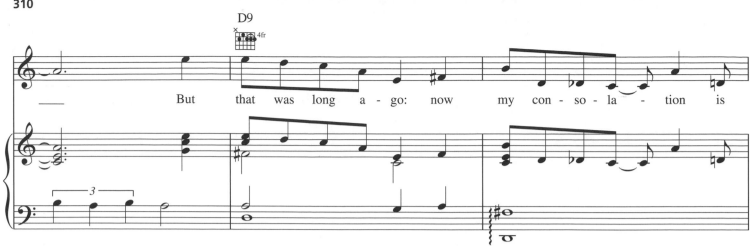

But that was long a-go: now my con-so-la-tion is

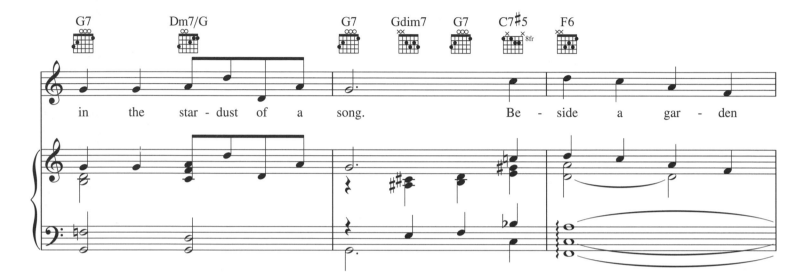

in the star-dust of a song. Be-side a gar-den

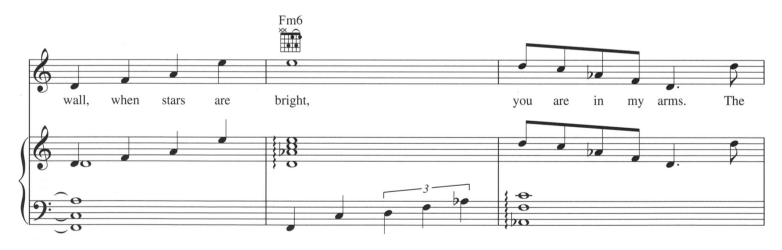

wall, when stars are bright, you are in my arms. The

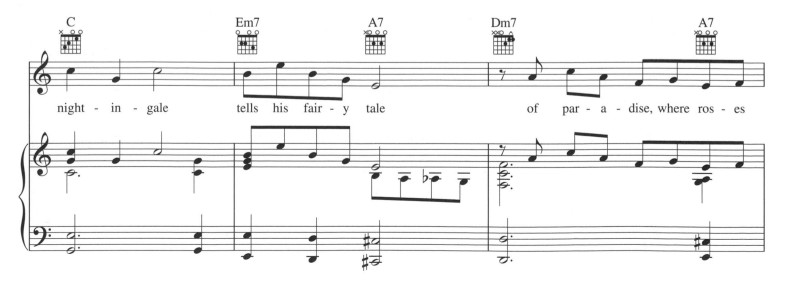

night-in-gale tells his fair-y tale of par-a-dise, where ros-es

LOVE THEME FROM "ST. ELMO'S FIRE"

from the Motion Picture ST. ELMO'S FIRE

Words and Music by
DAVID FOSTER

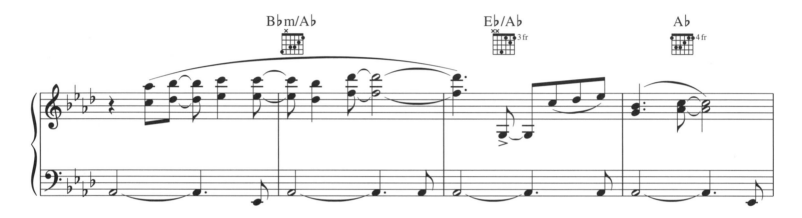

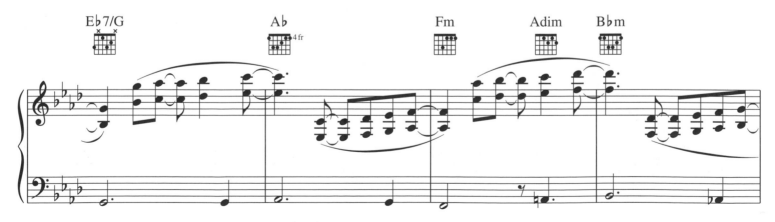

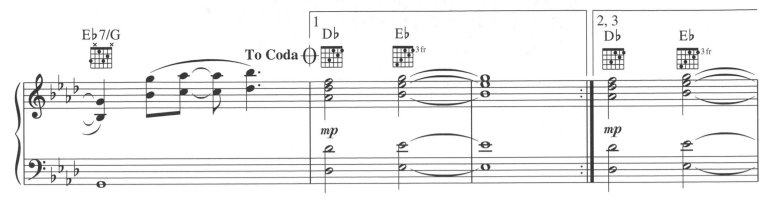

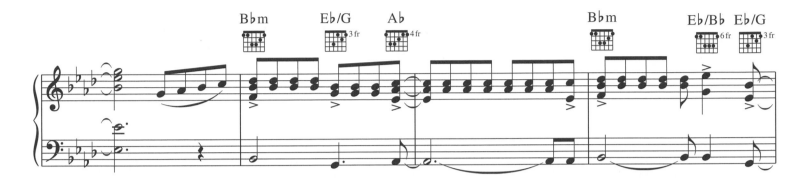

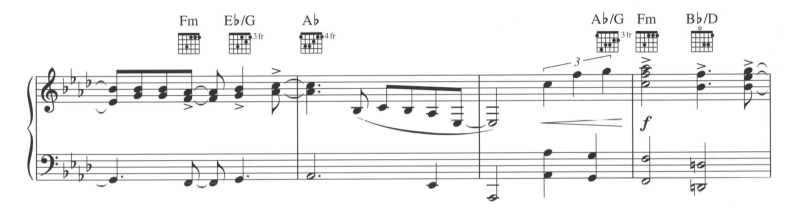

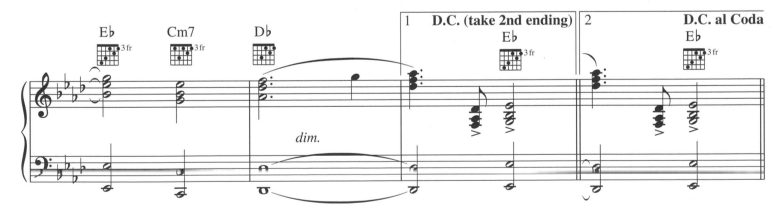

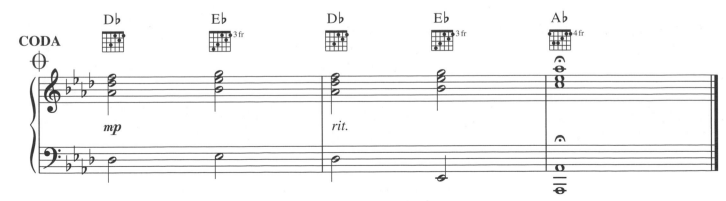

STAR TREK® THE MOTION PICTURE

Theme from the Paramount Picture STAR TREK: THE MOTION PICTURE

Music by JERRY GOLDSMITH

Moderately fast March tempo

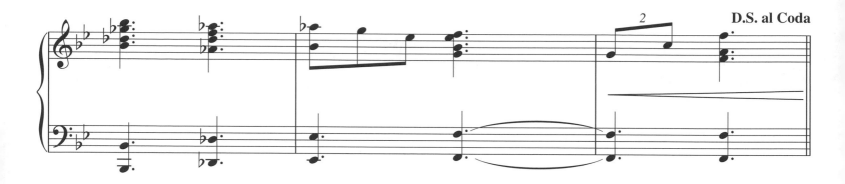

D.S. al Coda

CODA

Slowly, expansively

mp

With pedal

mf

Tempo I

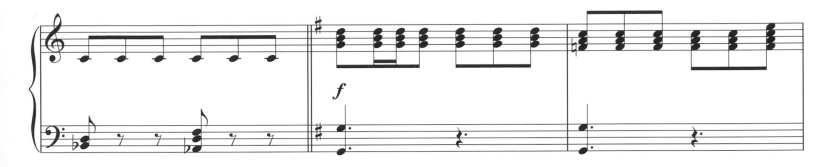

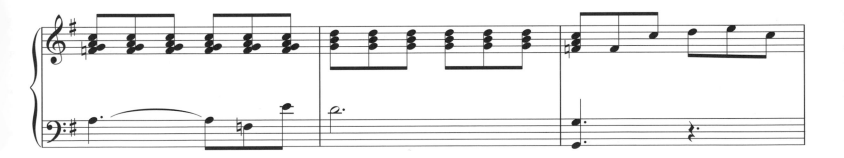

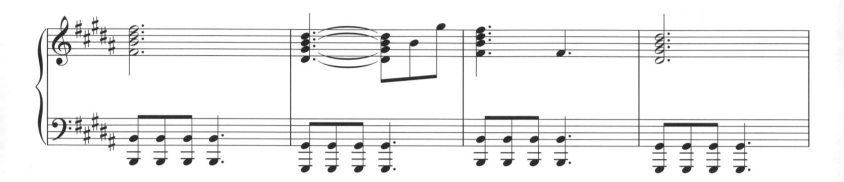

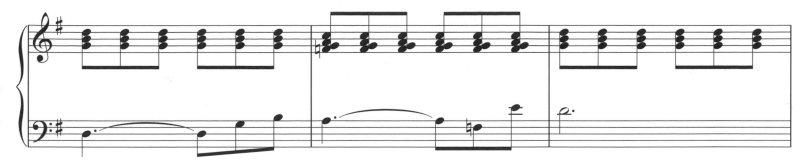

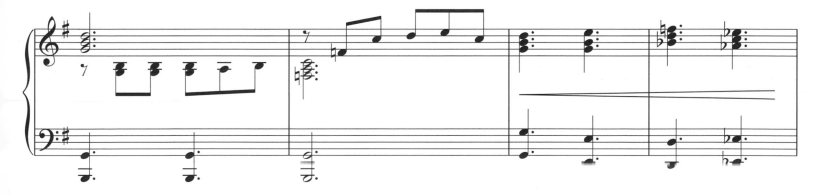

THE STRIPPER

from THE STRIPPER

Music by DAVID ROSE

Blues tempo

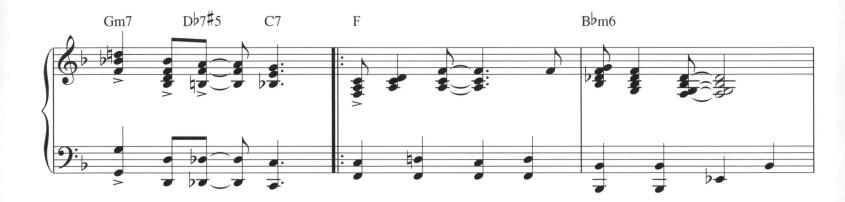

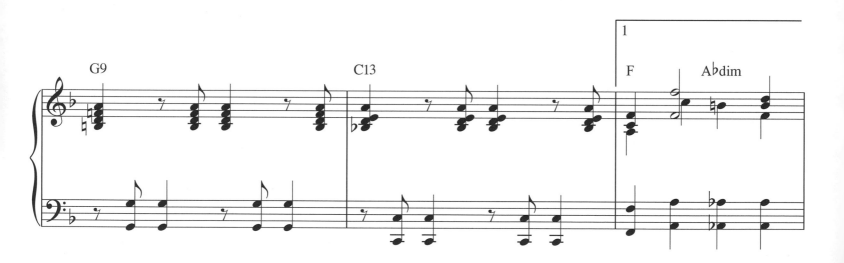

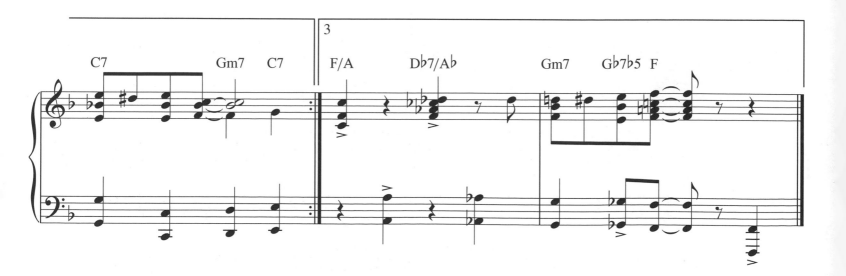

TAKE MY BREATH AWAY
(Love Theme)
from the Paramount Picture TOP GUN

Words and Music by GIORGIO MORODER
and TOM WHITLOCK

Watch-ing ev-'ry mo-tion in ___ my fool-ish lov-er's game; ___ on this end-less o-cean, fi-

Watch-ing, I keep wait-ing, still ___ an-tic-i-pat-ing love, ___ nev-er hes-i-tat-ing to ___

Watch-ing ev-'ry mo-tion in ___ this fool-ish lov-er's game; ___ haunt-ed by the no-tion some-

-n'lly lov - ers know no shame._____
_____ be - come the fat - ed ones._____
- where there's a love in flames._____

Turn - ing and re - turn - ing to_____
Turn - ing and re - turn - ing to_____
Turn - ing and re - turn - ing to_____

_____ some se - cret place in - side;_____
_____ some se - cret place to hide;_____
_____ some se - cret place in - side;_____

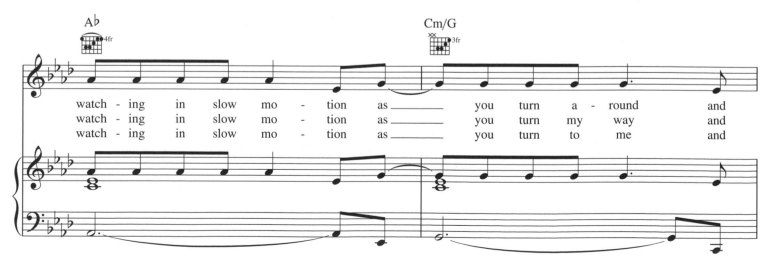

watch - ing in slow mo - tion as_____ you turn a - round and
watch - ing in slow mo - tion as_____ you turn my way and
watch - ing in slow mo - tion as_____ you turn to me and

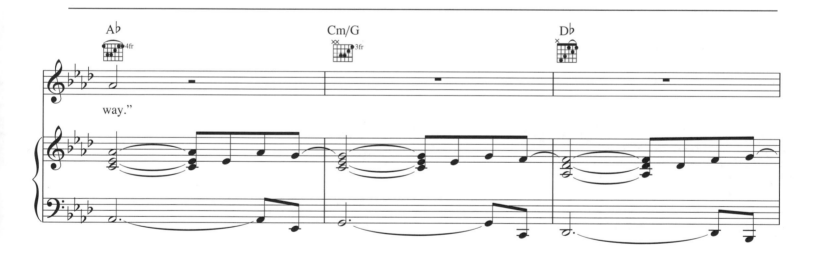

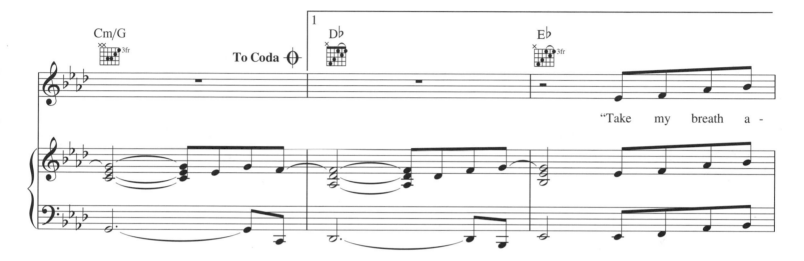

Through the hour-glass I saw you. In time, you slipped a-way.

When the mir-ror crashed, I called you and turned

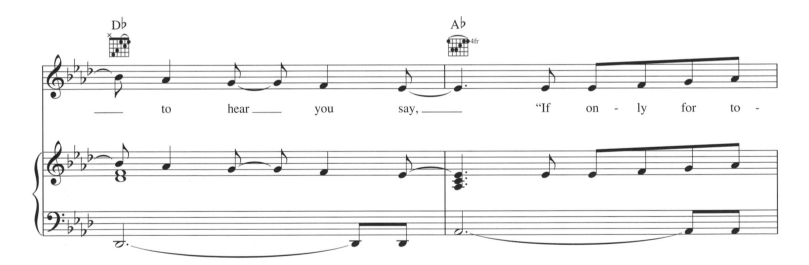

to hear you say, "If on-ly for to-

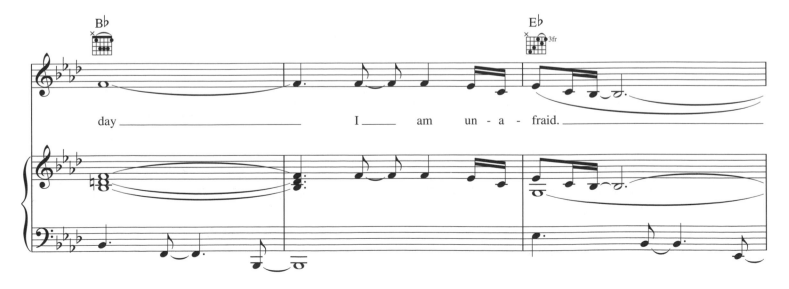

day I am un-a-fraid.

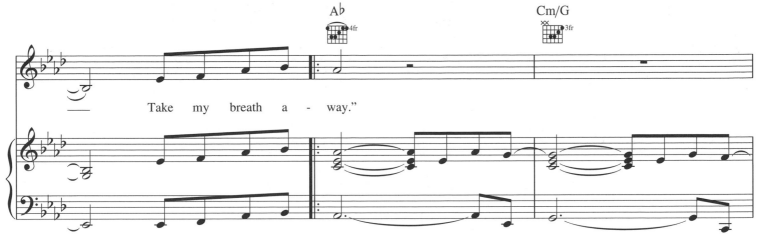

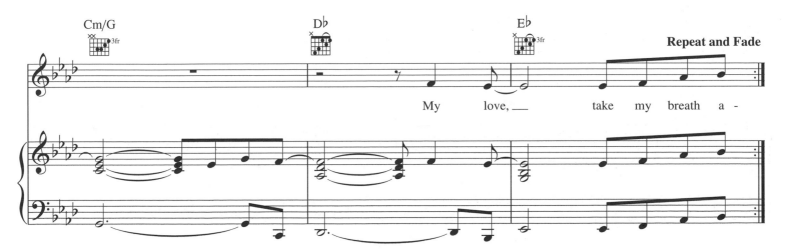

SWINGING ON A STAR

from GOING MY WAY

Words by JOHNNY BURKE
Music by JIMMY VAN HEUSEN

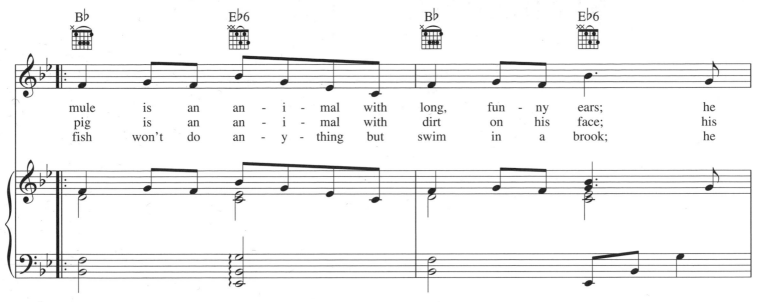

mule | is | an | an - i - | mal | with | long, | fun - ny | ears; | he
pig | is | an | an - i - | mal | with | dirt | on | his | face; | his
fish | won't | do | an - y - | thing | but | swim | in | a | brook; | he

kicks | up | at | an - y - | thing | he | hears. _____ | His
shoes | are | a | ter - ri - | ble | dis - | grace. _____ | He's
can't | write | his | name | or | read | a | book. _____ | To

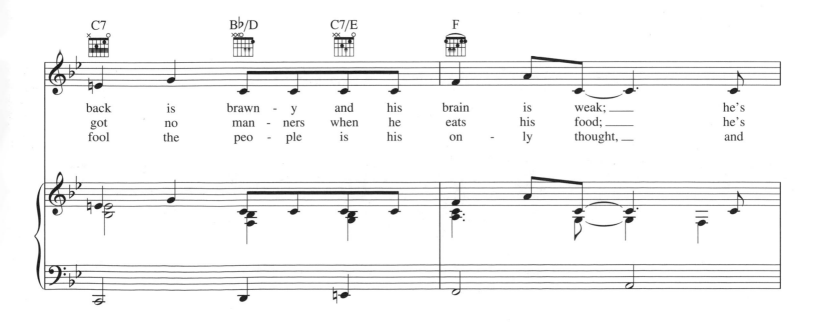

back | is | brawn - y | and | his | brain | is | weak; ____ | he's
got | no | man - ners | when | he | eats | his | food; ____ | he's
fool | the | peo - ple | is | his | on - ly | thought, __ | and

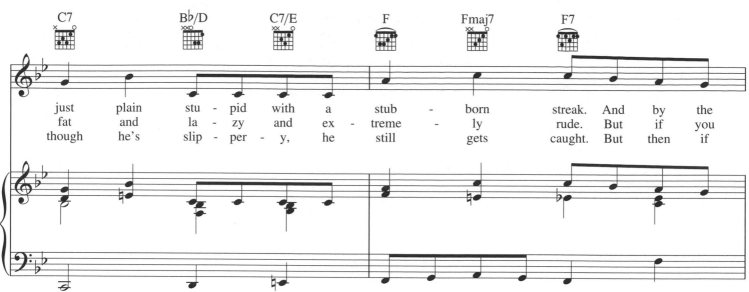

just plain stu - pid with a stub - born streak. And by the
fat and la - zy and ex - treme - ly rude. But if you
though he's slip - per - y, he still gets caught. But then if

way, if you hate to go to school, you may grow up to be a
don't care a feath - er or a fig, you may grow up to be a
that sort of life is what you wish, you may grow up to be a

mule. _____ Or would you like to swing on a star, car - ry
pig. _____ Or would you like to swing on a star, car - ry
fish. _____ And all the mon - keys aren't in the zoo; ev - 'ry

moon - beams home in a jar, _____ and be bet - ter off than you
moon - beams home in a jar, _____ and be bet - ter off than you
day you meet quite a few. _____ So you see, it's all up to

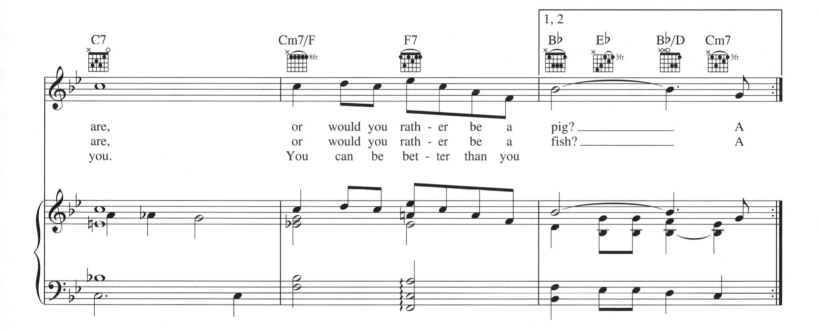

1, 2

are, or would you rath - er be a pig? _____ A
are, or would you rath - er be a fish? _____ A
you. You can be bet - ter than you

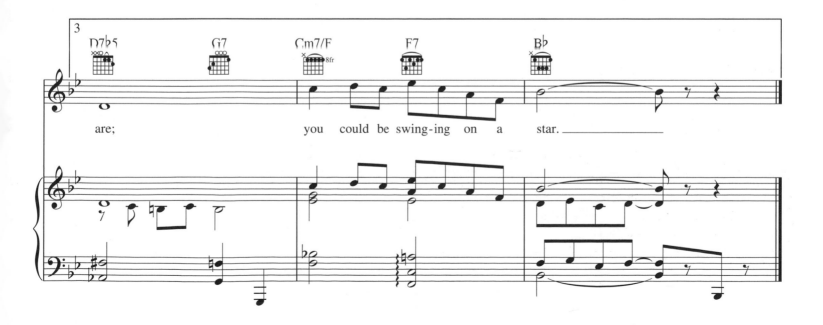

3

are; you could be swing - ing on a star. _____

Tammy

from TAMMY AND THE BACHELOR

Words and Music by JAY LIVINGSTON
and RAY EVANS

THAT'S ENTERTAINMENT
from THE BAND WAGON

Words by HOWARD DIETZ
Music by ARTHUR SCHWARTZ

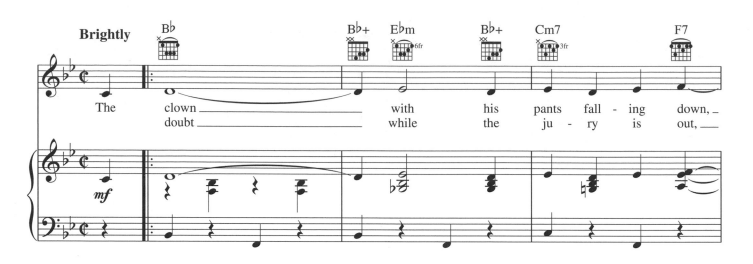

The clown _____ with his pants fall-ing down, __
doubt _____ while the ju-ry is out, __

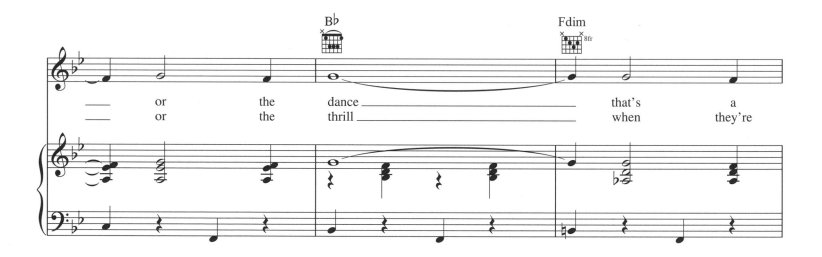

__ or the dance _____ that's a
__ or the thrill _____ when they're

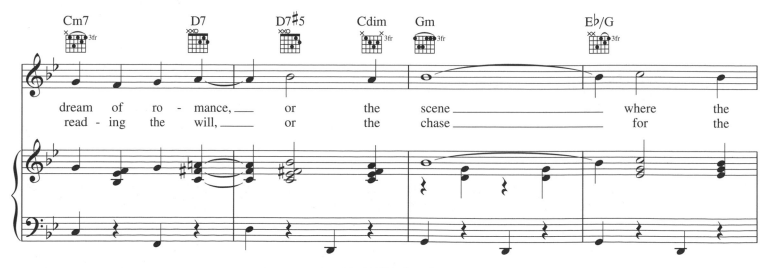

dream of ro-mance, __ or the scene _____ where the
read-ing the will, __ or the chase _____ for the

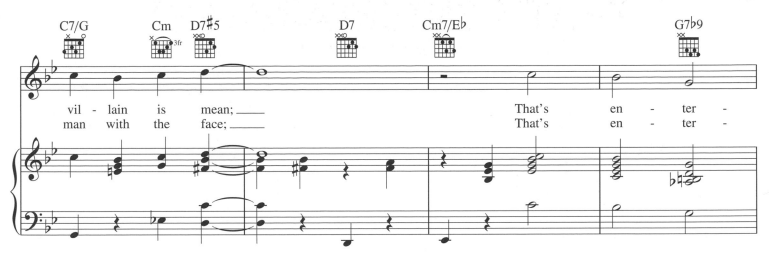

vil - lain is mean; _____ That's en - ter -
man with the face; _____ That's en - ter -

tain - ment! _____ The lights _____ on the
tain - ment! _____ The dame _____ who is

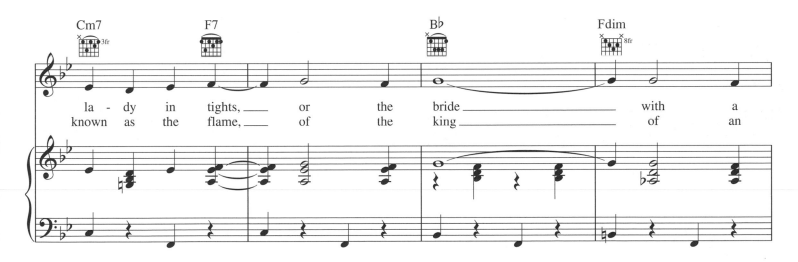

la - dy in tights, _____ or the bride _____ with a
known as the flame, _____ of the king _____ of an

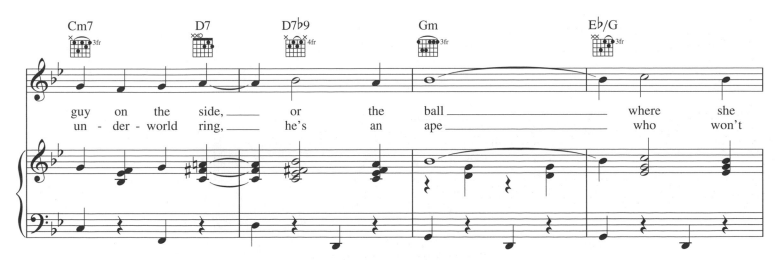

guy on the side, _____ or the ball _____ where she
un - der - world ring, _____ he's an ape _____ who won't

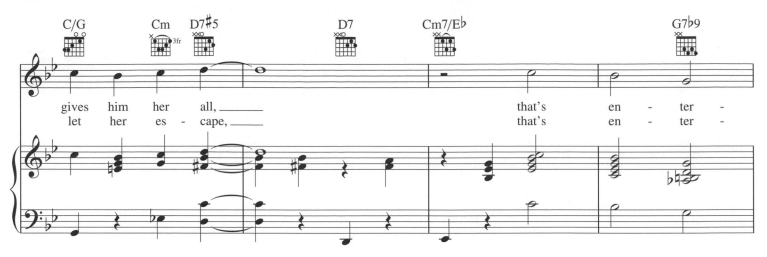

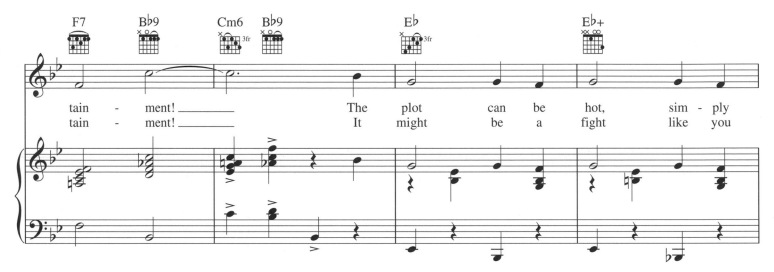

It can be Oe - di - pus Rex, ___
Some great Shake - spear - e - an scene, ___

___ where a chap kills his fa - ther, and
___ where a ghost and a prince meet and

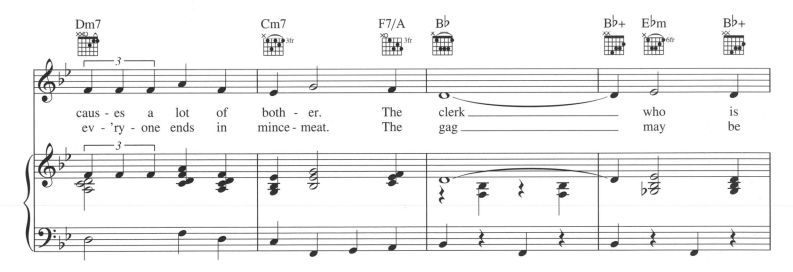

caus - es a lot of both - er. The clerk ___ who is
ev - 'ry - one ends in mince - meat. The gag ___ may be

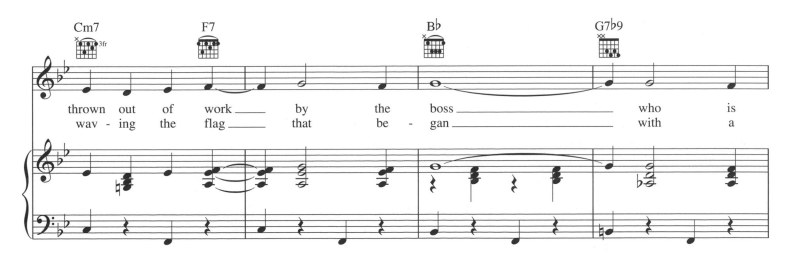

thrown out of work ___ by the boss ___ who is
wav - ing the flag ___ that be - gan ___ with a

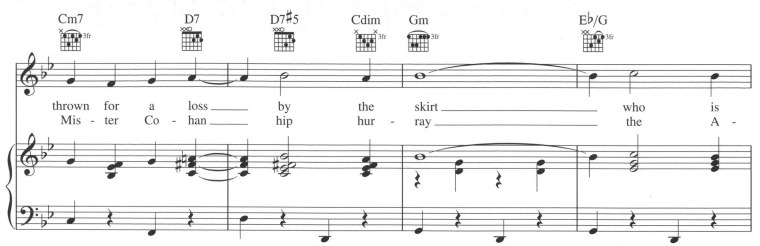

thrown for a loss _____ by the skirt _____ who is
Mis - ter Co - han _____ hip hur - ray _____ the A -

do - ing him dirt; _____ The world is a stage, the
mer - i - can way; _____ The world is a stage, the

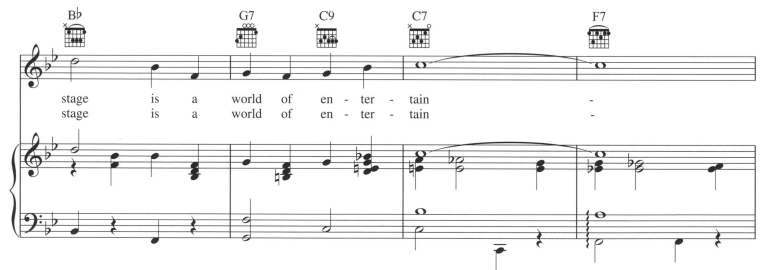

stage is a world of en - ter - tain -
stage is a world of en - ter - tain -

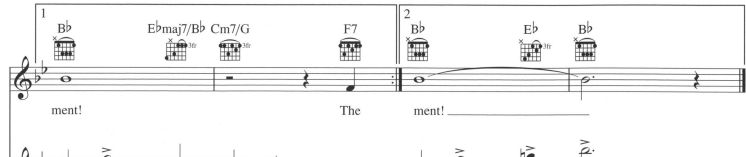

ment! The ment! _____

THREE COINS IN THE FOUNTAIN
from THREE COINS IN THE FOUNTAIN

Words by SAMMY CAHN
Music by JULE STYNE

Three coins in the foun-tain, each one seek-ing hap-pi-ness, thrown by three hope-ful lov-ers, which one will the foun-tain bless? Three hearts in the foun-tain,

each heart long-ing for its home, there they lie in the foun-tain some-where in the heart of Rome.

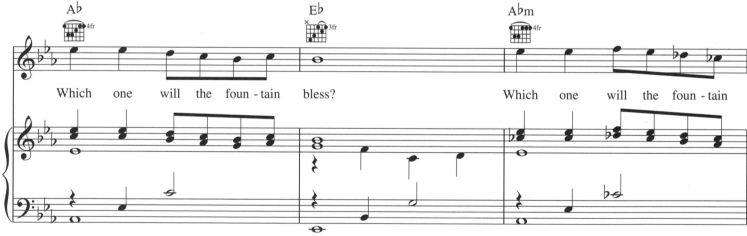

Which one will the foun-tain bless? Which one will the foun-tain bless?

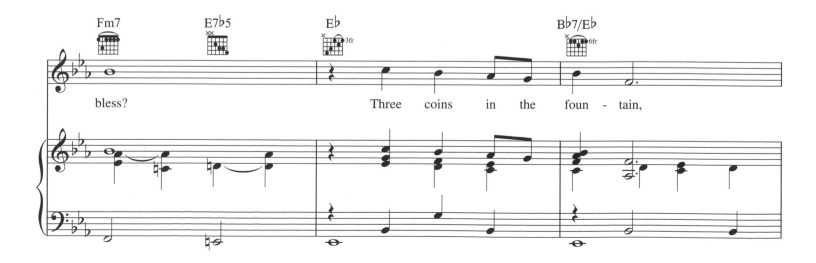

Three coins in the foun-tain,

(I've Had)
THE TIME OF MY LIFE
from DIRTY DANCING

Words and Music by FRANKE PREVITE,
JOHN DeNICOLA and DONALD MARKOWITZ

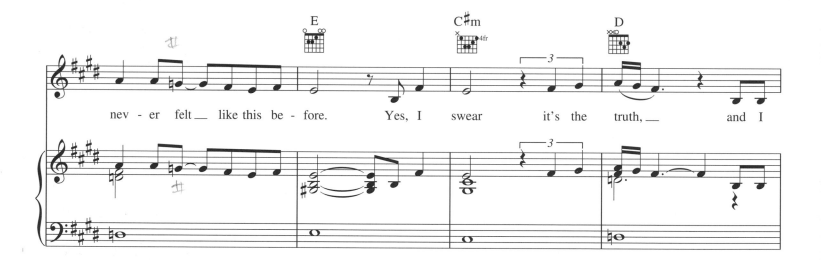

owe it all to you. _____

Male: I've been wait-ing for so long; _____ now I've

fi - n'lly found some-one __ to stand by me. *Female:* We saw the

writ - ing on the wall _____ as we felt this mag - i - cal __ fan - ta -

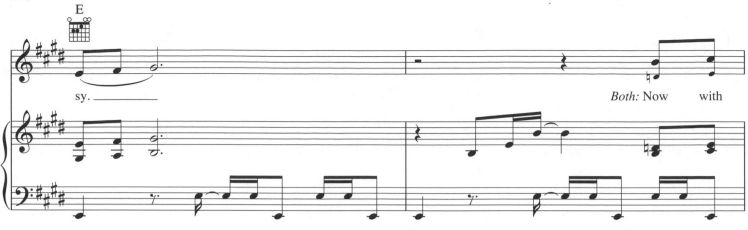

sy. _____ *Both:* Now with

pas - sion in our eyes _____ there's no way we could _ dis - guise _____ it se - cret -

ly. _____ So we

take each oth - er's hand _____ 'cause we seem to un - der - stand _ the ur - gen -

fore. Yes, I swear it's the truth, _____ and I owe it all to you. _____

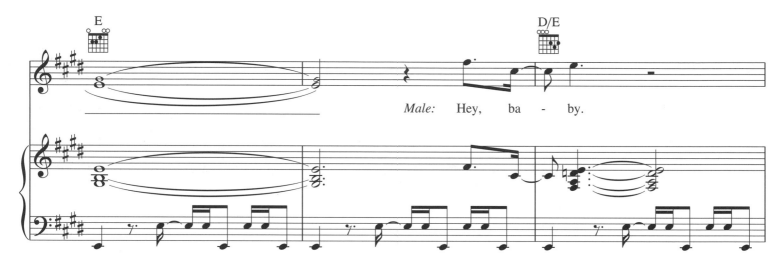

Male: Hey, ba - by.

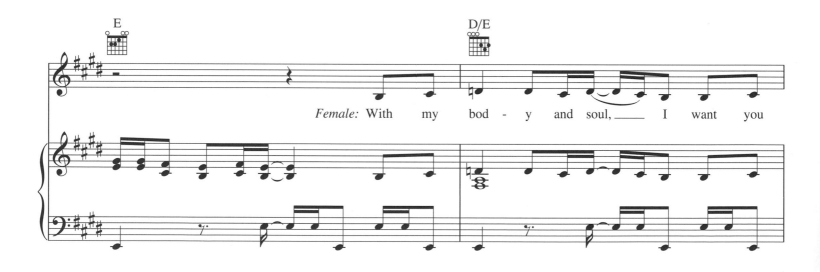

Female: With my bod - y and soul, _____ I want you

more than you'll ev - er know. _ *Male:* So we'll

just let it go;___ don't be a - fraid to lose con - trol.___

Female: Yes, I know what's on ___ your mind when you say stay with me to-

night.___ *Male:* Stay ___ with me. Just re - mem - ber, you're the

one thing ___ *Female:* I ___ can't get e - nough of. *Male:* So I'll tell you

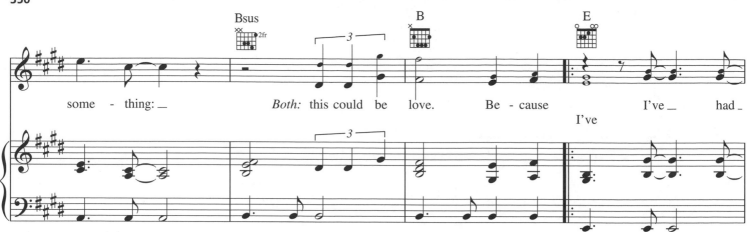

some - thing: ___ *Both:* this could be love. Be - cause I've ___ had ___ I've

___ the time of my life. ___ No, I nev - er felt ___ this way be -
had the time of my life. ___ And I've searched through ev -'ry o - pen

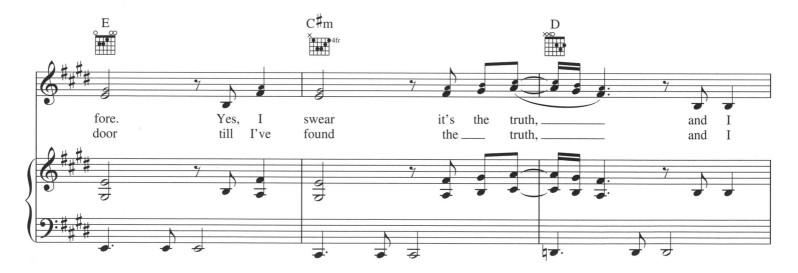

fore. Yes, I swear it's the truth, ___ and I
door till I've found the ___ truth, ___ and I

owe it all to you. ___ 'Cause ___
owe it all to you. ___

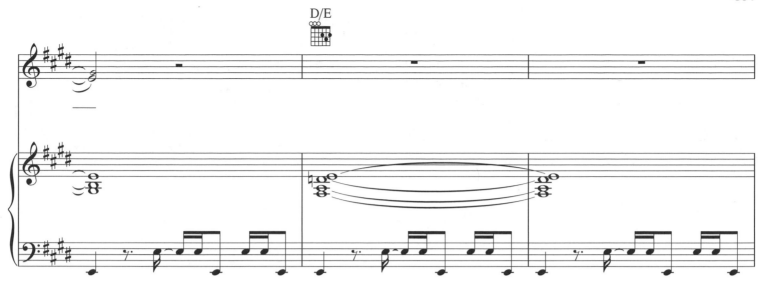

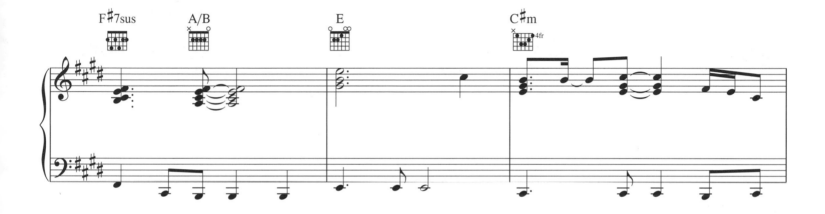

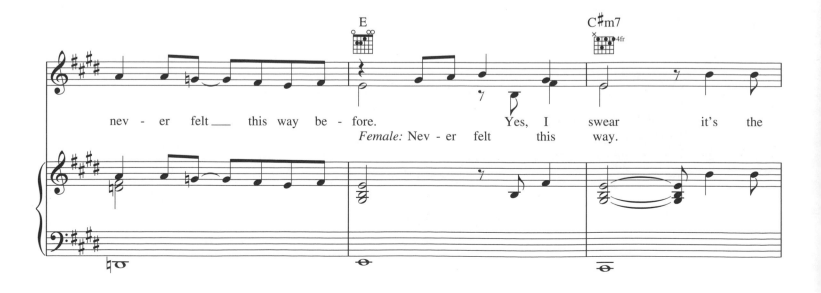

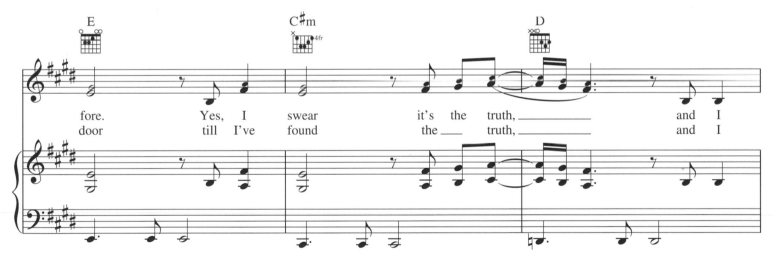

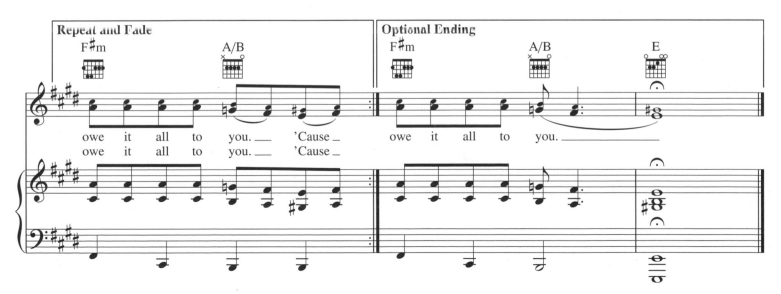

TO SIR, WITH LOVE

from TO SIR, WITH LOVE

Words by DON BLACK
Music by MARC LONDON

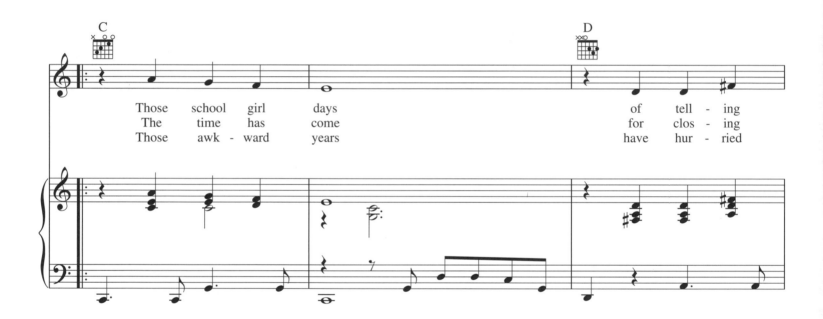

Those school girl days   of tell - ing
The time has come   for clos - ing
Those awk - ward years   have hur - ried

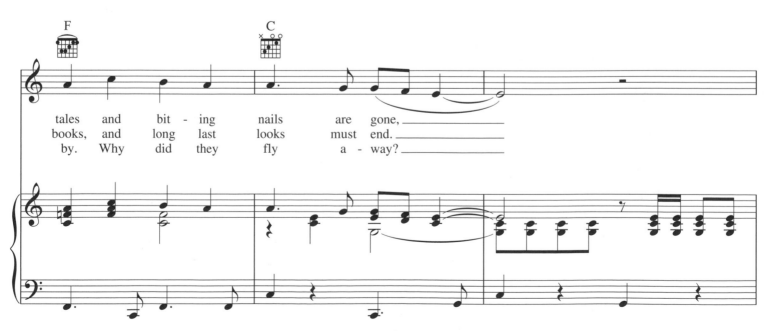

tales and bit - ing nails are gone, _____
books, and long last looks must end. _____
by. Why did they fly a - way? _____

but in my mind   I know they
And as I leave,   I know that
Why is it, sir,   chil - dren grow

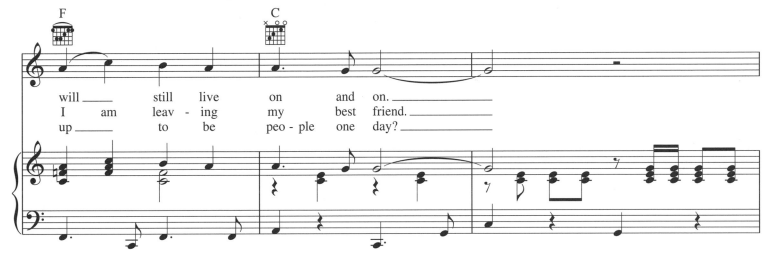

will ____ still live on and on. ____
I am leav - ing my best friend. ____
up ____ to be peo - ple one day? ____

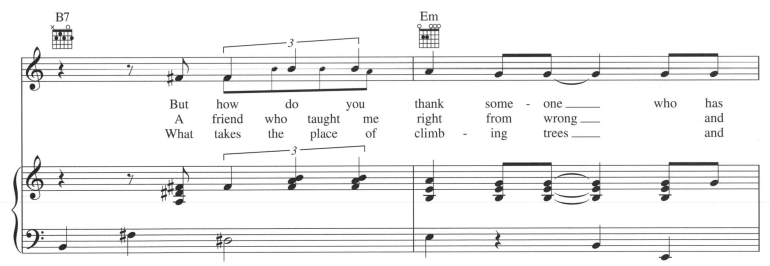

But how do you thank some - one ____ who has
A friend who taught me right from wrong ____ and
What takes the place of climb - ing trees ____ and

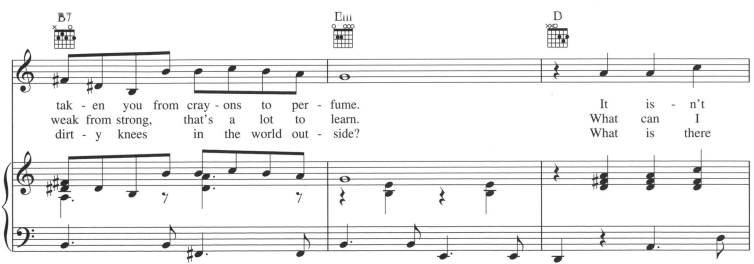

tak - en you from cray - ons to per - fume.
weak from strong, that's a lot to learn.
dirt - y knees in the world out - side?

It is - n't
What can I
What is there

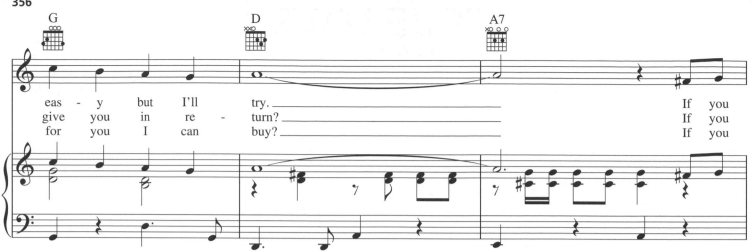

easy but I'll try. _____ If you
give you in re - turn? _____ If you
for you I can buy? _____ If you

want - ed the sky I'd write a - cross the sky in let - ters that would
want - ed the moon I would try to make a start, but
want - ed the world I'd sur - round it with a wall; I'd scrawl these

soar a thou - sand feet high "To sir, with
I would rath - er you let me give my heart to sir, with
words with let - ters ten feet tall: "To sir, with

love." _____
love. _____

love." _____

TRUE LOVE
from HIGH SOCIETY

Words and Music by
COLE PORTER

Moderately slow

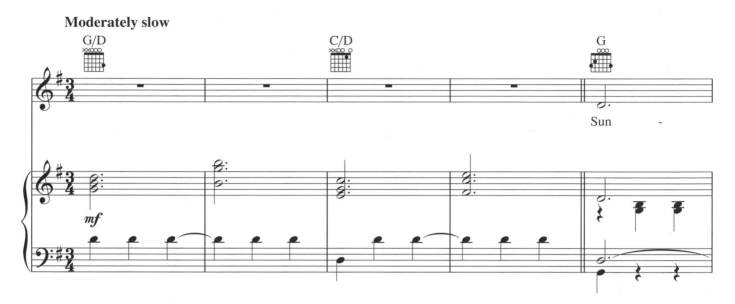

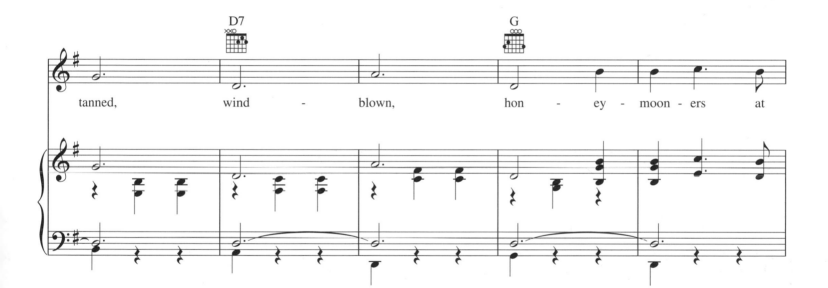

par. Oh, how luck - y we are. _____ While I

give to you and you give to me true

love, true love. So, on and on it will

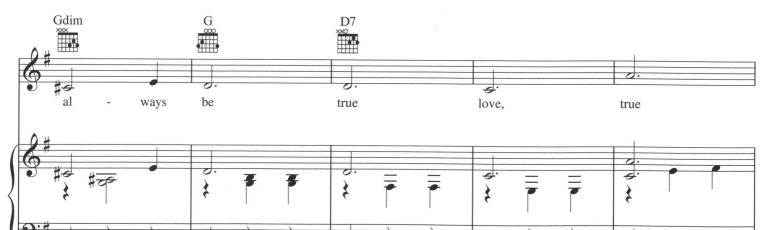

al - ways be true love, true

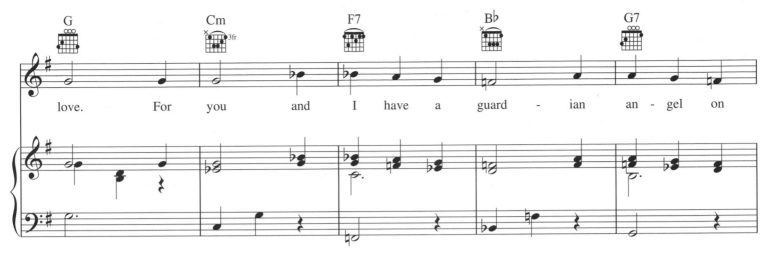

love. For you and I have a guard - ian an - gel on

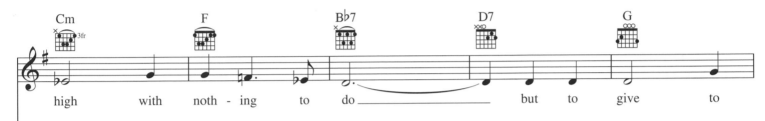

high with noth - ing to do _____ but to give to

you and to give to me love for - ev - er

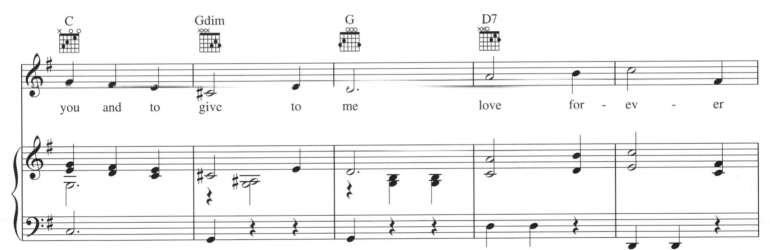

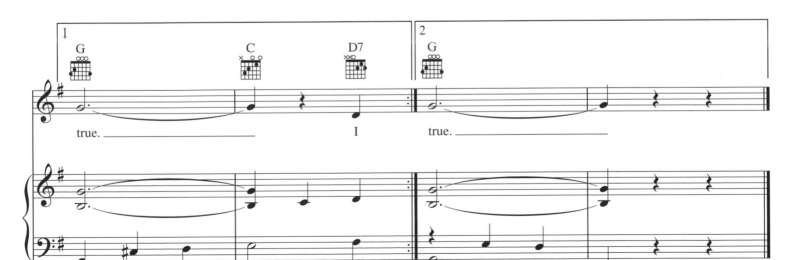

true. _____ I true. _____

TOMORROW
from the Musical Production ANNIE

Lyric by MARTIN CHARNIN
Music by CHARLES STROUSE

The sun - 'll come out _____ to - mor - row,

bet your bot - tom dol - lar that to - mor - row _____ there'll be

sun! Jus' think - ing a - bout _____ to - mor - row

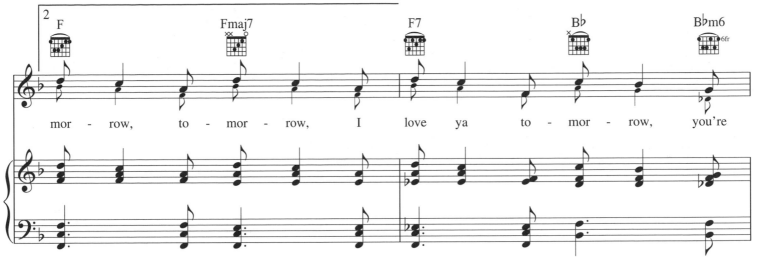

mor - row, to - mor - row, I love ya to - mor - row, you're

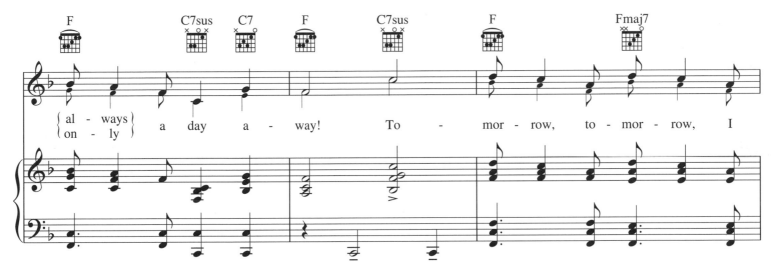

{al - ways} {on - ly} a day a - way! To - mor - row, to - mor - row, I

love ya to - mor - row, you're {al - ways} {on - ly} a day a -

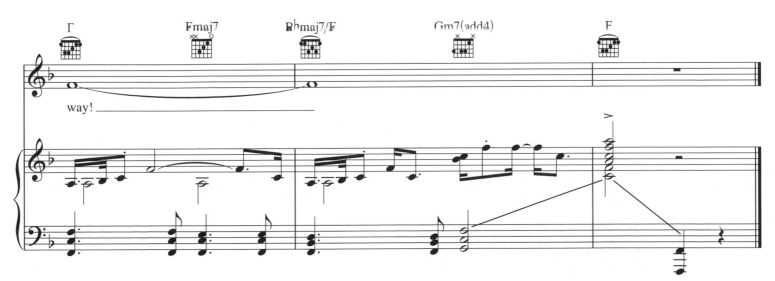

way! _____

UNCHAIN MY HEART

from RAY

Words and Music by BOBBY SHARP
and TEDDY POWELL

Bright Rhumba

* *Recorded a half step lower.*

WHAT THE WORLD NEEDS NOW IS LOVE

from BOB & CAROL & TED & ALICE

Lyric by HAL DAVID
Music by BURT BACHARACH

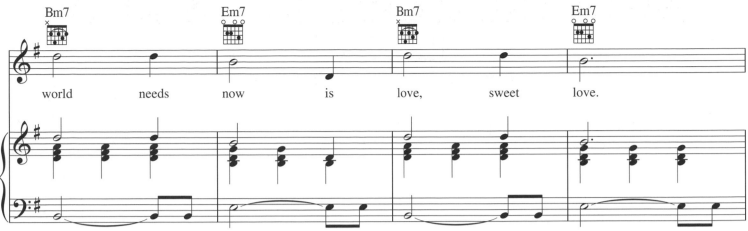

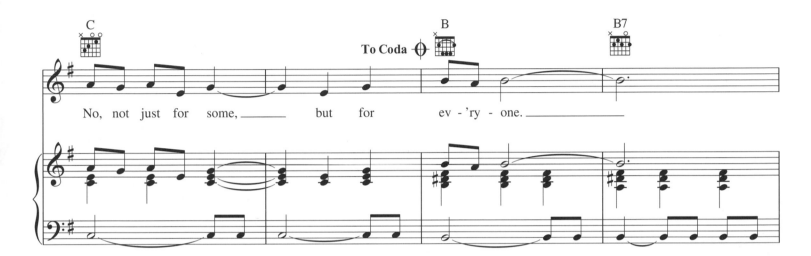

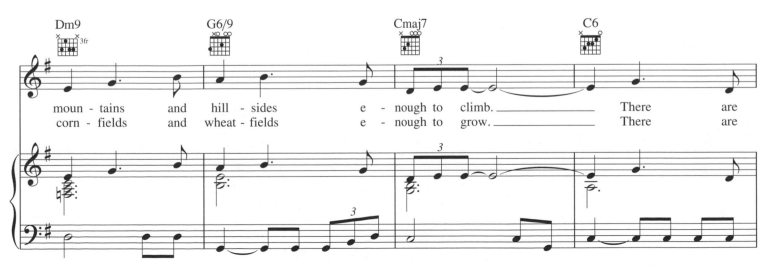

o - ceans and riv - ers e - nough to cross,_____ e - nough to last ___
sun - beams and moon - beams e - nough to shine,_____ oh, lis - ten, Lord, _

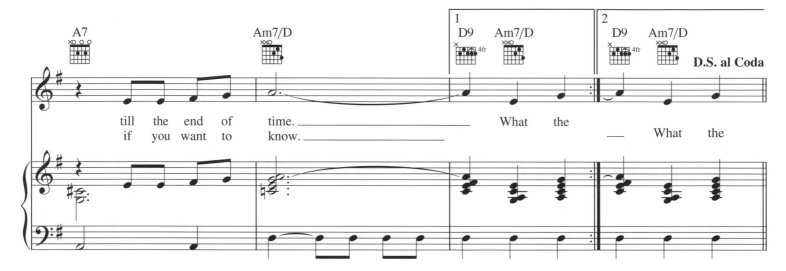

till the end of time._____ What the
if you want to know._____ ___ What the

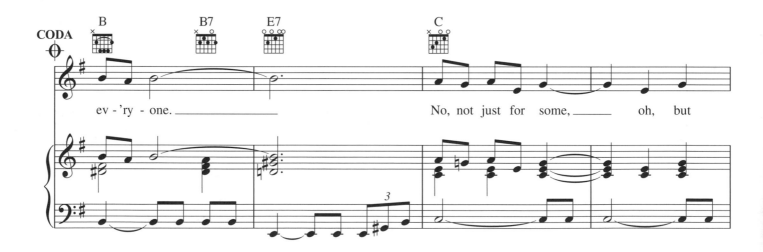

ev - 'ry - one._____ No, not just for some,_____ oh, but

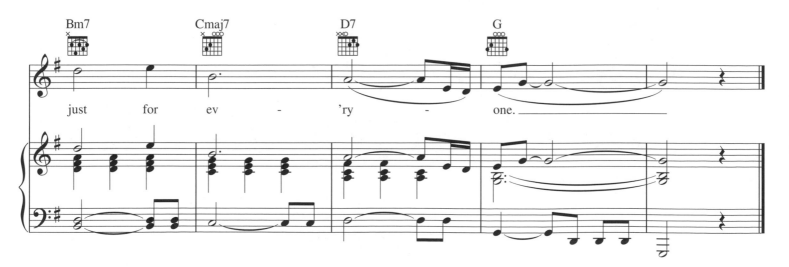

just for ev - 'ry - one._____

WHEN I FALL IN LOVE

featured in the TriStar Motion Picture SLEEPLESS IN SEATTLE

Words by EDWARD HEYMAN
Music by VICTOR YOUNG

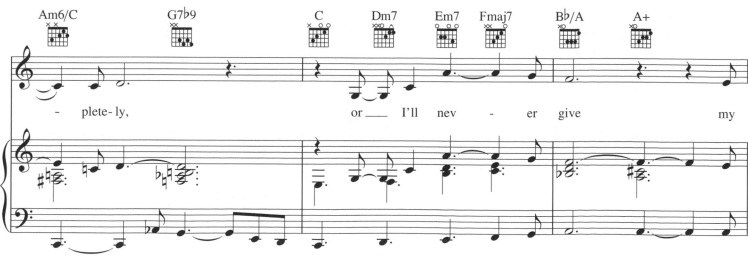

heart. _____ Don't let me give my heart. _____ And ___ the

mo - ment I can feel _____ that ___ you feel __ that _____ way,

too, _____ I feel that ___ way, ___ too, is when I fall _____ in

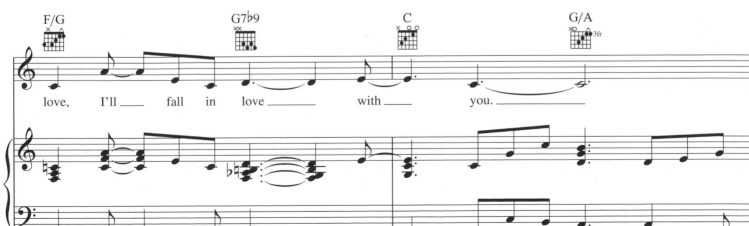

love, I'll ___ fall in love _____ with ___ you. _____

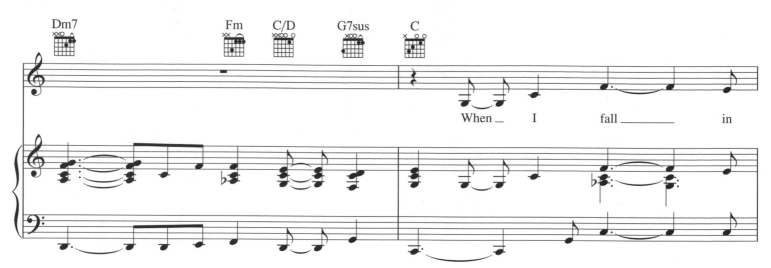

When __ I fall _____ in

love, _____ it ____ will be _____ for -

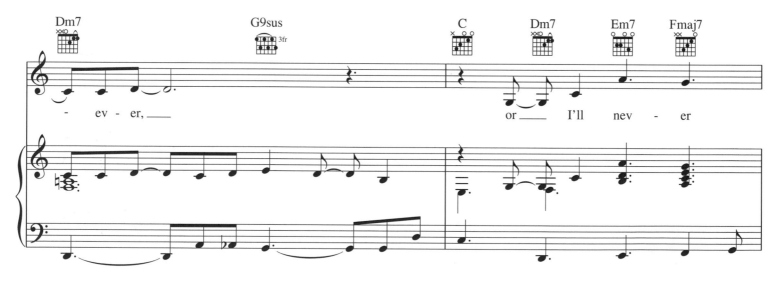

- ev - er, ____ or ____ I'll nev - er

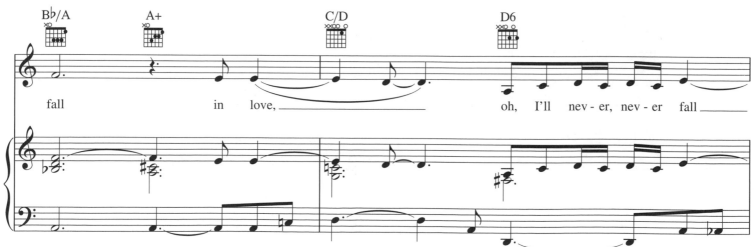

fall in love, _____ oh, I'll nev - er, nev - er fall _____

in love. In a rest - less world like

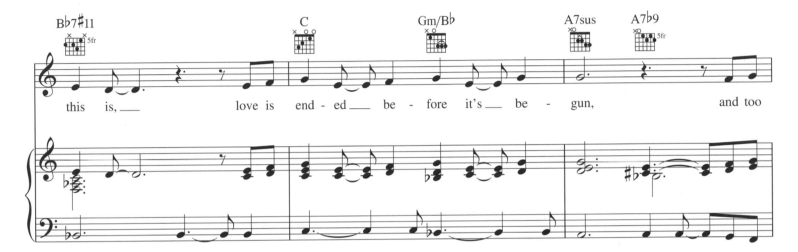

this is, love is end - ed be - fore it's be - gun, and too

man - y moon - light kiss - es seem to

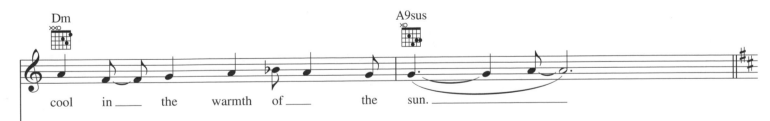

cool in the warmth of the sun.

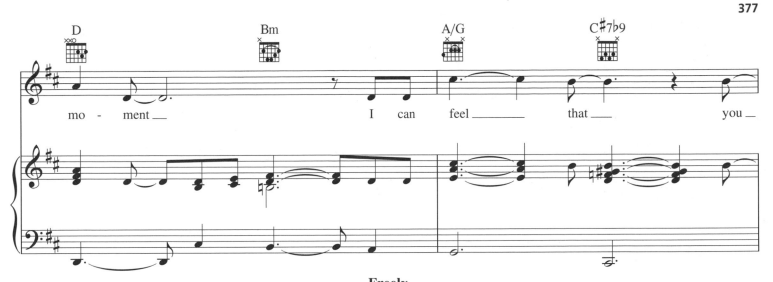

mo - ment ___ I can feel ___ that ___ you ___

Freely

___ feel ___ that ___ way, ___ too, _____ is

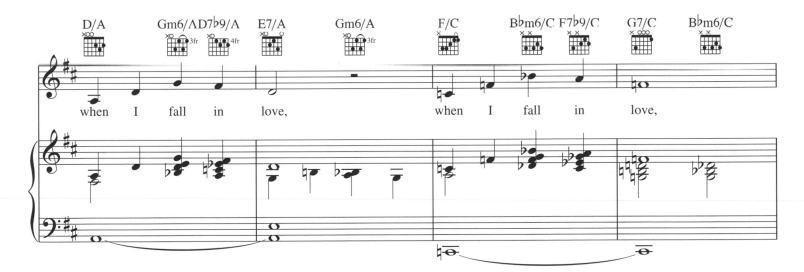

when I fall in love, when I fall in love,

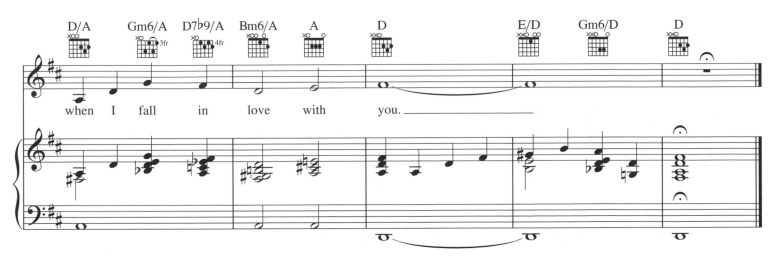

when I fall in love with you. _____

WHEN YOU WISH UPON A STAR

from Walt Disney's PINOCCHIO

Words by NED WASHINGTON
Music by LEIGH HARLINE

WHERE IS LOVE?

from the Columbia Pictures - Romulus Film OLIVER!

Words and Music by
LIONEL BART

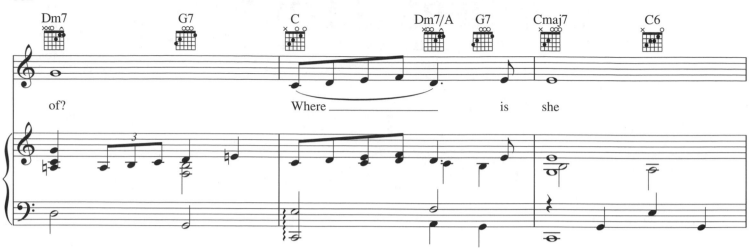

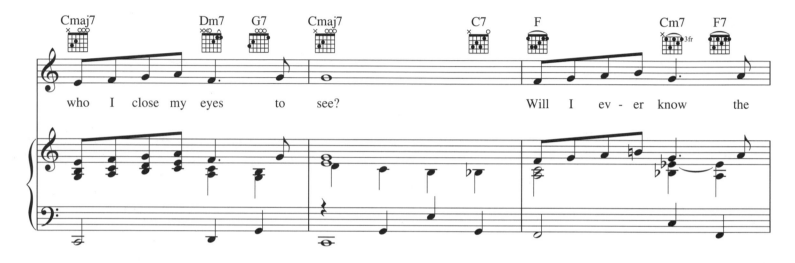

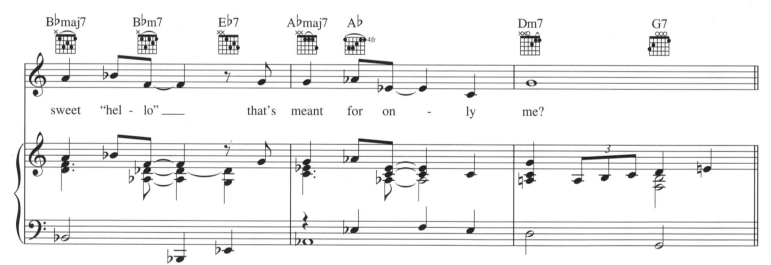

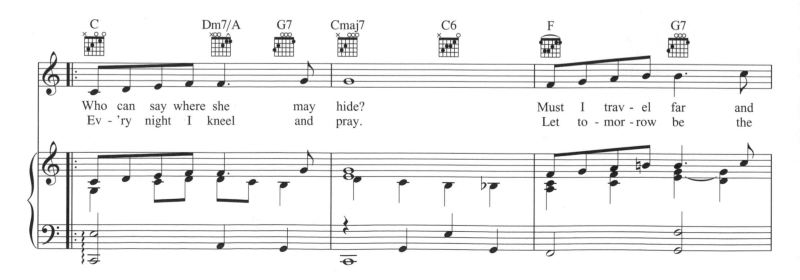

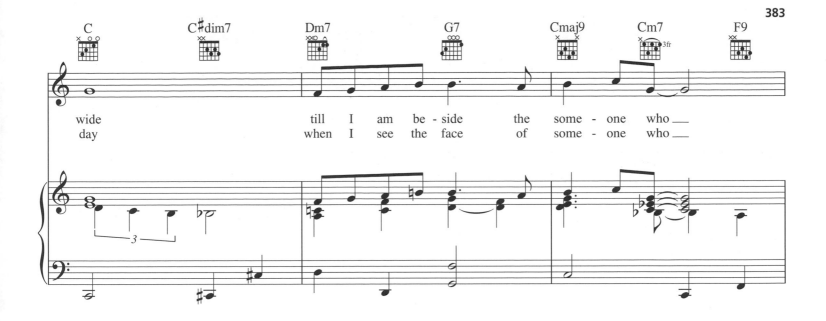

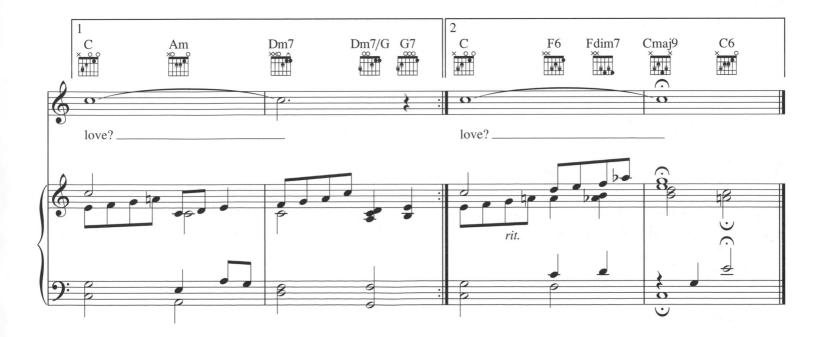

WHERE IS YOUR HEART

(The Song from Moulin Rouge)
from MOULIN ROUGE

Words by WILLIAM ENGVICK
Music by GEORGE AURIC

Moderately

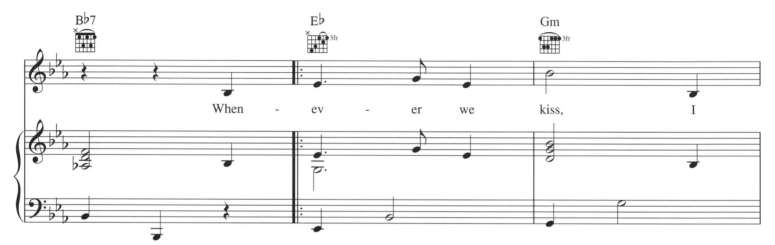

When - ev - er we kiss, I

wor - ry and won - der. Your lips may be

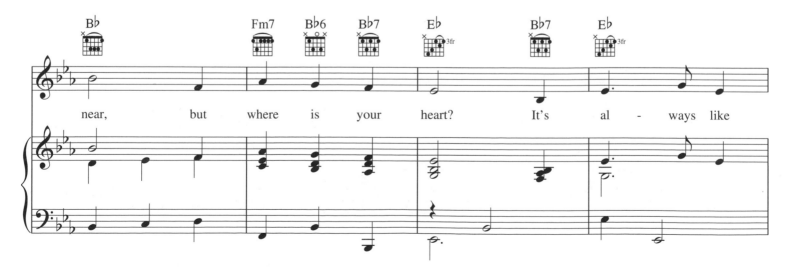

near, but where is your heart? It's al - ways like

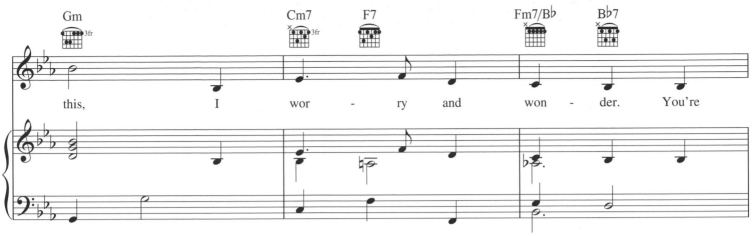

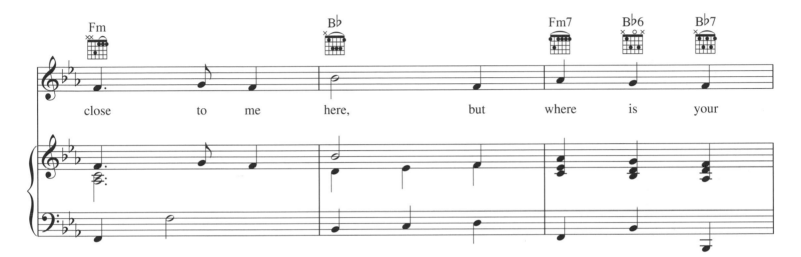

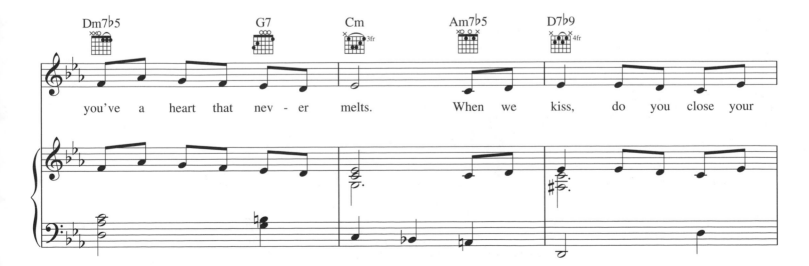

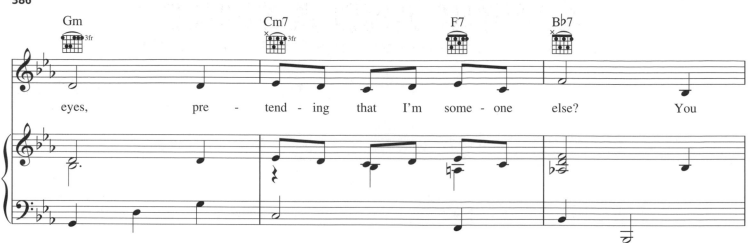

eyes, pre - tend - ing that I'm some - one else? You

must break the spell, this cloud that I'm un - der. So

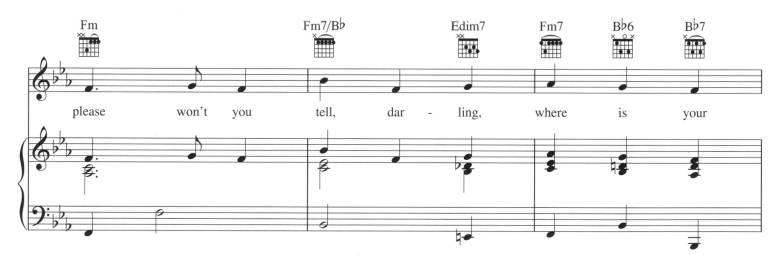

please won't you tell, dar - ling, where is your

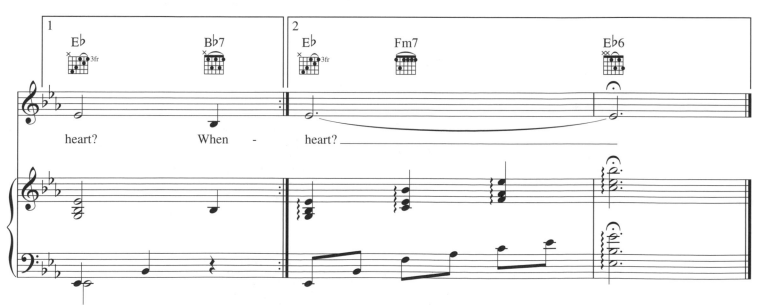

heart? When - heart? _____

A WINK AND A SMILE

featured in the TriStar Motion Picture SLEEPLESS IN SEATTLE

Music by MARC SHAIMAN
Lyrics by RAMSEY McLEAN

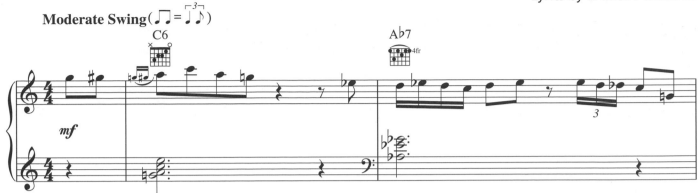

I re-mem-ber the days __ of just keep-ing time, __ of
Instrumental solo ad lib.

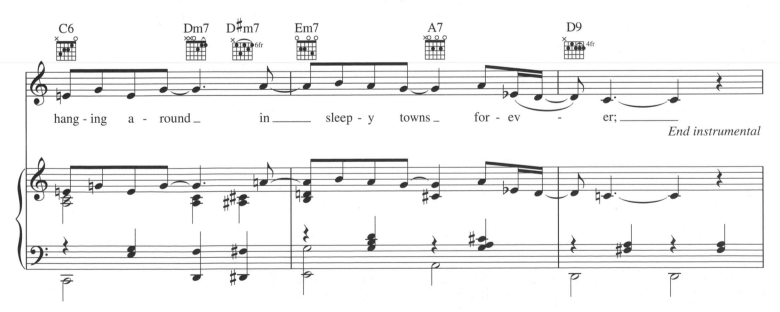

hang-ing a-round __ in __ sleep-y towns __ for-ev - er; __
End instrumental

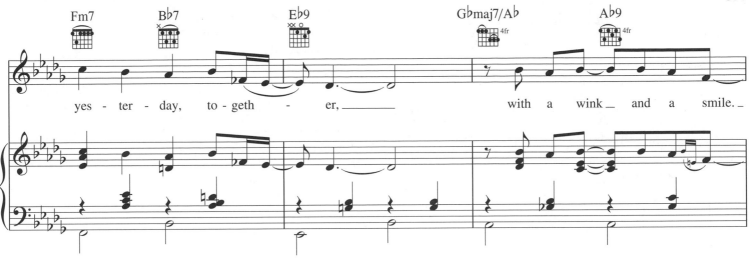

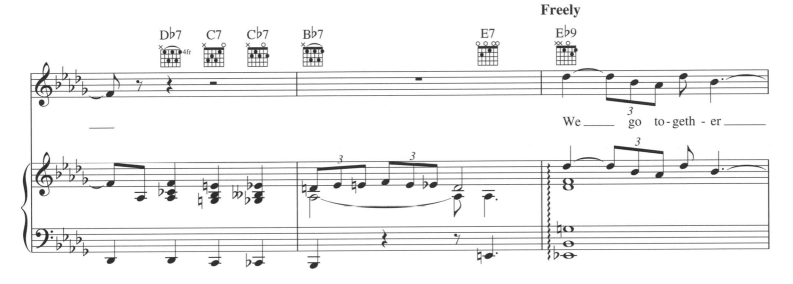

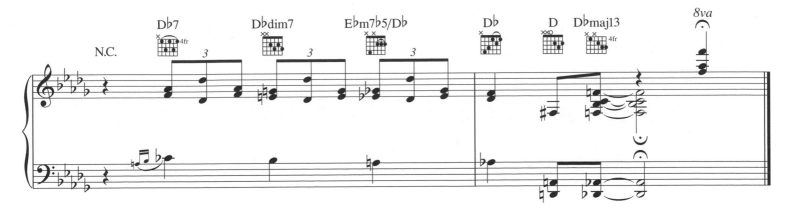

A WHOLE NEW WORLD

from Walt Disney's ALADDIN

Music by ALAN MENKEN
Lyrics by TIM RICE

I can o-pen your eyes, take you won-der by

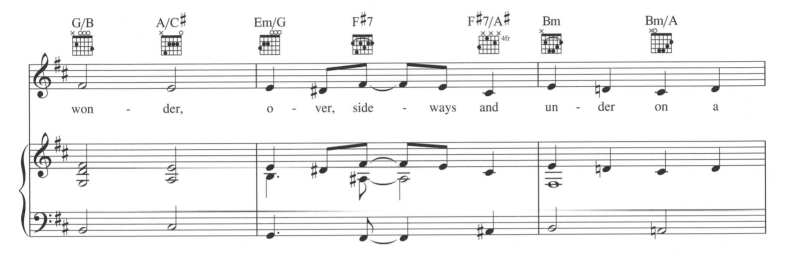

won - der, o - ver, side - ways and un - der on a

mag - ic car - pet ride. ___ A whole new world, ___

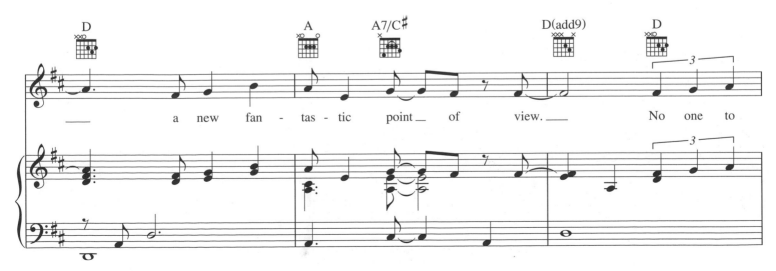

___ a new fan - tas - tic point ___ of view. ___ No one to

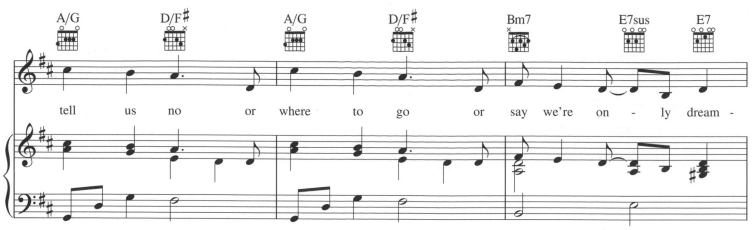

tell us no or where to go or say we're on - ly dream -

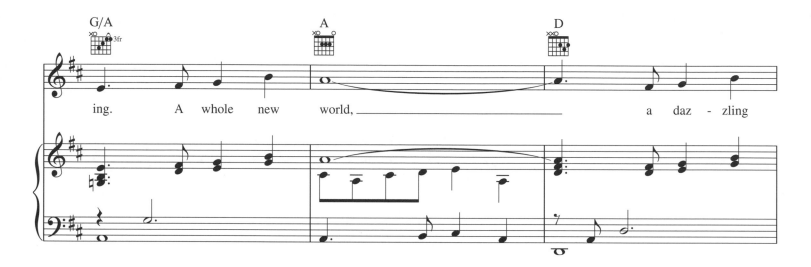

ing. A whole new world, _____ a daz - zling

place I nev - er knew. ___ But when I'm way up here, it's

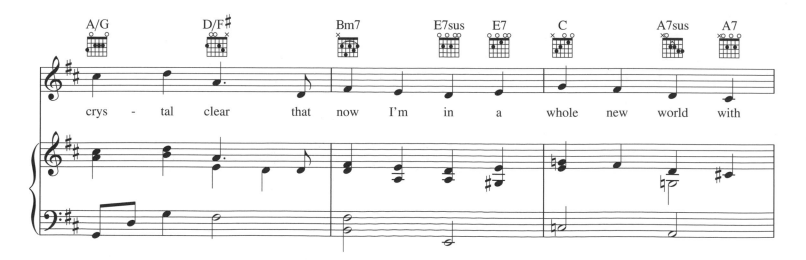

crys - tal clear that now I'm in a whole new world with

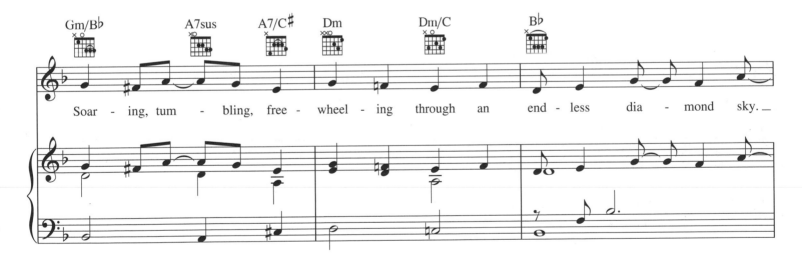

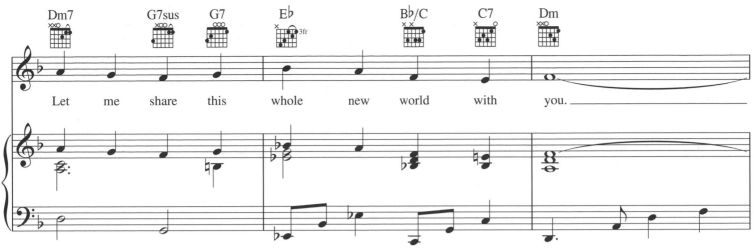

Let me share this whole new world with you. _____

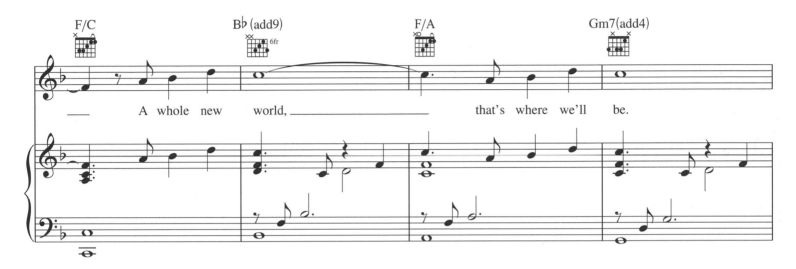

____ A whole new world, _____ that's where we'll be.

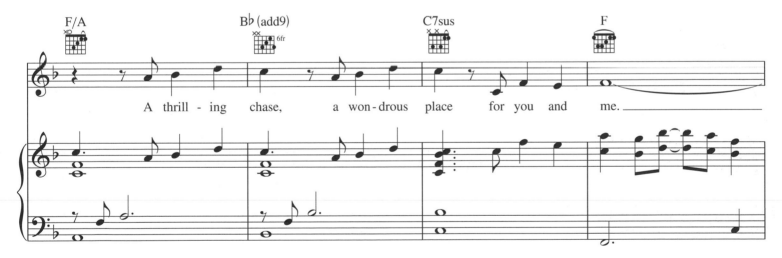

A thrill-ing chase, a won-drous place for you and me. _____

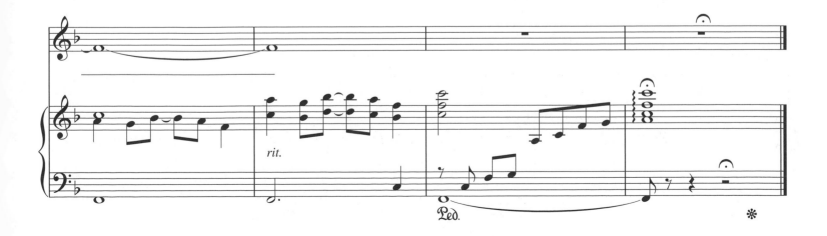

THE WINNER TAKES IT ALL

from MAMMA MIA!

Words and Music by BENNY ANDERSSON
and BJÖRN ULVAEUS

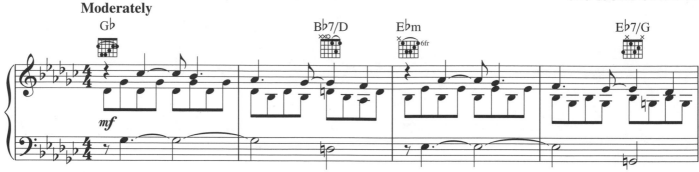

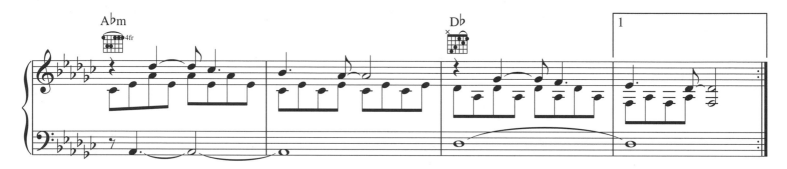

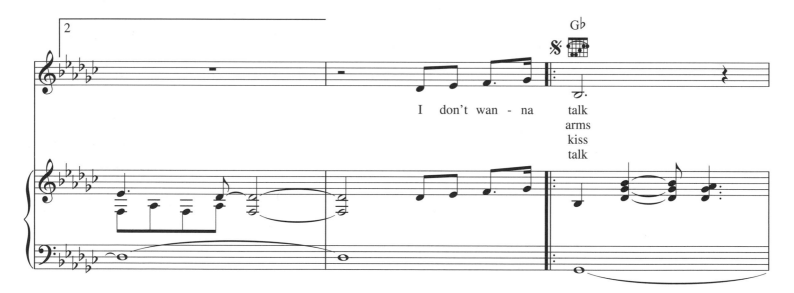

I don't wan-na talk
arms kiss
talk

a - bout things we've gone through,
think - ing I be - longed there,
like I used to kiss you,
if it makes you feel sad,

though it's hurt - ing
I fig - ured it made
does it feel the
and I un - der-

me,
sense,
same
stand

now it's his - to - ry.
build - ing me a fence,
when she calls your name?
you've come to shake my hand.

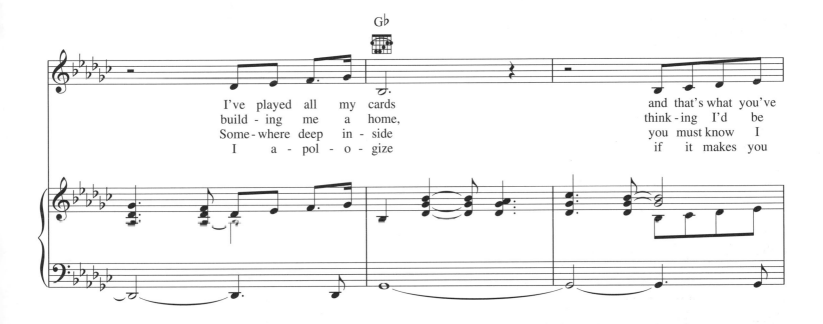

I've played all my cards
build - ing me a home,
Some - where deep in - side
I a - pol - o - gize

and that's what you've
think - ing I'd be
you must know I
if it makes you

done, too,
strong there,
miss you,
feel bad

noth - ing more to say,
but I was a fool,
but what can I say,
see - ing me so tense,

no more ace to play.
play - ing by the rules.
rules must be o - beyed.
no self con - fi - dence.

The win - ner takes it
The gods may throw a
The judg - es will de -
The win - ner takes it

all,
dice,
cide,

the los - er stand - ing small
their minds as cold as ice,
the likes of me a - bide,

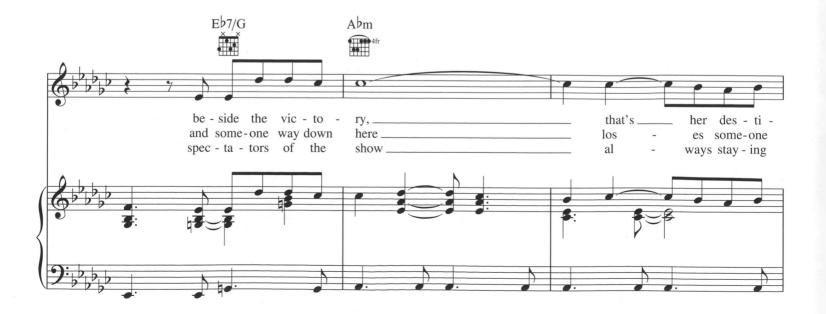

be - side the vic - to - ry,_____ that's _____ her des - ti -
and some - one way down here _____ los - es some - one
spec - ta - tors of the show _____ al - ways stay - ing

ny. _____ I was in your
dear. _____
low. _____ The win-ner takes it
The game is on a-

all, the los-er has to fall, it's sim-ple and it's
gain, a lov-er or a friend, a big thing or a

plain, _____ why should I com - plain. _____
small, _____ the win - ner takes it all. _____

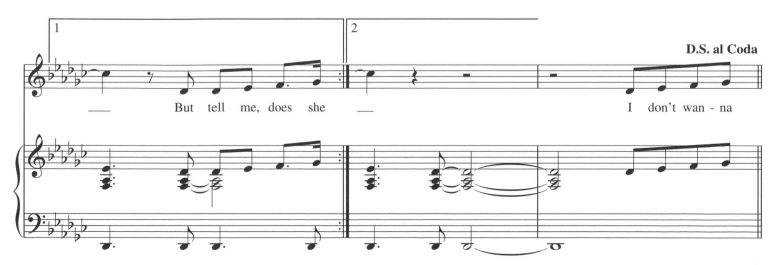

But tell me, does she _____

I don't wan - na

D.S. al Coda

YOU ARE THE MUSIC IN ME

from the Disney Channel Original Movie HIGH SCHOOL MUSICAL 2

Words and Music by
JAMIE HOUSTON

Moderately fast Rock

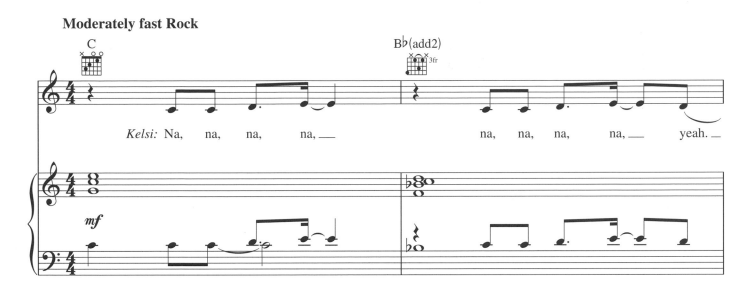

Kelsi: Na, na, na, na, ___ na, na, na, na, ___ yeah. ___

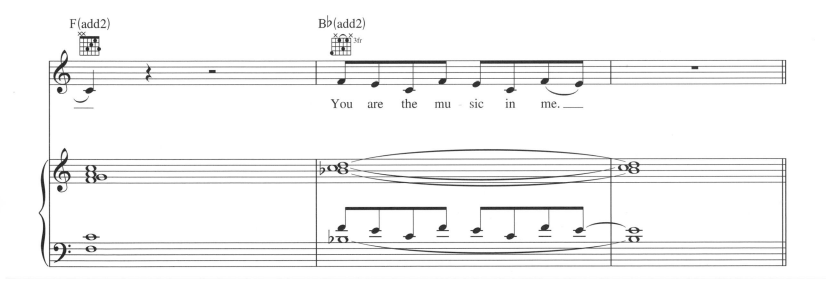

You are the mu-sic in me. ___

You know, the words, ___ "once up-on a time" make you lis-

Kelsi & Gabriella:
When you dream, there's a chance you'll find a lit-tle laugh-

-ter or "hap-py ev-er af-ter." *Gabriella & Troy:* You're a har-mo-ny to the

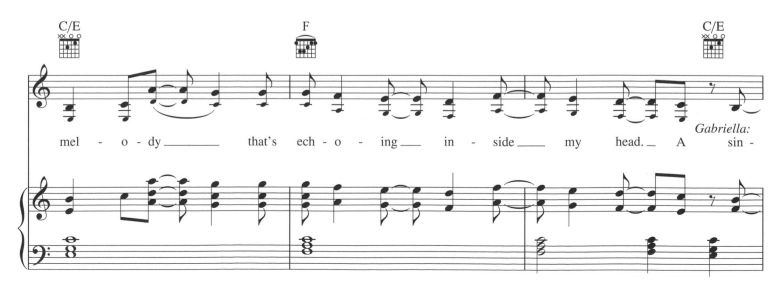

mel-o-dy that's ech-o-ing in-side my head. *Gabriella:* A sin-

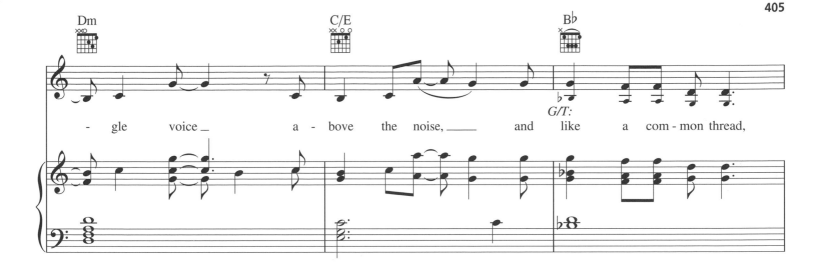

-gle voice _ a - bove the noise, ___ and like a com - mon thread,

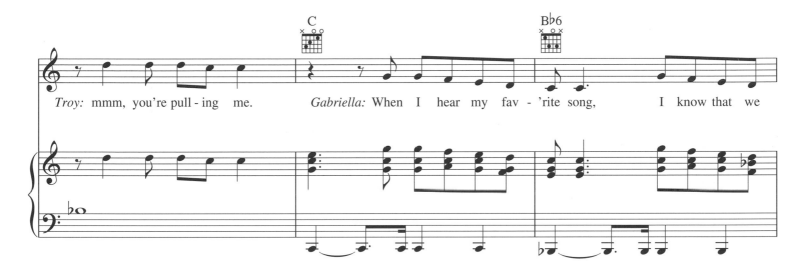

Troy: mmm, you're pull - ing me. *Gabriella:* When I hear my fav - 'rite song, I know that we

be - long. *Troy:* Oh, ___ you ___ are the mu - sic in me.

Yeah, it's liv - ing in all of us, *Gabriella:* and it's brought us here ___

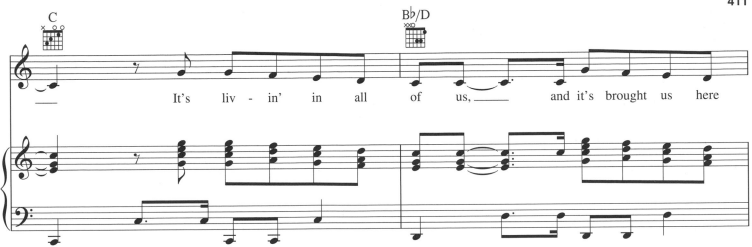

It's liv-in' in all of us, _____ and it's brought us here

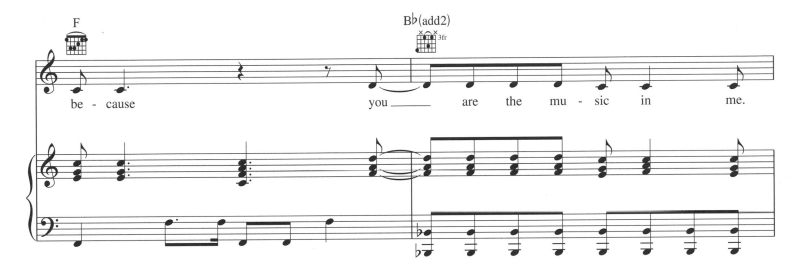

be - cause you _____ are the mu - sic in me.

Na, na, na, na. Na, na, na, na, na. Na, na, na, na. You _____

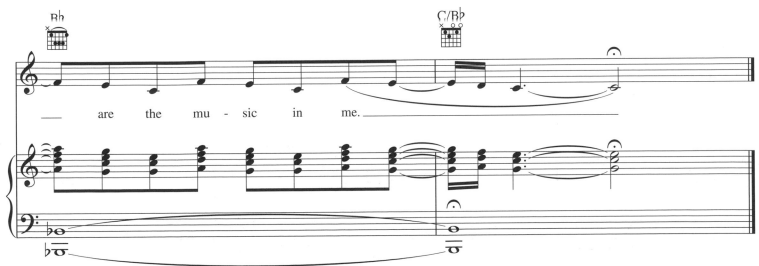

_____ are the mu - sic in me. _____

WONDERFUL COPENHAGEN

from the Motion Picture HANS CHRISTIAN ANDERSEN

By FRANK LOESSER

Moderate Waltz

Lyrics: I sail up the Skag-ge-rak, and sail down the Kat-te-gat thru the har-bor and up to the quay, and there she stands,

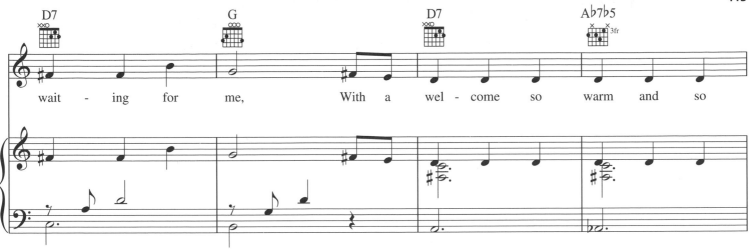

wait - ing for me, With a wel - come so warm and so

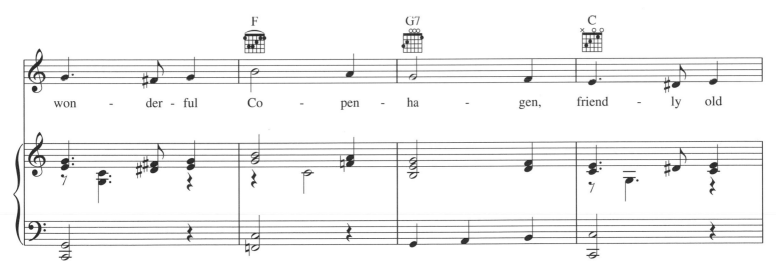

gay. _____ Won - der - ful,

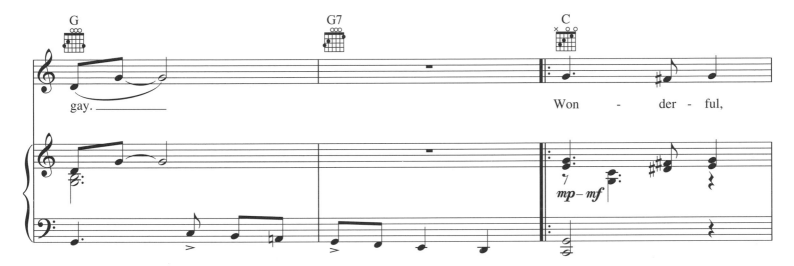

won - der - ful Co - pen - ha - gen, friend - ly old

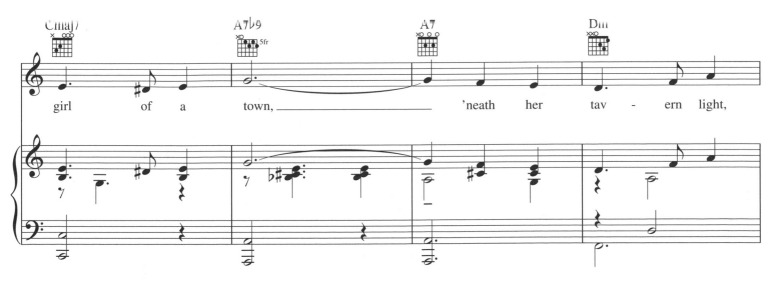

girl of a town, _____ 'neath her tav - ern light,

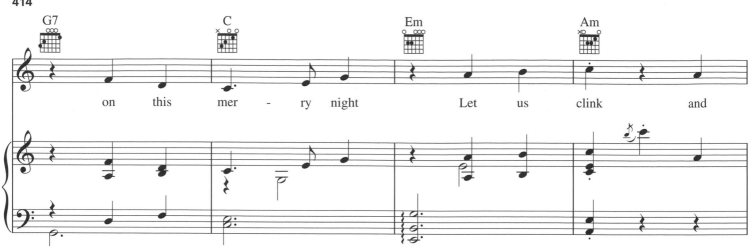

on this mer - ry night Let us clink and

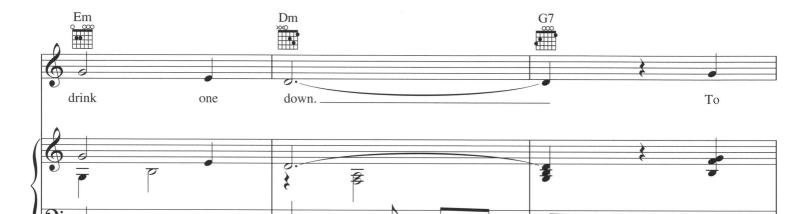

drink one down. _____ To

won - der - ful, won - der - ful Co - pen - ha - gen,

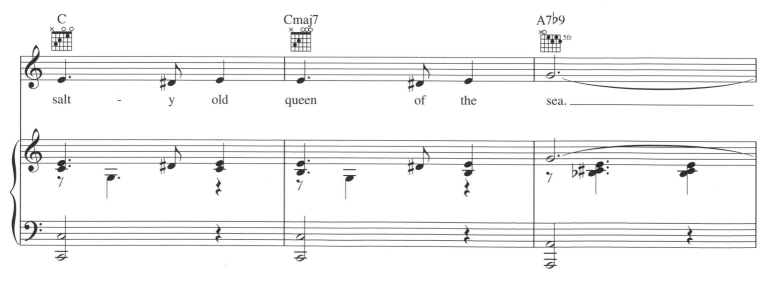

salt - y old queen of the sea. _____

YOU'D BE SO NICE
TO COME HOME TO
from SOMETHING TO SHOUT ABOUT

Words and Music by
COLE PORTER

It's not that you're fair-er, than a lot of girls just as pleas-in', that I doff my hat as a wor-ship-per at your shrine. ___ It's

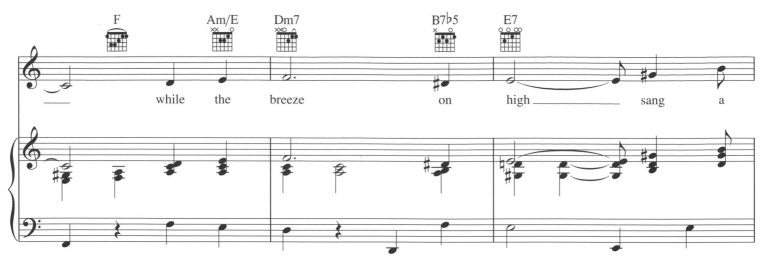

while the breeze on high _____ sang a

lull - a - by. _____ You'd be all that I could de-

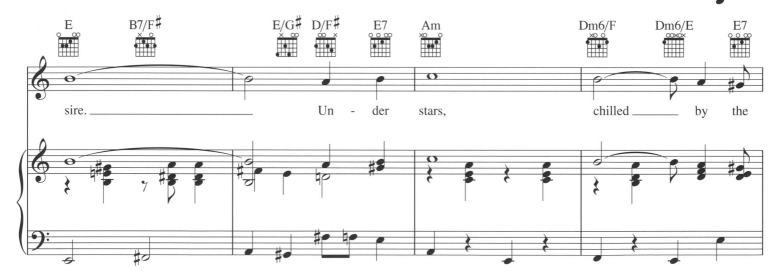

sire. _____ Un - der stars, chilled _____ by the

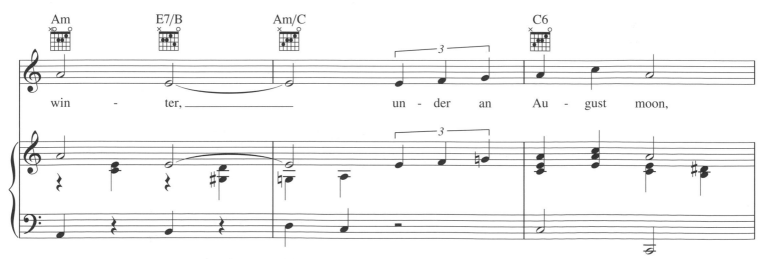

win - ter, _____ un - der an Au - gust moon,

YOU'LL BE IN MY HEART
(Pop Version)
from Walt Disney Pictures' TARZAN™

Words and Music by
PHIL COLLINS

Come stop your cry - ing; _ it will be all right. Just take my hand,

hold it tight. _____ I will pro-tect you from all a-round _ you.

I will be here; don't you _ cry. For one so small you
Why can't they un-der-stand the

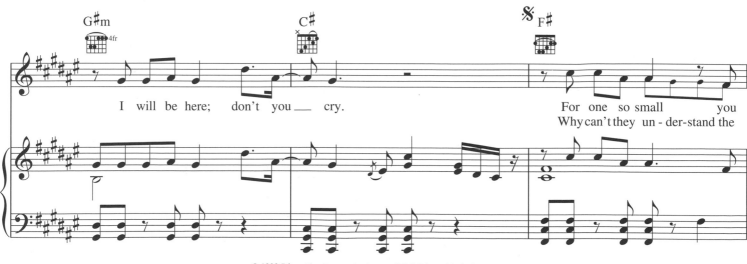

seem so ___ strong. ___
way we ___ feel? ___

My arms will hold you, ___ keep you
They just don't trust ___ what they

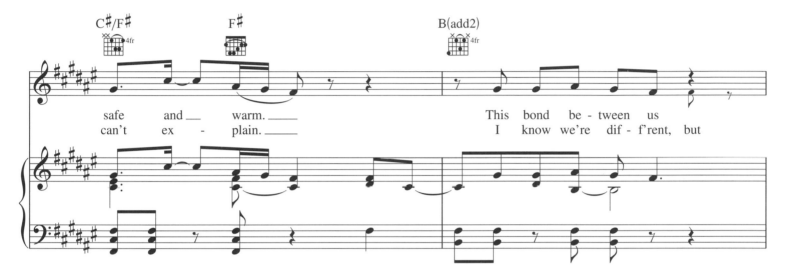

safe and ___ warm. ___
can't ex - plain. ___

This bond be - tween us
I know we're dif - f'rent, but

can't be bro - ken.
deep in - side ___ us

I will be here; don't you ___ cry.
we're not that dif - fer - ent at all. ___

'Cause
And

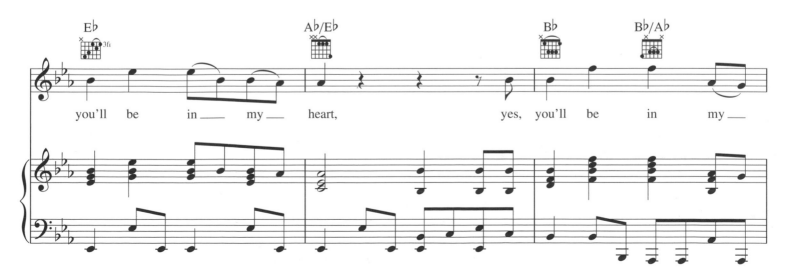

you'll be in ___ my ___ heart,

yes, you'll be in my ___

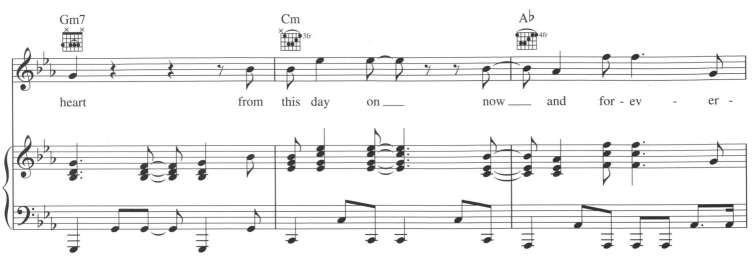

heart — from this day on — now — and for-ev - er -

more. You'll be in — my —

heart no mat-ter what — they — say. You'll

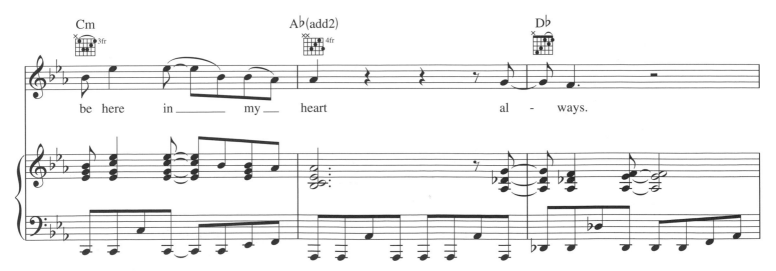

be here in — my — heart al - ways.

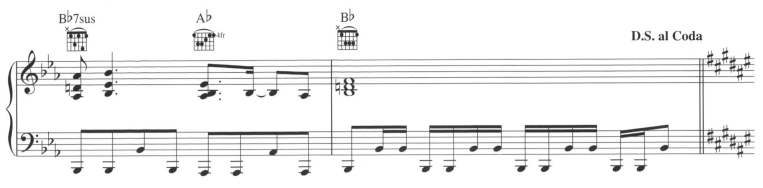

D.S. al Coda

Don't lis - ten to them, ____ 'cause you
des - ti - ny calls _ you, you

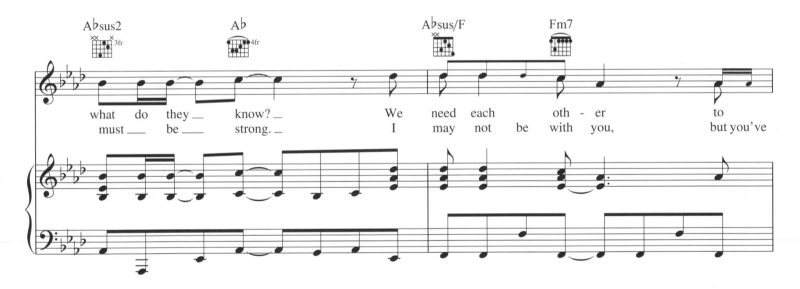

what do they _ know? _ We need each oth - er to
must _ be _ strong. _ I may not be with you, but you've

have, to _ hold. }
got to hold _ on. }
They'll _ see _ in time, I ____

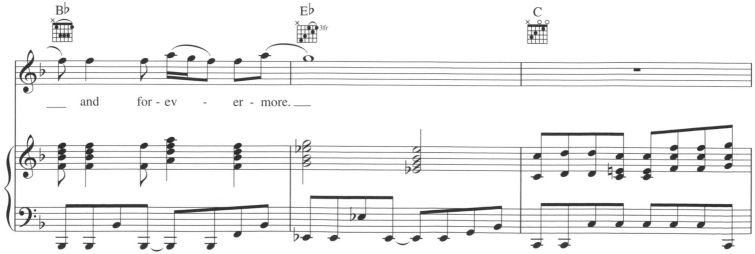

You'll be in _____ my ____ heart (You'll be here ___ in my heart.) ___ no mat-ter what __ they __

say. (I'll be with you.) You'll be here in _____ my __ heart (I'll be there.) al-

- ways. Al - ways, _____

I'll be with you. I'll be

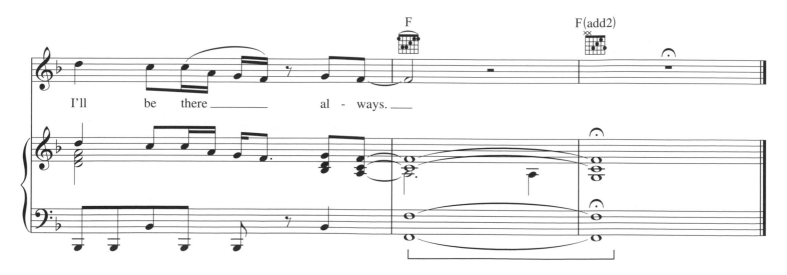

YOUNG AT HEART

from YOUNG AT HEART

Words by CAROLYN LEIGH
Music by JOHNNY RICHARDS

Fair-y tales ___ can come true, ___ it can hap-pen to you ___ if you're

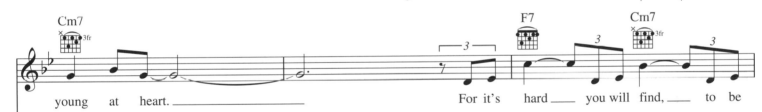

young at heart. _____ For it's hard ___ you will find, ___ to be

nar-row of mind ___ if you're young at heart. _____ You can

ZIP-A-DEE-DOO-DAH
from Walt Disney's SONG OF THE SOUTH

Words by RAY GILBERT
Music by ALLIE WRUBEL

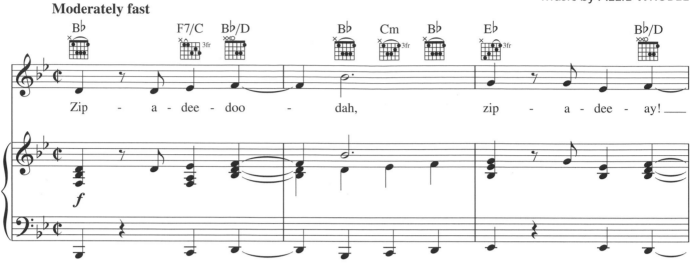

Zip - a - dee - doo - dah, zip - a - dee - ay! ___

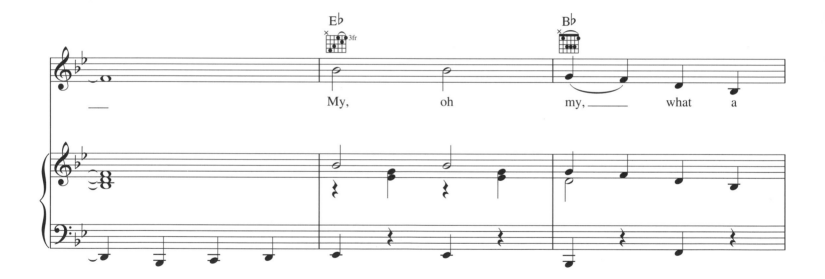

___ My, oh my, ___ what a

won - der - ful day! ___ Plen - ty of sun -

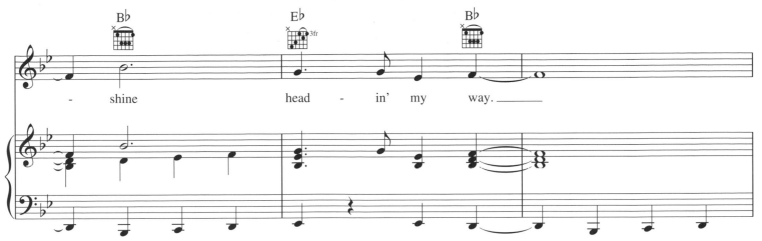

-shine head - in' my way. _____

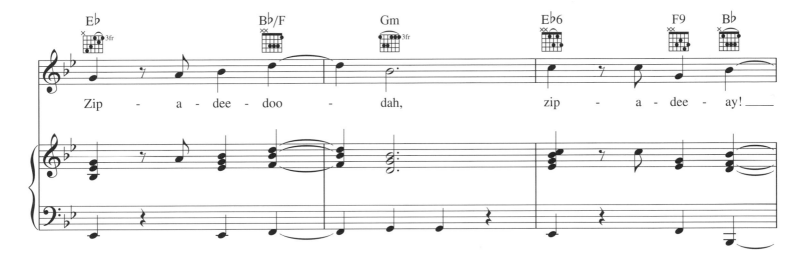

Zip - a - dee - doo - dah, zip - a - dee - ay! _____

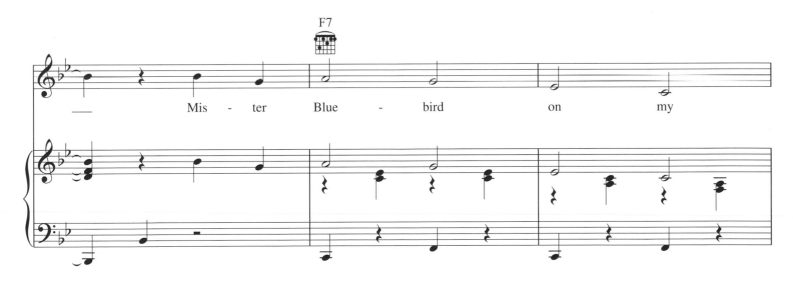

_____ Mis - ter Blue - bird on my

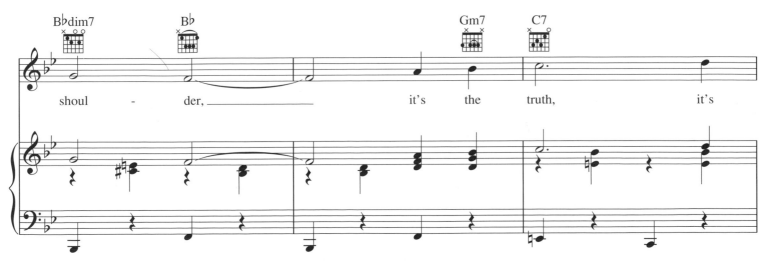

shoul - der, _____ it's the truth, it's

"act - ch'll" ev - 'ry - thing is "sat - is - fact - ch'll."

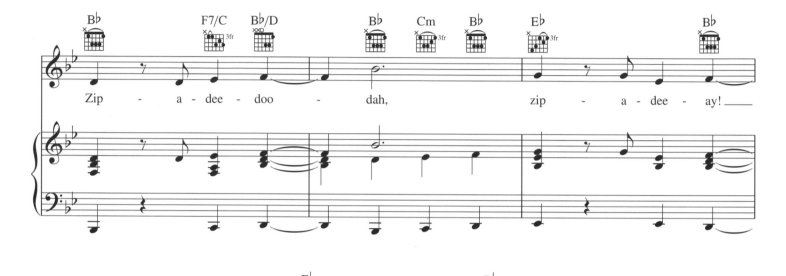

Zip - a - dee - doo - dah, zip - a - dee - ay! _____

_____ Won - der - ful feel - ing,

won - der - ful day! _____